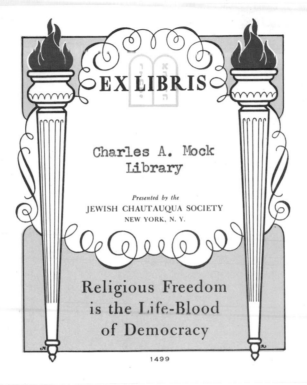

Here and there, Christians in different lands are taking into their souls the conflict between the historic Christian defamation of Jews and the gospel requirement of love. YOUR PEOPLE, MY PEOPLE chronicles the accomplishments and limitations of such efforts as the Vatican Council pronouncement on the Jews, movingly reports recent encounters between Jews and Christians in this country and abroad, appraises such thinkers as Reinhold Niebuhr, Gregory Baum, Edward Flannery, Rosemary Ruether, Abraham Heschel, Friedrich Heer, and Harvey Cox, and summarizes much of the current literature in the field.

In a final section the author wrestles constructively and affirmatively with the question of whether we may continue to have faith in God in a world after the death camps, as he also enumerates Christian acts of justice for Jews. Dr. Eckardt provides an original ethical and theological position which, in critical refinement of his earlier writings, affirms the integrity of a humanizing Christian faith and at the same time fully honors Judaism and Jewish peoplehood.

YOUR PEOPLE, MY PEOPLE is the single most comprehensive study yet available of the entire range of contemporary Jewish-Christian relations.

About the author

A. Roy Eckardt is a leading American Christian thinker in the field of Jewish-Christian relations. Now Professor and Chairman of the Department of Religion Studies at Leheigh University, he has taught at Duke University, The City College of New York, and other schools. A clergyman in the United Methodist Church since 1944, he was editor of the *Journal of the American Academy of Religion* and served as president of the Academy. Among other honors, he has served as the vice-president of Christians Concerned for Israel, and received the Distinguished Alumnus Award from Brooklyn College in 1963. A frequent contributor to professional and lay journals, he is the author of *Elder and Younger Brothers* and *Encounter with Israel* (with Alice Eckardt) among other books, and has edited several volumes, including *The Theologian at Work*.

YOUR PEOPLE, MY PEOPLE

Your people shall be my people.
Ruth 1:16

Let us speak the truth in love.
Ephesians 4:15

*It is not the unbelieving who invite
"damnation" but the unloving.*
Joseph Fletcher

BOOKS BY A. ROY ECKARDT
Your People, My People
Christianity in Israel (editor)
The Theologian at Work (editor)
Elder and Younger Brothers
The Surge of Piety in America
Christianity and the Children of Israel

WITH ALICE ECKARDT
Encounter with Israel

Your People, My People

The Meeting of Jews and Christians

A. ROY ECKARDT

QUADRANGLE
The New York Times Book Company

Library of Congress Catalog Card Number: 73-90162
International Standard Book Number: 0-8129-0412-5

Design by Emily Harste

Production by Planned Production

For
DOROTHY AND JAMES PARKES
in thankfulness and admiration

Contents

Preface

The theme of this volume is the meeting of Christians and Jews in the world after Auschwitz, with special emphasis upon the moral demand for Christian brotherliness. The assessment is made from a Christian and Protestant standpoint. That Jews and Christians do meet in our global neighborhood is inevitable; the only questions are what are the terms of the meeting, and what human bonds or alienations result?

It would not be defensible for a Christian writer to emphasize recent changes for the better within Christendom in equal balance with moral and theological judgments against Christendom. Such "evenhandedness" would be either unjust or unnecessary—the first, because there is a gross inaccuracy in asserting that the Christian attitude toward, and treatment of, Jews have now become as good as they have earlier been evil; the second, because this book is itself a witness, even if a poor one, that for all their abiding sins, Christians may champion love and justice for the Jewish people.

I pretend to no definitive or final answers to a number of questions that arise in these pages, such as the exact relationship between Christian antisemitism[1] and other forms of anti-

---

[1] The usage "antisemitism" appears throughout this book. I agree with James Parkes that "anti-Semitism" is incorrect and misleading; it wrongly

semitism, the loci of authority in our religious and intellectual life, the issue of hope versus hopelessness in the human journey, and the ultimate theological significance of the re-emergence of the State of Israel. I do trust that the reflections I offer will help readers of varied persuasions to think their own way through these and other moral and spiritual dilemmas.

I acknowledge the kindness of several journals for permitting me to adapt some writings of mine to the purposes of this study: *The Christian Century, Christianity and Crisis, Christian News From Israel* (Jerusalem), *Commentary, Congress bi-Weekly, Emuna* (Cologne), *In de Waagschaal* (Utrecht), *Jewish Spectator, Journal of the Central Conference of American Rabbis, Journal of Church and State, Midstream, Religion in Life,* and *Women's American ORT Reporter.* All of these materials have been radically altered and updated. Much of the text has not been published before, and none of it has appeared in this revised form. Chapter 10 was composed jointly with my wife, Alice L. Eckardt.

I express thanks to generous hosts and patient audiences in this country and abroad with whom I have discussed some of the themes presented here. Over the past few years these meetings extended from various church and synagogue groups to the following larger institutions: the American Institute of Holy Land Studies (Jerusalem), American Jewish Committee (Jerusalem), Boston College, Briarcliff College, Dropsie University, Ecumenical Theological Research Fraternity (Jerusalem), Hampshire College, Israel Interfaith Committee, the Methodist Theological School in Ohio, the New School for Social Research, Northwestern University (Goldman Lecture),

---

implies a movement against an imagined "Semitism." On the meaning of the term "antisemitism," the root of the English word lacks preciseness. In the *Random House Dictionary,* the sole definition of "antisemite" is "a person who is hostile to Jews." I would only suggest adding the qualifying words, "because they are Jews." That Arabs are reputedly a Semitic people lessens in no way the power of antisemitism among them. A German word that is not readily subject to semantic gameplaying is *Judenfeindschaft,* enmity toward Jews.

Seton Hall University, Stern College for Women of Yeshiva University, and the United Christian Council in Israel. At the following conferences, too, I have shared ideas now presented here: the Annual Conference of the American Academic Association for Peace in the Middle East held at the Massachusetts Institute of Technology, 1969; the 1971 Symposium on Jewish–Christian Relations, sponsored by the J. M. Dawson Studies In Church and State at Baylor University and the Anti-Defamation League of B'nai B'rith; the 1971 Consultation on the Church and the Jewish People, World Council of Churches, in Zürich; the 1972 Colloquium on Christian–Jewish Relations sponsored by the University of Miami and the American Jewish Committee; the 1972 International Scholars Conference on the German Church Struggle and the Holocaust, Wayne State University; and, in 1973, the Conference on Jewish–Christian Relations and the Curriculum, sponsored by the North American Academy of Ecumenists and the National Conference of Christians and Jews, held in Philadelphia. I utilized some of the materials in this book in a course in the history and theology of Jewish–Christian relations at the College of the City of New York in the spring of 1973, working in collaboration with my wife and Professor Irving Greenberg. Not least, I offer a special word of gratitude for encouragement and help received from my friend Solomon S. Bernards. Most capably, Martine Bucha readied the manuscript for publication.

I was reading the proofs of this book on the very day (October 6, 1973) that Arab nations renewed the all-out effort to destroy Israel; it is possible to include only an immediate and brief response: The Christian world was very largely silent and complicitous before the Nazi genocide of Jews. Christian silence and "evenhandedness" amidst the attempted second Holocaust of 1967 are well known. With the Yom Kippur War of 1973, Christians and the churches faced the choice either of collaborating yet another time in the unceasing effort to annihilate the Jewish people, or of condemning and fighting the evil. To the extent that Christian collaborationism prevails once more, a new fact will have afflicted our conscience: consent to the wicked blasphemy of utilizing the holiest day of the Jewish year to the end of destroying Jews.

A. Roy Eckardt

Lehigh University

Part One
THE CHRISTIAN PREDICAMENT

1

Guilt

I am hardly alone in writing and speaking of Christian guilt for the evil treatment of Jews throughout Christian history, culminating in the Holocaust of the Nazi period and continuing until today.[1]

Some observers may wonder whether calls for the acknowledgment of Christian guilt have become, at best, an obsession and, at worst, an incantation. And is it not morally too late for all this business? Indeed, is it not *reprehensible* to confess our sins today, now that there is complete safety in speaking out? (Admittedly, stubborn and widespread exceptions to such safety continue in Communist and Arab lands.) Perhaps the latter-day reaction against Christian self-defensiveness is itself no more than delayed but instinctive shame. Perhaps the new Christian "repentance" has as its hidden motivation no more than a self-centered and hence despicable salving of conscience. Or, it may be that in "quiet desperation," yet without awareness of our real motives, we Christians are simply casting about for supportive allies in an

[1] One peculiarity I can claim is, perhaps, unfortunate: My repeated emphasis upon the fact of Christian guilt and my manner of presentation sometimes seem to prompt hearers (as in a recent instance in Detroit) to accuse me of self-flagellation, rather than to take seriously the requirement of penitence.

essentially post-Christian age. Or, alternatively, perhaps our guilt is in truth infinite, and demands, therefore, continuous vocalization broadcast to an undetermined future.

Critical reactions from cynical Christians and from cynical Jews to recent admissions of Christian guilt include references to the cheapness of talk, the hollowness of the breast-beating of hopelessly dilatory confessors, their unrepressed fascination with destruction and killing, their deification of the slain (Raul Hilberg), their concocting of a series of incantations, etc., etc. The one response to such charges that we are entitled to offer here is to propose that the very same psychological interpretation and the very same moral judgment upon sin be extended to cover the motivations and behavior of every man, including the cynics themselves. Withal, the stern truth remains that despite scattered and valiant efforts, a spirit of contrition has hardly managed to penetrate the world Christian community.[2]

It is sometimes asserted, with respect to the German situation, that every individual German living today ought to feel guilt for the persecution and slaughter of Jews during the Nazi period. It is insisted by others that any such imputing of universal guilt is immoral, since many persons, and in particular those born since Hitler's time, cannot possibly be held accountable in this way. Here is a profound moral issue that transcends any single epoch or group of human beings. The issue manifests itself with varying seriousness throughout the entire history of Christian relations with Jews. The problem is not amenable to any either–or intellectual reckoning, and the moral dilemma involved stands beyond any final solution. How can we hope ever to disclose fully the hidden depths of human motivation? The venerable and overall moral predicament of man involves at one and the same time the blameworthiness that attaches in principle to his moral freedom and the innocence that accompanies his social, historical,

---

[2] A. Roy Eckardt, "The Jewish–Christian Dialogue: Recent Christian Efforts in Europe," *Conservative Judaism*, 19:3 (Spring, 1965), 15–16.

or natural fate. Yet the persistence of that predicament as a subject for soul-searching discussion may itself testify that the overall human situation compounds both these elements. The emphasis upon blameworthiness recognizes the mystery of human and social solidarity in sin, yet it tends to obscure necessary moral distinctions among relative goods and among relative evils. The emphasis upon innocence honors the indispensable distinction between good and evil, yet it tends to ignore the mystery of corporate sin.

Are we deprived of all moral principles for assessing what in a few churches after the Second Great War seemed almost to become a ritual, a program of guilt? Surely the preparation and issuance of church pronouncements carry no great price, and may even enhance the personal reputations of the signatories. And it is quite possible that one or another of the parties involved may also seek to promote certain national or group interests. Yet we are not forced totally to deny the worth of public statements by Christian bodies or church leaders. Everything depends upon what is said, the way it is said, the timing involved, and the extent of consequent efforts to put the words into living practice.

The obligation remains of how to make ourselves aware of the divine judgment and mercy, so that having been confronted in some way by the purposes of the hidden God, our lives may be transformed and the future influenced. For this, no one way is final or perfect. Confessions of guilt are required just as long as there is need for genuine and general repentance to take root in human hearts. Needless to say, this means the hearts of people outside Germany as well as those inside, and it applies to the drafters of statements and the writers of books as much as to anyone else. In H. David Leuner's words, "without confession of guilt, confession of faith remains unconvincing and suspect. . . . That the confession of a guilt that has become tradition is embarrassing, and is especially difficult to make because it is demanded of an often all too self-confident religious group, should not be denied, but it does not change the fact that it is urgently necessary and has unfortunately not yet taken place."[3] We have a long way to go before there is any danger that the cup of our repentance may overflow.

It is acknowledged within Christian faith that the state of penitence is no more than a preliminary to the positive healing of the Holy Spirit. No act of man is wholly able to purge away either evil or its lasting consequences. Every human being who says "I am sorry" knows in moments of absolute honesty that his penitence is not absolutely pure. While the words would probably never be expressed without a sincere desire to restore a broken relationship and to serve the other's welfare, neither would they be uttered at all were not the interests of the self also at stake.

Whatever its surface function or conscious intention or seeming redundance, any confession of penitence for the wronging of other human beings must at the very least call us to continued searching of conscience. In principle, the drive to make amends is a good thing. At its fount is the restlessness of men who, unknowingly or knowingly, seek after God. Nothing in the Christian ethic contradicts the wish to gain or to restore a nation's—or, for that matter, a church's —self-respect. Indeed, without mutual self-respect, human equality and justice are unattainable.

Furthermore, the persuasion of guilt has at least two facets. It can spring out of ordinary human relations. But it can issue as well from explicit faith in God. In Western culture a public act of group penitence is still in some way a fruit of faith, of the acknowledging of a judgment that transcends any human judgment. In an important sense, the Christian church has a moral right to speak with authority to its membership about sin and guilt in a way that cannot be demanded or even wistfully hoped for among secular institutions. Ideally, Christians will assent to the righteous judgment of God as voiced through the church.

[3] H. David Leuner, "From Mission to Dialog—Rethinking the Relation of Christians and Jews," *Lutheran World,* 10:4 (Oct., 1963), 387.

2

The Churches, Antisemitism, and the Holocaust

This chapter concentrates upon ways in which traditional Christian antisemitism helped to make the Nazi Holocaust possible. Elements of opposition to antisemitism in Christian history and the Christian tradition are not touched. Though we must not forget those Christians who during the Holocaust and at other times sacrificed their lives or their reputations for the sake of Jews, we should hardly be doing honor to them by tampering with or hiding the dominating truth.

Objectively speaking, the Christian tradition is ambivalent toward Judaism and the Jewish people. On the one hand, there is love and gratitude toward Jews because of their stewardship of sacred history and the gift of Jesus to the world; on the other hand, there is a negativistic stance based on the Jews' repudiation (allegedly) of their own gift. We might have hoped that these two impulses would exert at least equal force. The truth is, though, that any theoretical equality of the two opposite impulses has never been attained in practice. Across the centuries of Christendom, the scales have been weighted on the side of enmity toward things Jewish, not on the side of acceptance and thankfulness.

I

The New Testament is so central to the Christian faith that the question of antisemitism in those writings is of utmost seriousness and relevance; it demands extra and careful attention.

The Catholic theologian Rosemary Ruether asserts that the decree on the Jews issued by Vatican Council II was carefully framed so as to preclude the raising of any questions concerning antisemitic attitudes within the New Testament. She argues that antisemitism is deeply rooted in the Christian gospel of the New Testament.[1] The Catholic New Testament scholar Dominic M. Crossan is not as negativistic as Ruether, but neither is he entirely happy with the relevant documents. Crossan concludes that the term "the Jews" as employed by Saint John is "a very dangerous symbolic term, and one cannot but wonder if it might be a root of anti-Semitism in the Christian subconscious."[2]

On the Protestant side, Alan T. Davies, in arguing that there is no anti-Judaism without some measure of hostility to Jews, attests that anti-Judaism inheres in any ideology that considers the New Testament sacrosanct, as does Protestant biblicism. With specific reference to antisemitism, Davies maintains that such biblicism is quite as dangerous as the persisting, dogmatic traditionalism of historic Catholicism.

[1] Rosemary Ruether, "Theological Anti-Semitism in the New Testament," *The Christian Century,* 85:7 (Feb. 14, 1968), 191–96. Friedrich Heer asserts that the Second Vatican Council did nothing essential to bring about real amends for Christian guilt toward Jews [*God's First Love: Christians and Jews Over Two Thousand Years* (New York: Weybright and Talley, 1970), p. 247.] Subsequent events and trends within the Catholic Church raise doubts over the complete justice of Heer's assertion. Cf. Rose Thering, "Survey Report of Catholic Institutions' Implementation of Vatican II Statement on the Jews" (unpublished), prepared for the Theological Consultation, "Toward a Theology of Israel," Seton Hall University, October 25–28, 1970.

[2] Dominic M. Crossan, "Anti-Semitism and the Gospel," *Theological Studies,* 26:2 (June, 1965), 199. Crossan insists, however, that the only proper translation for John's special use of the phrase "the Jews" is "those among the authorities of the Jews who constantly opposed Jesus."

Passages in the New Testament that are tainted with antisemitism have been put to exactly the same antisemitic use as patristic calumnies against Jews.[3] Another Protestant scholar, Robert E. Willis, is persuaded that until the Christian church performs acts of repentance for scriptural passages that convey anti-Judaic and antisemitic images, innuendos, and nuances, the church will continue to show that it has not been seriously affected by its continuing complicity "in the perpetuation of anti-Semitism and its nascent presence within the Christian community today."[4]

What judgments are we to make? It is absurd to contend that the New Testament is, in essence, an antisemitic document. Nevertheless, to shut our eyes to the antisemitic proclivities of Christian Scripture is indefensible. For example, we have the apostle Paul's statement to the Christians at Thessalonika: ". . . You suffered the same things from your own countrymen as they did from the Jews, who killed both the Lord Jesus and the prophets, and drove us out, and displease God and oppose all men by hindering us from speaking to the Gentiles that they may be saved—so as always to fill up the measure of their sins. But God's wrath has come upon them at last" (I Thess. 2:14–16).

It is well known that over the course of the New Testament years, with particular reference to the four Gospels, culpability for the fate of Jesus was increasingly shifted from the Romans to the Jews. The reputed Jewish responsibility for opposition to Jesus is chronicled in less and less discriminate fashion. Yet already in Mark, usually considered the earliest Gospel, "the chief priests and the scribes" and "the whole council" conspire to kill Jesus, and "the multitude" demands his crucifixion (14:1, 11, 43ff., 55, 64; 15:11–15). Matthew's primary contribution lies in initiating the claim of

---

[3] Alan T. Davies, *Anti-Semitism and the Christian Mind: The Crisis of Conscience after Auschwitz* (New York: Herder and Herder, 1969), pp. 104, 110–111, 112.

[4] Robert E. Willis, "A Perennial Outrage: Anti-Semitism in the New Testament," *The Christian Century*, 87:33 (Aug. 19, 1970), 992.

an eternal curse laid upon the Jewish people: "His blood be on us and our children" (27:25). The development climaxes in the Gospel of John, which, significantly, has long served as preeminent companion and inspiration to Christian piety. While in Mark the challenge to Jesus for symbolically destroying the Temple comes only from "the high priests, the Scribes, and the elders" (11:27), in John "the Jews" make the challenge (2:18–20). In the Synoptic Gospels, conflicts over Sabbath healings involve only the authorities (cf. Mark 3:26; Luke 6:6–11; Matt. 12:9–10, 13–14); in John, the cripple whom Jesus heals is reproached by "the Jews" (5:10).[5]

The practical and fateful imbalance referred to at the beginning of this chapter is conspicuous in John. That Gospel's attestation that salvation comes from the Jews (4:22) is drowned out by a series of accusations: It is "the Jews" who are stirred to persecute Jesus, "the Jews" determine to kill him, "the Jews" seek to stone him, "the Jews"—insisting that they "have no king but Caesar"—succeed in getting Pontius Pilate to hand Jesus over to be crucified, against Pilate's desire to release Jesus (5:16–18; 10:31; 19:12–16; see also 6:41; 7:1, 13; cf. Mark 15:11; Matt. 27:20). Reputedly, Jesus himself tells "the Jews" that they are not children of God but are, by deliberate choice, children of the devil (8:42–47).

It is always difficult to assess the inner spiritual states of men, especially men who lived long ago. Perhaps John was led astray by detractors of Jews. His Gospel reflects the changed atmosphere at the turn of the century, a difference for which there is earlier evidence as well: the schism between the Jewish and Christian communities, and the church's felt need to propitiate the Romans. It is conceivable that could John and the others have foreknown the terrible uses to which their Gospels were to be put, they would have destroyed their scrolls or radically altered them.

---

[5] See Crossan, "Anti-Semitism and the Gospel," p. 194.

An explanation of how and why a human being is led to say or do something does not in itself erase culpability for the act. *Tout comprendre, c'est tout pardonner* may be a very fine watchword for God; it is doubtful whether human community would endure under such counsel. Again, the possible sincerity of the Johannine author or the other evangelists is hardly a mitigating factor; few men have been more sincere in their convictions respecting Jews than Adolf Hitler.

It is often maintained that racism is a modern phenomenon.[6] Yet if it is the nature of racism to fabricate an essential defect in the *being* of the out-race,[7] the roots of racism are discernible in past ages. For one powerful ally of racism is indiscriminateness. A fateful consideration is that so many New Testament passages resort to the indiscriminate phrase "the Jews."

Gregory Baum, conceding that the Gospel of John has been called upon to justify contempt for the Jewish people, yet insists that the historical and religious context of these seemingly hostile passages forbids us to speak of antisemitism in John.[8] A possible rejoinder to Baum is grounded in this principle of moral reasoning: While the context of any assertion is relevant when discriminate or qualified judgments are tendered, the context becomes totally irrelevant once indiscriminate or unqualified judgments are made. The truism, "some Americans are killers," is not in and of itself an instance of anti-Americanism. But the indiscriminate proposition, "*the* Americans are killers," simply cannot be redeemed through taking refuge in a historical context. Thus, when the Gospel of John again and again makes indiscriminate, hostile judgments against "*the* Jews" as Jews, it is impossible to separate the Gospel from antisemitism. Hostility to "the Jews"

[6] George D. Kelsey, *Racism and the Christian Understanding of Man* (New York: Scribner, 1965), pp. 19–23.

[7] Ibid., pp. 32–33 and *passim*.

[8] Gregory Baum, *Is the New Testament Anti-Semitic?* (Glen Rock, N.J.: Paulist Press, 1965), p. 136.

is, indeed, the single meaning of antisemitism. The article "the" is as decisive as the word "Jews," or more so.

We have already alluded to the tendency, as time went by during the New Testament period, to make less and less discriminate Jewish blame respecting opposition to Jesus and the fate of Jesus. It is highly ironic that the more seriously we take the developing historical context of the New Testament, the more indisputable are the evidences therein of *Judenfeindschaft*, enmity toward Jews.[9] Indiscriminate, unqualified judgments are inseparable from the allegation of a defect-in-being.[10]

Saint Paul's assertion—already an indiscriminate one despite its earliness—that the Jews killed Jesus may be likened in structure to such a hypothetical sentence as "the Americans killed President Kennedy," containing as the latter sentence does a logical and psychological insinuation that Mr. Kennedy was not an American. So, too, the phrase "the Jews killed Jesus," which is hardly a hypothetical assertion from the standpoint of Christian detractors of Jews, almost seems to insinuate that Jesus was not a Jew. It is no accident that this very conclusion was to be reached in Christian theology, as exemplified in the insistence within the Faith Movement of German Christians in our century that Jesus could not have been a Jew but was instead a member of the pure, Aryan race, maligned and murdered by the Jewish race.

While we are required to point up, analytically and historically, certain independently antisemitic proclivities within the New Testament, the really fateful consideration is that these documents came to constitute, for the church, the divinely willed and God-provided instrument for persecuting

---

[9] A. Roy Eckardt, *Elder and Younger Brothers: The Encounter of Jews and Christians* (New York: Scribner, 1967; Schocken, 1973), pp. 124–125. Cf., more generally, pp. 122–129.

[10] Due to the absence of such judgments within the Hebrew Bible, we have to emphasize that there is no antisemitism in the so-called Old Testament—insinuations by real-life antisemites to the contrary notwithstanding.

Jews. Without Christendom's later decision to transubstantiate the human words of the New Testament writers into the Word of God, the evil would have been infinitely less. Because the New Testament is the primordial Christian authority, the one accepted, honored, and disseminated by all Christian communions, that material must remain the primary focus of the entire problem of Christian hostility to Jews. The New Testament remains the major dogmatic and existential barrier to any victory over antisemitism. However, it is most doubtful that the Christian church will ever surrender the claim that the New Testament, and the "events" it recounts, constitutes the unique history of salvation and indeed the Word of God, and, accordingly, that it comprises the "gospel truth" which stands in judgment upon all other alleged truth. Christendom retains an indestructibly vested interest in the "Jewish rejection of Christ." The slander must be preserved, for without it, the whole ideological edifice of the churches would crash to the ground.

Those who seek to declare the New Testament innocent of antisemitism[11] are hard put to explain how New Testament Christianity could have become a foundation reference for Christian antisemitism through the ages. Every instance of Christian antisemitism in postbiblical history is directly or indirectly traceable to the events or reputed events recorded in the New Testament. The foundations of Christian antisemitism and the church's contribution to the Nazi Holocaust were laid 1900 years ago; the line from the New Testament through the centuries of Christian contempt for Jews to the gas ovens and crematoria is unbroken. This is why no responsible moral assessment of either the writer of John or of the other New Testament evangelists can turn its back on the calumnies they circulated. For the historical consequences of these slanders were persecution and, finally, mass murder.

[11] Cf., Baum, *Is The New Testament Anti-Semitic?*, p. 16 and *passim.*

II

Let us turn to the postbiblical developments.

Christian churchmen and theologians carried forward and brought to destructive fulfillment the process initiated in the New Testament period. In early Christianity, the posture with respect to Jews was primarily apologetic—an effort to defend the integrity of the gospel. However, as the years passed and the church became more and more gentile in character, an increasingly polemical stance was taken. It was destined to issue, at last, in what Jules Isaac has aptly called "the teaching of contempt,"[12] contempt for the Jewish people and for Judaism.

By the middle of the second century, Jewish Christians who remained faithful to the Torah were considered heretics by the church.[13] With respect to the Christian attitude toward the faith of Jews who remained Jews, a foremost means for developing and perpetuating Christian antisemitism has been anti-Judaism. Isaac numbers among the themes of "the teaching of contempt" the "degenerate state of Judaism at the time of Jesus."[14] That accusation was infinitely compounded after the time of Jesus, for, reputedly, "the Jews" had manifested a devilish form of degeneracy by rejecting and putting to death their own Savior. A tendency to depict the Jewish people as a whole as the murderers of Christ came to condition the thinking of the church fathers. Judaism was soon identified as the work of the devil and the Jews were thought

[12] Jules Isaac, *The Teaching of Contempt: Christian Roots of Anti-Semitism* (New York: Holt, Rinehart and Winston, 1964). See also Isaac's fuller, definitive study, *Jesus and Israel,* trans., Sally Gran, ed., with a foreword by Claire Huchet Bishop (New York: Holt, Rinehart and Winston, 1971).

[13] James Parkes, *Judaism and Christianity* (Chicago: University of Chicago Press, 1948), .p. 113. D. R. A. Hare emphasizes that Jews played a very minor role in the persecution of Christians, with particular reference to persecution by the Romans ("The Relationship Between Jewish and Gentile Persecution of Christians," *Journal of Ecumenical Studies,* 4:3 (Summer, 1967), 446–456.)

[14] Isaac, *The Teaching of Contempt,* Part II.

to be destined for eternal torment. These were the judgments of such personages as Tertullian, Origen, Cyprian, and Augustine.[15]

A most important early source, and a model for similar efforts later, is the *Dialogue With Trypho* by Justin Martyr, a second-century church historian and philosopher. A more descriptive title would be *Diatribe Against Trypho*. Justin typified the attitude that Judaism was something at once comic and contemptible.[16] He turns the entire Torah into a quarry from which Christian prooftexts may be mined—thus initiating a procedure that was to become definitive in the church's exegesis. He puts into the mouth of Trypho this summary-parody of Judaism: "first be circumcised, and then observe what ordinances have been enacted for the Sabbath and the feasts, and the new moons of God, and in a word do all the things which have been written in the Law, and then, perhaps, you may obtain mercy from God." Then Trypho is made to consider what he holds valid in the Law now that the Temple has been destroyed. He answers that it remains "to keep the Sabbath, to be circumcised, to observe months, to be washed if you touch anything prohibited by Moses, and after sexual intercourse."[17]

The third-century Epistle to Diognetus, following in the tradition of Justin, is more scurrilous: The sacrifices of the Jews "are absurd . . . their scruples about the Sabbath ridiculous, their vaunting of circumcision nonsense, and their festivals folly."[18]

In the patristic literature a significant ideological strategy

[15] A. Roy Eckardt, *Christianity and the Children of Israel* (New York: King's Crown Press, 1948), p. 1.

[16] James Parkes, *The Conflict of the Church and the Synagogue: A Study in the Origins of Antisemitism* (Cleveland and New York: World Publishing Co.; Philadelphia: The Jewish Publication Society of America, 1961), pp. 70, 100.

[17] *Trypho*, pp. viii, xlvi, as cited in Parkes, *The Conflict of the Church and the Synagogue*, pp. 99–101.

[18] *Epistle to Diognetus*, pp. iii and iv, as cited in Parkes, *The Conflict of the Church and the Synagogue*, p. 101.

developed. By way of background, two considerations must be kept in mind. First, as James Parkes writes, "little by little the Church was read back into the whole of Old Testament history, and Christian history was shown to be older than Jewish history in that it dated from the creation,[19] and not from Sinai, or even Abraham. Continual references to Christ were found in the Old Testament, and it was 'the Christ of God' who 'appeared to Abraham, gave divine instructions to Isaac, and held converse with Moses and the later prophets.' "[20] The second consideration is that the church carried forward, of course, the Judaic teaching of Yahweh as at once wrathful and merciful. The outcome can be readily guessed: God's rejection is visited upon the Jews for their sin; God's acceptance encompasses the Christians for their faithfulness. Almost all Christian polemic before the Middle Ages has as its main source "the denunciations of the prophets, and the exhortations and condemnations of the Law. The Jews were made to pay dearly for the unflattering honesty of their prophets and sages. Every weakness denounced, every failure exposed, every sin castigated, was seized on with relish by Christian preachers; while every word of praise or comfort was appropriated to its own history by the Christian Church."[21]

The church historian Eusebius of Caesarea (260–340) refined this ideology further through a distinction between the term "Hebrew" and the term "Jew." The "Hebrews" are all the virtuous figures of the Old Testament. Eusebius treats them as preincarnation Christians. The "Jews" are all the evil people of the Old Testament. The gravity of Eusebius's views lay in his great influence at the very time that the church was gaining the power to enforce her denunciations of the

[19] Eusebius, *Ecclesiastical History,* I, iv.
[20] Parkes, *The Conflict of the Church and the Synagogue,* p. 100. Parkes is quoting Eusebius, *Ecclesiastical History,* Part I, p. iv.
[21] Parkes, *Judaism and Christianity,* p. 115.

Jews by means of imperial legislation.[22] Christianity, the erstwhile *religio illicita,* became a *religio licita,* and then entered into direct alliance with the Roman *imperium,* with dire consequences for the Jewish people.

Morally speaking, the lowest point of the patristic period was reached with John Chrysostom (345–407), an influential church leader at Constantinople and a celebrated orator. At Antioch in 387 Chrysostom preached a series of eight sermons that horribly reviled "the Jews." The major source of Chrysostom's anti-Jewish polemic, together with other Christian writers, was the New Testament.[23] In the following passage Chrysostom resorts both to the New Testament and to the strictures of the prophets (specifically Jeremiah):

I know that a great number of the faithful have for the Jews a certain respect and hold their ceremonies in reverence. This provokes me to eradicate completely such a disastrous opinion. I have already brought forward that the synagogue is worth no more than the theater. Here is what the prophet says, and the prophets are more to be respected than the Jews [*sic*]: "But because you have a harlot's brow, you refused to blush" (Jer. 3:3). But the place where the harlot is prostituted is the brothel. The synagogue therefore is not only a theater, it is a place of prostitution, it is a den of thieves and a hiding-place of wild animals, . . . not simply of animals, but of impure beasts. We read: "I abandon my house, cast off my heritage" (Jer. 12:7). Now if God has abandoned them, what hope of salvation have they left? They say that they too worship God; but this is not so. None of the Jews, not one of them, is a worshiper of God. It was the Son of God who told them: "If you knew the Father, you would know me also, but you know neither me nor my Father" (cf. John 8:19). Since they have disowned the Father, crucified the Son, and rejected the Spirit's help, who would dare to assert that the synagogue is not a home of demons! God is not worshiped there; it is simply a house of idolatry . . . The Jews live for their bellies,

[22] Ibid., p. 116. The relevant works of Eusebius are *Preparatio Evangelica* and *Demonstratio Evangelica.*

[23] Frederick M. Schweitzer, *A History of the Jews Since the First Century A.D.* (New York: Macmillan, 1971), p. 115.

they crave for the goods of this world. In shamelessness and greed they surpass even pigs and goats . . . The Jews are possessed by demons, they are handed over to impure spirits . . . Instead of greeting them and addressing them as much as a word, you should turn away from them as from the pest and a plague of the human race.[24]

I have alluded to the transformation of the church's political status. Christendom's most powerful weapon against the Jews became, not argument, but legislation. Again I cite James Parkes:

While most of the legislation aimed at preventing Jews from coming to any prominent position in the official, commercial or social life of the Empire, other laws definitely excluded them from certain professions and occupations, and the combined effect of what was an attack on their citizenship and their legal equality with other citizens was a blow from which Jewry has not yet recovered. For it led to the long period of ghetto life, of political impotence and social ostracism which was only partially lifted by the emancipation of the nineteenth century. Even the internal affairs of the Jewish community were the subject of legislation. Their judicial autonomy and certain tax immunities were abolished, new synagogues were forbidden to be built, the circumcision of slaves became a crime, and even the conduct of service in synagogues came under the regulations of Justinian.[25]

The very first law passed under Christian influence in the Roman Empire (Oct. 18, 315) stipulated the consigning to the flames of Jews who acted to prevent other Jews from becoming Christians and of Christians who joined the "evil sect" of Judaism.[26] If it is true that the laws against Jews were one constituent part of legislation aimed against false belief, the idea of the Christian emperors that civil peace demands religious conformity cannot be excused on the ground that this was a universal assumption of the time. For the idea was a peculiarly Christian one, without equal in either rabbinic

---

[24] John Chrysostom, *Patrologia Graeca,* vol. 48, cols. 847, 848, 852, as cited in Baum, *Is the New Testament Anti-Semitic?*, p. 18.

[25] Parkes, *Judaism and Christianity*, p. 119.

[26] Ibid., as cited.

Judaism, Roman jurisprudence, or Greek culture.[27] And the telling consequence of the tacit alliance between imperial legislation and the unique, theological denunciations of Jews and Judaism was repeated outbreaks of violence. With the disappearance of erstwhile Roman law, the Jewish people were deprived of any political or civil status. The effects of rightlessness upon the Jewish soul cannot be overstressed.[28] In the Charter of King John of France (1361) these words appear: "Jews have no country or place of their own in all Christendom where they can live and move and have their being, except by the purely voluntary permission and good-will of the lord or lords under whom they wish to settle to dwell under them as their subjects, and who are willing to receive and accept them to this end"[29]—a description that could still be applied to Jews as recently as 1947.

Hundreds of years of Christian preaching taught the populace to believe the vilest tales about Jews.[30] The massacres of the First Crusade became inevitable. For by that time the Jews were considered "part of the infidel army dwelling in the very heart of Christendom."[31] The foremost pope, Innocent III, and the foremost theologian, Thomas Aquinas, could agree with the early fathers of the church that guilt for the crucifixion demanded perpetual servitude for Jews.[32] Christian antisemitism rose in ferocity with the Black Death of the fourteenth century and then climaxed in the fanaticism of fifteenth-century Spain.[33]

Was not the Jew, after all, the chosen weapon of that instigator of all unbelief, the devil? Was not the Jew infecting and annihilating the blessed truth of the gospel? Joshua

---

[27] Ibid., p. 120.
[28] Ibid., p. 124.
[29] Ibid., cited p. 125.
[30] Ibid., p. 124.
[31] Peter Schneider, *Sweeter Than Honey* (London: SCM Press, 1966), p. 34.
[32] Eckardt, *Christianity and the Children of Israel*, p. 2.
[33] Schneider, *Sweeter Than Honey*, p. 33.

Trachtenberg's *The Devil and the Jews* fully and sadly documents the relation between the medieval notion of the demonic, antihuman Jew and modern antisemitism.[34] Charges included utilization of Christian blood in Jewish ceremonials, practice of sorcery, resort to poisoning, desecration of the host, and ritual murder. Trachtenberg comments: "The most vivid impression to be gained from a reading of medieval allusions to the Jew is of a hatred so vast and abysmal, so intense, that it leaves one gasping for comprehension. . . . [The Jew is consistently represented] as the epitome of everything evil and abominable, for whom in particular the unbounded scorn and contumely of the Christian world [are] reserved. . . ." Writing at the height of the Nazi terror, Trachtenberg concludes:

The Christian religion is in disfavor today among certain leading antisemitic circles whose consuming aim it is to destroy all Christian values; among others hatred of the Jew is preached in the name of a hypocritical and false Christianity. Whatever their attitude toward the teaching and the church of Jesus, this one offshoot of medieval Christian fanaticism, antisemitism, makes them kin. The magic of words has transmuted a pernicious medieval superstition into an even more debasing and corrosive modern superstition. Antisemitism today is 'scientific'; it would disdain to include in the contemporaneous lexicon of Jewish crime such outmoded items as satanism and sorcery. . . . [Yet] to the modern antisemite, of whatever persuasion, the . . . [Jew's] aim still is to destroy Christendom, to conquer the world and enslave it to his own . . . devilish ends.[35]

The Protestant Reformation was hardly a blessing for Jews. Martin Luther shifted his position by 180 degrees. Early on, he castigated the "papists" for maltreatment of the Jewish people. He even asked to be identified with Jews: "I hereby bid my beloved papists, if they should tire of calling me a

[34] Joshua Trachtenberg, *The Devil and the Jews: The Medieval Conception of the Jew and its Relation to Modern Anti-Semitism* (Cleveland and New York: World Publishing Company (Meridian Books), 1943; Philadelphia: Jewish Publication Society of America, 1961).

[35] Ibid., pp. 12, 219–220.

heretic to begin to revile me as a Jew." Once the church was delivered from papist errors, Jews would come to the Christian faith. But when, following upon the break with Rome, the overwhelming body of Jews showed no intention of becoming Christians, Luther turned savagely on them. He wrote, "[for 1500 years] we senseless heathen, having not been God's people, now are God's people. That makes the Jews senseless and foolish and because of it they have ceased to be God's people. . . ." What are we to do with the Jews, now that they are revealed as "obstinate, disobedient, murderers of the prophets, arrogant, usurers, and full of every vice"? Christians must, among other things, take this "rejected and damned people," set their synagogues and schools ablaze, destroy their homes, confiscate their prayer books, forbid their rabbis to teach, disallow their usury, take all their possessions, and compel them to work by the sweat of their brow as children of Adam ought to do.[36] (Note the evidence of extrabiblical influences upon Luther.)

Other Protestant reformers retained the traditional Christian position of hostility toward Jews. Thus, John Calvin asserted that the folly of the Jews "in the present age, in expecting an earthly kingdom of the Messiah, would be . . . extraordinary, had not the Scriptures long before predicted that they would thus be punished for their rejection of the gospel. For it was consistent with the righteous judgment of God to strike with blindness the minds of those, who, rejecting the light of heaven when presented to them, kept themselves in voluntary darkness. . . . Thus [the light] will remain covered and concealed to them, till they are converted to Christ, from whom they now endeavour as much as they can to withdraw and divert it."[37] Martin Bucer advocated a stern policy toward the Jewish people, including the segregation of

[36] As cited in Eckardt, *Christianity and the Children of Israel*, pp. 94–95n; Eckardt, *Elder and Younger Brothers*, p. 11n.

[37] John Calvin, *Institutes of the Christian Religion* (Philadelphia: Presbyterian Board of Christian Education, 7th American ed., 1936), vol. I, p. 488.

Jews from Christians. There is evidence that the Protestant leadership compelled Jews to attend Christian preaching services, as had their Catholic counterparts.[38]

It was a Protestant, John Andrew Eisenmenger, who in 1700 wrote *Judaism Revealed,* a notorious attack on the Talmud. In the 1880s, just at the onset of modern political antisemitism, the Lutheran Court Chaplain, Adolf Stöcker, led the German antisemitic movement from Berlin, as meantime the Catholic priest Augustus Rohling disseminated anti-Jewish propaganda in his preaching and writing. A specialty of Rohling was the accusation of ritual murder. The only surprising element in modern religious antisemitism, though not involving anything substantively new, was the successful resurrecting of the ritual murder charge among Roman Catholics and Eastern Orthodox Christians in central and eastern Europe. Between 1880 and 1945 there were as many instances of the accusation as during the entire Middle Ages. The legend "was revived because it was still of great value to nineteenth-century political antisemitism to be able to rely on an unbroken tradition of religious hostility, which could be exploited for political ends."[39]

III

In Christian Europe three alternatives were made available to Jews: conversion to Christianity, expulsion, death.

---

[38] K. S. Latourette, *A History of the Expansion of Christianity* (New York: Harper, 1939), vol. III, p. 59.

[39] Parkes, *Judaism and Christianity,* pp. 136–139. In illustration of the continuing spillover from the above kind of charge, an article published December 24, 1971 in *Al-Hawadath* (Beirut) states that "residents of the Saad and Sa'id quarters of Jerusalem near the Jewish Mea Shearim quarter prevent their children from leaving the house lest they be kidnapped by the Jews and their blood used for kneading dough for matzot." And in mid-February, 1972 the Egyptian daily *Al-Akhbar* described Passover, which is "conducted amid the letting of blood from a non-Jew." Then "they take part of the flesh of the man and mix it with matzot. The slaughter is done by the rabbi himself. . . . This is our enemy and this is his character. . . ."

Raul Hilberg writes: "The missionaries of Christianity had said in effect: You have no right to live among us as Jews. The secular rulers who followed had complained: You have no right to live among us. The German Nazis at last decreed: You have no right to live. . . . The process began with the attempt to drive the Jews into Christianity. The development was continued in order to force the victims into exile. It was finished when the Jews were driven to their deaths. The German Nazis, then, did not discard the past; they built upon it. They did not begin a development; they completed it."[40]

Professor Hilberg, in showing the many parallels between Christian canonical–legal measures and Nazi measures, includes these examples: prohibition of intermarriage and of sexual relations between Christians and Jews, Synod of Elvira, 306, and the Law for the Protection of German Blood and Honor, Sept. 15, 1935; Jews not allowed to hold public office, Synod of Clermont, 535, and the Law for the Re-establishment of the Professional Civil Service, April 7, 1933; Jews not allowed to be on the streets during Passion Week, 3d Synod of Orleans, 538, and the Decree authorizing local authorities to bar Jews from the streets on certain days, Dec. 3, 1938; the marking of Jews' clothing with a badge, 4th Lateran Council, 1215, and a parallel decree of Sept. 1, 1941; compulsory ghettos, Synod of Breslau, 1267, and the comparable order by Heydrich, Sept. 21, 1939; adoption by a Christian of the Jewish religion defined as a heresy, Synod of Mainz, 1310, and the decision placing Christians who adopt Judaism in jeopardy of being treated as Jews, June 26, 1942; Jews not permitted to obtain academic decrees, Council of Basel, 1434, and the Law Against Overcrowding of German Schools and Universities, April 25, 1933.[41]

The Christian church is marked by a twin affliction: the authority of a New Testament containing antisemitic elements,

[40] Raul Hilberg, *The Destruction of the European Jews* (Chicago: Quadrangle, 1961), pp. 3–4.
[41] Ibid., pp. 5–6.

and a long and dreary postbiblical heritage. Each of these reinforces the other, and each finds ready exemplification in our own time. Ellen Flesseman-Van Leer thus sums up the outlook respecting Jews on the part of theologians within the Faith Movement of German Christians: ". . . Are they not the people who crucified Jesus . . . and [who] still place themselves in the fiercest opposition to Him? Therefore God hates them and all good Christians must hate them too, and therefore the anti-Semitic laws, and even persecutions are perfectly all right, a work pleasing in the sight of God."[42] When the first Nazi measures against Jews were instituted, the propagandist Julius Streicher could malevolently identify what was happening as Jewish punishment for Golgotha. Hermann Diem, a Christian opponent of the crimes, attests that the sentiment, "His blood be on us and our children," created confusion among his fellow-Christians in Germany. "For it was with precisely the same watchword that the church in her whole history . . . had not only explained and justified but also sponsored the hatred of Jews. . . . The seed that we ourselves had sown had sprung up, and we stood disconcerted before its terrible fruits."[43]

Julius Streicher could tell the tribunal at Nürnberg that Martin Luther ought to have been standing in his place as the accused, for he, Streicher, was merely putting into effect Luther's counsel respecting the Jews.[44] Many theologians of the German Christian Movement "justified the right to racial discriminations within the Christian Church by recalling Luther's polemic against the Jews."[45] When, in April of 1933, two bishops raised with Adolf Hitler the issue of his policy toward Jews, he promised them that he would do to the Jews what Christian preaching and teaching had been saying for

---

[42] As cited in Eckardt, *Christianity and the Children of Israel,* p. 101.

[43] As cited in Eckardt, *Elder and Younger Brothers,* p. 11.

[44] Ibid.

[45] Paul B. Means, *Things That Are Caesar's* (New York: Round Table Press, 1935), p. 196. An example of such utilization of Luther is Erich Vogelsang.

almost two thousand years.[46] Right up to his death Hitler was able to enjoy the support of responsible leaders of both the Catholic and the Evangelical churches.[47] Hitler could die a Catholic in good standing—i.e., the Church did not act to excommunicate him[48]—as Hermann Göring could die an Evangelical.

We all know that Nazism was a resolute and demonic foe of the Christian ethic of love. As Jacob Bernard Agus writes, "the bitterly anti-Christian animus of the Nazi ideology is clear and indisputable."[49] This fact does not, alas, negate the truth that the soil for the persecutions of Jews had been fatefully prepared by centuries of "the teaching of contempt."

In his famous Advent sermons in Munich, Michael Cardinal von Faulhaber could say that "after the death of Christ, Israel was dismissed from the service of Revelation. She had not known the time of her visitation. She had repudiated and rejected the Lord's Anointed, had driven Him out of the city and nailed Him to the Cross. Then the veil of the Temple was rent, and with it the covenant between the Lord and His people. The daughter of Zion received the bill of divorce, and from that time forth Assuerus wanders, forever restless, over the face of the earth." When the World Jewish Congress sought to thank the Cardinal for his sermons—they do contain judgments against Nazism—he indignantly declined the gesture, for he had no desire to speak in defense of present-day Judaism.[50] These sermons remind us that it was not only the Faith Movement of German Christians that called re-

---

[46] Schweitzer, *A History of the Jews,* p. 222.

[47] Heer, *God's First Love,* p. 296.

[48] Ibid., p. 311. Hitler's writings were never placed on the Index.

[49] Jacob Bernard Agus, *Dialogue and Tradition: The Challenge of Contemporary Judeo-Christian Thought* (New York: Abelard-Schuman, 1971), p. 275.

[50] As cited in a paper by Charlotte Klein, "The Theological Dimensions of the State of Israel" (unpublished), presented before the Theological Consultation, "Toward A Theology of Israel," Seton Hall University, Oct. 25–28, 1970.

peated attention to the (alleged) Jewish rejection of Christ;[51] they serve also to remind us of the tragedy of the Christian resistance movement in Europe in the 1930s and 1940s. The tragedy lay in the double burden the movement was forced to bear: fighting against Nazi teachings and policies while also struggling against many of the church's own teachings and policies.

The indictment may be summarized with aid from Friedrich Heer's massive documentation: Behind the Christian world's callous indifference to the fate of Jews in the twentieth century lies an acquiescence that Christians have sought "to conceal from their own conscience." It was this very indifference and tacit approval that enabled Hitler to turn Europe into a Jewish graveyard. The roots of the Christian world's failure to oppose Nazi policies lay in its own ambivalence toward the Jewish people. The Christian theologians had "proved" Jewish guilt a thousand times. The helpers and sympathizers of Hitler were everywhere, but especially in the churches. Both actively and passively, Christians assisted in the extermination of Jews. In the 1940s the Church of Rome was to prove incapable, *intellectually and spiritually,* of keeping even the Jews of the City of Rome from the murderers' hands. "As in the sixteenth and seventeenth centuries, the principal country in Europe to give shelter to the Jews was Islamic Turkey." The United States refused to relax its immigration laws. Such happenings as the abortive Bermuda Refugee Conference in the spring of 1943 served to strengthen Hitler's persuasion that the world really did not care what happened to "the Jews," and to fortify his resolve to liquidate them.[52]

While the present part of our exposition does not extend beyond the Holocaust, we may cite one episode from after the War, by way of a reminder that the denigration of Jews hardly ceased with the Holocaust, and that the continuity of

---

[51] Cf. Eckardt, *Christianity and the Children of Israel,* p. 100.
[52] Heer, *God's First Love,* pp. 171, 321, 324, 341, 361.

the Christian antisemitic tradition was not abrogated by the death camps. Richard Crossman provides the following report of his interview with the Bishop of Vienna and a certain Jesuit in 1946:

The bishop began by stating that the Church did not fight the Jews but only the Jewish spirit of materialism. [Article 24 of the NSDAP platform said; "The party . . . fights the spirit of Jewish materialism. . . ."] The solution of the Jewish problem was the conversion of the Jews to the true faith. That was the task of his Jesuit colleague.

The Jesuit took up the story. In a cold monotone he pointed out that the chief cause of anti-Semitism in the view of the Church was the behavior of the Jewish community and he went on to tell in great circumstantial detail how the officials of the Jewish community in Vienna had collaborated with the Gestapo. . . .

I turned to the old bishop . . . and asked him whether there was a future for the Jews in Austria. "Of course we don't actually want to drive them out," he said. "That would be unchristian."[53]

It is true that the Bishop and his Jesuit friend were not coveting the "racial purity" that the "German Christians" sought. Yet we have to wonder what the honest attitude of these two men would be toward such Jews as they might convert—not to mention toward Jews refusing conversion. It must be remembered, in any event, that since 1945 antisemitic acts and pronouncements have been legion in lands "whose way of life has been formed by Christian principles."[54]

Lamentably, it is only with fairly recent historiography that the centuries-long and traditional Christian maltreatment of Jews has been granted the attention it requires. Such "liberal Christian" historians as Kenneth Scott Latourette managed almost totally to avoid the truth.[55] Now, thankfully, we have the formidable work of Alan T. Davies, Willehad P. Eckert, Edward H. Flannery, Eva Fleischner, Franklin H. Lit-

---

[53] Richard Crossman, *Palestine Mission: A Personal Record* (New York: Harper, 1947), p. 93.

[54] Heer, *God's First Love*, p. 3.

[55] Cf. Kenneth Scott Latourette, *A History of Christianity*, (New York: Harper, 1953).

tell, John M. Oesterreicher, James Parkes, John T. Pawlikow-
ski, Frederick M. Schweitzer, Karl Thieme, and other Christian scholars. But, of course, these efforts have come only
subsequent to Christendom's long historical preparation for
the Holocaust of the Jews. The Nazis simply gave practical
application to the theological and moral findings of the church,
with the aid of a technology not previously available to
Christendom.

3

On History's Greatest
Perversion of Justice

The question of responsibility for the trial and death of Jesus, an issue that has already engaged us in the context of Christian antisemitism, requires separate and careful attention. It is one thing to say that Jews do not "accept" Jesus as the Christ; it is infinitely more serious to assert that they killed the Son of God.

I

According to traditional Christian ideological literature —sometimes hostile to historical truth, sometimes indifferent to it, sometimes ignorant of it—the singular culprits behind the trial and death of Jesus of Nazareth were indeed "the Jews." The writer of Mark, (probably) the earliest Gospel, "already damned the Jews unreservedly with responsibility for Jesus' death. . . ."[1] Pontius Pilate became wholly "innocent of the blood of this righteous man" (Matt. 27:25), while the Jewish people reportedly called down Jesus' blood upon themselves and their children. Mr. Justice Haim Cohn refers to

[1] Haim Cohn, *The Trial and Death of Jesus* (New York: Harper & Row, 1971), p. 261. Copyright © 1971 by Haim Cohn. Quotations in this chapter reprinted by permission of the publisher.

the Matthean tradition of an eternal curse laid on the Jewish people for their guilt: "It was the Jewish self-arraignment invented by Matthew that became the theological, or pseudo-theological, basis of never-ending persecution and tyranny."[2]

The beginnings of a change in the above allegations were made possible by an elementary historical-critical finding to which we made reference in Chapter 2: In successive chronological levels of the New Testament itself, blame for the apprehension and crucifixion of Jesus is increasingly shifted from the Roman *imperium* to the Jewish leaders and people. In accordance with this finding, a number of church representatives and Christian scholars came to concede joint responsibility for Jesus' trial and death. The Jews of the time were party to the affair, but Roman complicity was present as well and was, indeed, the decisive factor. Furthermore, the conception of collective guilt was repudiated, while in some Christian circles the Jewish "denial" of Christ even gained a kind of moral sanction as representing God's utilization of human acts in the salvation of the world (cf. Rom. 11).

In the development of modern historiography one step remained: the judgment that the Jewish people of the day had nothing whatever to do with Jesus' fate. Thus, in Haim Cohn's formidable work, *The Trial and Death of Jesus,* the *reductio ad absurdum* of any and all Jewish responsibility for the trial and death of Jesus is consummated, and upon a solid historico-jurisprudential foundation. This conclusion extends as well to the imputation of coresponsibility. The Jews were, in a word, "wholly innocent."[3]

---

[2] Ibid., p. 275; cf. pp. 262, 321. Cohn is a justice in the Supreme Court of Israel. As he points out, in truth Pontius Pilate would never have declared his innocence to a Jewish crowd, while the crowd's "acceptance" of responsibility would not only have comprised an act of effrontery to Rome bordering upon criminal contempt, but would have "amounted to a presumption of judicial authority, as if the crowd knew better than any judge, and an imperial one at that, where innocence lay and where guilt (ibid., p. 270).

[3] Ibid., p. 328. As Cohn makes clear in his introduction, the data before us ought long since "have put conscientious legal observers on the

Using Cohn's argumentation, let us pursue the matter of culpability for Jesus' death.

II

The great challenge is how to arrive at reliable findings from pervasively unreliable reports. Haim Cohn simply grasps the nettle, in the way of an honest historian. It is evident, for one thing, that no accurate account of either Jewish or Roman law is obtainable through the Gospel reports. Further, "the potential unauthenticity and the manifest inconsistency" of those reports must "give the legal historian cause and justification to reject narratives which cannot be supported by law or reason, and accept only what is reasonable or corroborated by legal customs and practices of the time." Nevertheless, Cohn argues forcefully that the events are subject to reconstruction. Clearly, the all-determining element must be our independent knowledge of the entire historical epoch involved. We must keep at the fore the truth that the evangelists, writing a generation and more after the occurrences, portrayed the Jewish leaders and people not on the basis of the facts of the time, but as a result of rabbinical hostility toward them *in their own day*.[4] In actuality, Cohn's assumptions in regard to New Testament documents are, in places, quite circumspect and conservative. Note his readiness to entertain prima facie validity concerning a given tradition, provided that it is put forward by all four Gospel writers. Another test is "objective reasonableness," the consideration that the reported events

---

alert, rather than dazzle them, with the rest of Christianity, into a belief that no legal argument could shake." Lamentably, that belief remains so strong that "the largest concession which even the great liberals among the hierarchy of the Catholic Church would nowadays be prepared to make would be to absolve the Jewish people as a whole, and the Jews of later generations, from a guilt which—they hold—attaches irrevocably to the Jews whom the Gospels accuse of an active part in the trial" (ibid., pp. xi–xii).

4 Ibid., pp. xiii, xviii, 138.

"could indeed, in the given and known circumstances, have happened in the way and the setting described."[5] Although Cohn is quick to acknowledge that mere conceivability cannot guarantee that a reputed event actually took place, he interposes an all-important distinction:

We are concerned not so much with the historicity of the events as with the evidentiary worth of the tradition. Once accepted as potentially valid testimony, each tradition will be the starting point from which the further inquiry may proceed, the nucleus around which the potentially true story will have to be retold. For example, that Jesus was arrested, if accepted as a practically uncontested starting point, will at once invite the questions by whom, on whose orders, and for what purpose. . . . If we start from the premise that the reports are biased and tendentious, it is only by testing every detail against the background of conditions of life at the time, including laws and customs as we know them from independent sources, that we may succeed in winnowing the reliable from the uncertain, the acceptable from the inadmissible.[6]

There is, in addition, the principle commended by historians that when an apologist for a given viewpoint chronicles as a fact something that damages his own case, we may presume authenticity at that particular point (cf. the admission in the indiscriminately anti-Jewish Gospel of John that a Roman cohort was involved in Jesus' arrest[7]). Much of Cohn's strength lies in his quite consistent refusal to argue from an absence of evidence and in his avoidance of question-begging. As a matter of fact, he succeeds in applying seemingly weighty concessions to the very building of his case—e.g., Jews *did* have an active part in the arrest of Jesus; the Great Sanhedrin *did* meet and the high priest Kaiaphas presided; the Sanhedrin *did* retain all the capital jurisdiction it had ever possessed under Jewish law; and, contrary to the total falsehood of John 18:31, the Jewish authorities *could* lawfully put people to death. The Great Sanhedrin would have

---

[5] Ibid., p. xix.
[6] Ibid., pp. xxi, xxii–xxiii.
[7] Ibid., p. 78; see also p. 231.

assembled as the council in charge of political affairs. "It was not just a Small Sanhedrin, which could have exercised jurisdiction in a criminal or capital case, but the Great Sanhedrin, which would not exercise such jurisdiction at all even if possibly competent to, if only for the reason that it was much too much taken up at the time with current and pressing political issues."[8]

In order to exemplify and to make more concrete Cohn's argument, let us concentrate upon the meeting of the Great Sanhedrin.[9] No issue is more critical than the Sanhedrin's action, from the standpoint of both truth and morality. For, as Cohn reminds us, the early Christian apostles could not have invented a better or more damaging weapon "than the slander of responsibility for the crucifixion"[10] as a means of undermining sanhedrial authority and of making people detest the Sanhedrin as well as all established authority (as opposed to the new authority of Christian faith).

What had happened to make the high priest insist that Jesus be brought to his palace in the middle of that memorable night? And why did the chief priests, elders, scribes, and all the council assemble there?

Cohn affirms that neither the character nor the prestige of the high priest was at stake, but, instead, the Sanhedrin itself, which "spoke for all sections and factions of the Jewish people. . . ." Hence, in allowing that this representative body did meet—and on its own initiative and for its own purposes—"we assume the burden of an 'admission against interest,' because we follow the evangelists in involving the Jews and Jewish authorities as a whole. . . ." At the same time, "it is inconceivable that a Jew would be delivered by a Jewish court to the Roman enemy for either trial or execution, whatever his crime," for this would have meant a confession of "inability or incompetence to maintain law and

---

[8] Ibid., pp. 24, 25, 26, 31, 32–33, 72, 95, 96.
[9] Ibid., chap. 5.
[10] Ibid., pp. 246–247.

order among the Jews." Indeed, the very idea that Jesus was given a "Jewish trial" on a charge of blasphemy, that he was convicted upon his own confession, and that he then received a capital sentence is entirely out of the question upon no less then seven well-established provisions of Jewish law.[11] For that matter, the Great Sanhedrin did not come together in order to conduct some kind of "preliminary investigation" of Jesus. Yet something extraordinary demanded that the body meet in emergency session. What was this? Just one answer is possible. There was only one thing that vitally concerned the entire Jewish leadership: how "to prevent the crucifixion of a Jew by the Romans, and, more particularly, of a Jew who enjoyed the love and affection of the people."[12]

It must be quickly stated that the above conclusion does not require any idealizing of motives. Realistic, political factors were very much at stake. The prime condition for the Sanhedrin's survival and effectiveness was that it retain the people's confidence and allegiance.[13] Any

considerations which may have prompted the leaders to get rid of a man of progressive and reformist aspirations and independent thinking, and a worker of miracles, such as Jesus was, were far transcended by their conviction . . . that any attempt at interference with Jesus would at once cause a "public uproar" (Mark 14:2). But the stage of such a conflict of motives would never actually be reached, as no individual success, no particular doctrine, and no religious or political aspirations could have any relevance as against the paramount necessity for the Jewish leadership to win and keep popular support. . . .

. . . It was not the personality of Jesus that would inspire his advocates as well as his adversaries to take their stand: if it was his personality, or the merit of his doctrines, that was an issue, the Sanhedrin might have been divided. But it was unanimous, because not the personal fate of Jesus, or the merit of his doctrines was at stake, but the standing and popularity of the Sanhedrin. . . .

[11] Ibid., pp. 95–96, 97–98, 105, 112, 116. On the impossible possibility of blasphemy, see especially ibid., pp. 53, 101, 102, 130, 131; and on the alleged "Son of Man" declaration, cf. p. 129.
[12] Ibid., pp. 106, 109, 110, 112, 114.
[13] Ibid., pp. 114, 115.

[The trial and crucifixion of Jesus would be] an outrage which the people would surely not suffer quietly; and it was essential that the leaders should be able to come forward and satisfy the people that they not only had no hand or part in the proceedings but, on the contrary, had done everything in their power to avert the tragedy.[14]

It is within the foregoing context that the "witnesses" before the Sanhedrin must be judged.[15] The same is the case with the critical question of why the high priest—and he, alone—rent his garments. The

Jewish leadership could not be expected to vouch for Jesus before the Roman governor unless he were ready and willing at least to bow to its authority and assure it of his loyalty.

. . . If the high priest rent his garments that night, it was because of his grief not to be able to make Jesus see his point, his anguish that Jesus ostensibly refused to cooperate and was moving stubbornly toward his disastrous fate, and, not least, that Roman oppression would claim another Jewish victim. . . . [Jesus'] declaration before the Sanhedrin that he was the Messiah (the "Christ"), while it was not a criminal offense, amounted to a rejection by Jesus of the offer made to him by the high priest and the Jewish leadership: cooperation between them would be possible only if they would accept his assertion and recognize his claim. This, of course, they could not and would not do, not only because they did not believe in him, and would have regarded their submission to his authority as a dereliction of duty and a transgression of law, but also because sanhedrial recognition of the messianic pretensions of Jesus would surely have meant, in the eyes of the people as well as of Pilate, a confirmation of the very charges of which Jesus stood accused before the Roman authorities. . . .

[And the Sanhedrin] all knew that he would be found guilty and sentenced to die—by virtue not of any sentence or judgment of theirs, but of what that governor would pronounce against him. The outcry, "He must die," was the natural and spontaneous reflex to the words which Jesus had spoken, sealing, as they did, his fate in the coming trial, from whose upshot there seemed no longer any possibility of rescuing him.[16]

[14] Ibid., pp. 116, 117–118.
[15] Ibid., see pp. 120–125.
[16] Ibid., pp. 125, 133–134, 137.

Cohn's exposition hardly surmounts every problem. Thus, the acceptance as a fact of Jesus' alleged messianic claim[17] has been severely questioned within New Testament scholarship itself. Behind this specific debate looms, of course, the whole mountain of controversy over the degree to which definitive agreement can ever be reached on the historicity or nonhistoricity of various New Testament passages. For all Cohn's immense contribution to our knowledge and understanding, and for all the elementary truth in the observation that Jesus "was sentenced solely because of the stand which he himself had chosen to adopt in his trial before Pilate,"[18] Jesus' behavior and point of view remain something of a mystery. It scarcely needs to be observed that our judgments respecting the events of Jesus' trial and death, and the motivations therein involved, cannot be separated from our interpretation of his own stance and intentions. We continue to be met by the importunate query: Why did the prophet of Nazareth go to his death—especially since he could probably have avoided that outcome?[19] However, it must be emphasized that this question and the differing answers to it are ultimately irrelevant to the assessment of Haim Cohn's specific argumentation. For the substance of Cohn's case is not at all contingent upon Jesus' point of view or actions. On the contrary, that case is amenable to all kinds of possible outlooks and decisions on Jesus' part. Cohn rightly concentrates upon the position of the Jewish authorities, for this is the only legitimate way to deal with the issue of Jewish responsibility. And the concern of the Jewish authorities lay with Jesus the Jew and the man, together with their own needs and interests; it did not lie with what Jesus may have taught or with how he may have wished to behave. For that matter, Cohn's (questionable) attestation that Jesus was "the best-loved and most popular of Jews"[20] is not a salient datum.

[17] Ibid., pp. 125–126.
[18] Ibid., p. 329.
[19] Ibid., see pp. 175, 185.
[20] Ibid., p. 116.

In the end, the very force and importance of Cohn's work are due to his fully allowing for differences between Jesus and his countrymen's leadership without falling into the gratuitous conclusion that some kind of religious or politico-religious rift thereby developed between them. As events turned out, the only real dispute was over Jesus' deliverance from or subjection to a Roman fate. The traditional Christian polemic fabricates Jewish culpability for that subjection. But Haim Cohn shows that the Jewish leaders must have wanted only Jesus' deliverance.

III

We continue to be subjected, nonetheless, to the portentous question of whether such scholarly achievements and lessons as Haim Cohn's will exert any real influence upon a Christian world religiously and emotionally conditioned to believe otherwise. I refer again to the persisting sway of Christian ideology: the subjecting of ideas and doctrines to the service of collective self-interest and to the propagating of a given point of view. The exasperating fact is that the only Christians who will be convinced by Cohn's and kindred demonstrations are the convincible, and these remain a relatively small and, more or less, hapless and unconvincing minority. The one long-range moral remedy is explicit Christian renunciation of New Testament falsehoods, their categorization as enemy of God's truth—although, as pointed out in Chapter 2, we may hardly have illusions about this eventuality. Yet the truth remains that the historical structure of Christianity is erected upon a Big Lie: "the Jews' " rejection and murder of Jesus Christ. Repeat a lie enough times and it becomes "the truth." The brainwashing has been so unrelenting and pervasive that even the nonbelievers among us readily accept the tale. And as long as the Lie is sustained, Christendom prepares the way for new persecutions.

In the course of a group meeting in Jerusalem not long ago, a church representative objected to me that Haim Cohn is, after all, a Jew and would "naturally" strive to "exonerate" his people. I found myself replying that an ad hominem judgment can scarcely qualify as a mature or valid answer to a work of scholarship. I continue to be disturbed by the episode. For behind the man's protest lay an insinuation that a necessary disjunction obtains between the truth and Mr. Justice Cohn's identity as a Jew. (I could of course have responded, and ought to have done so, that Cohn's conclusions are paralleled in the latest and most responsible Christian New Testament scholarship.[21])

The real issue is whether the dissemination of historical fact has any real power to overcome the sins and dispel the stereotypes of old. A research study sponsored by the Anti-Defamation League adjudges that in the United States today lack of education is the primary cause of continued antisemitism (although the analysts strive to counteract simplistic applications of this finding, in particular the notion that education is a cure-all).[22] A formidable difficulty here is that unnumbered purveyors of those elements of the New Testament tradition that are hostile to Jews and Judaism are anything but uneducated men. One major nemesis of Christianity is its utilization of educational resources themselves to propagate a normative Scripture that, in fundamental respects, helps compound man's inhumanity to man. The stumbling block comes when countless contemporary Christians, including scholars, are brought to a necessary choice between two conflicting criteria of validity—the literal claims of Christian Scripture and objective historical knowledge—they often subject the second to the first. As the "Word of God," the New Testament stands as the final judge of historicity. This is why we must conclude that any resolution of the Christian predicament must transcend mere "education." Or if that term is

---

[21] See, e.g., Joseph B. Tyson, *A Study of Early Christianity* (New York: Macmillan, 1973), pp. 373–380.

[22] Gertrude J. Selznick and Stephen Steinberg, *The Tenacity of Prejudice: Anti-Semitism in Contemporary America* (New York: Harper Torchbooks, 1969), pp. 184–193.

retained, we must speak of the "education" of the heart: a radical moral, social, and political transformation of Christendom. The church will have to be converted. Christians will have to be born again.

It is sad to note that in a year as late as 1972 the respected Christian quarterly *Theology Today* should have seen fit to represent as fact the fabrication of a "Jewish trial" of Jesus. Two contributors make precisely that charge: a Catholic theologian, Thomas F. O'Meara, and a Protestant jurist, James E. Wallace, the latter of whom is, of all things, Executive Officer of the Law and Society Association.[23] O'Meara portrays the Sanhedrin as "convinced *a priori*" that Jesus was "religiously and politically dangerous." He has Jesus convicted for dissent against the Roman Empire, and "capitally executed" by both "temple and state," two establishments "which had sold out to each other." Again, O'Meara writes: "A number of . . . (mainly Jewish) scholars argue that the trial before the Jewish council" was a fabrication. The words in parenthesis appear rather revealing. Just what is their function? What motivation lies behind their inclusion?

Suppose that the facts of Jewish law were now to be explained to these interpreters. Would they be willing to abandon or modify their argument? Perhaps. But perhaps not. It is noteworthy that O'Meara should reproduce an essential, traditional stereotype: "The Law of Pentateuch is fulfilled by a New Law. . . . Organizations 'of the kingdom' are to live now not by forced control [*sic*] but as service. Could man be superior to the laws of his religion?" And then O'Meara repeats the ancient slander: Motivated by "Jesus' attacks on temple and priesthood as absolutes," and confronted by Jesus' demand "that religious leaders be subject to the deepest imperatives of a truly human ethic," the Sanhedrin turned him over to Pilate for execution.

[23] Thomas F. O'Meara, "The Trial of Jesus in An Age of Trials," *Theology Today*, 28:4 (January, 1972), 451–465; James E. Wallace, "The Trial of Jesus: A Legal Response," ibid., 466–469.

Is there really any way to bring to an end the absurdities of Christian apologists who are constitutionally committed to driving a wedge between Jesus and "the Jews"? It is as if hundreds of years of critical scholarship had never been. Are such spokesmen as O'Meara and Wallace eligible for reeducation? In principle, the answer will turn upon which motivation wins: the honoring of truth or the retaining of an ideology that must insist upon Jewish blameworthiness for Jesus' apprehension and death.

Anton Preisinger, director of the Oberammergau Passion Play, has sought to defend a refusal to engage in any substantive alteration of the play's traditional text by asserting: "We cannot change what the Bible says. At times it does use hard words about the Jews."[24] Here is the Christian predicament in a nutshell. On the one hand, Preisinger is quite correct in his (unintended) identification of the New Testament as the actual culprit. On the other hand, he completely obscures the real issue, which is bound ineluctably to the very decision to stage a "passion play" based upon the New Testament: How can the Christian community agree to serve as an accomplice in the recapitulating of the most terrible prevarication history has ever witnessed? How, indeed, can the Christian churches in all conscience reenact the "events" of "Passion Week" year after year? It does not help in the slightest to attribute relative innocence to the New Testament reporters through pointing out, for example, that in desiring to propagate their faith, they were simply trying to make friends with the Romans. Nor does it help to point out that the evangelists would never have dreamed of or condoned the unspeakable sufferings their fictitious accounts were going to make possible. As Haim Cohn writes, "perversion of truth in a trial report has this in common with judicial murder, that just as perverted justice, even if eventually redressed, cannot bring a hanged convict to life again, so perverted truth, how-

[24] As reported in *Newsweek,* June 1, 1970.

ever it be corrected afterward, cannot give breath a second time to the multitudes murdered on the grim strength of it."[25]

IV

True religion can never be grounded upon false history. On its part, the Jewish conscience has ever remained steadfastly clear of everything connected with the trial and death of Jesus. However grievously and often Jews have been reminded of their reputed guilt as "deicides," their own self-judgment has remained unassailable.[26] The closing words of *The Trial and Death of Jesus* stand, therefore, as an incarnation of divine judgment. (Divinity is born, I suggest, at the meeting place of righteousness and historical truth.)

Hundreds of generations of Jews, throughout the Christian world, have been indiscriminately mulcted for a crime which neither they nor their ancestors committed. Worse still, they have for centuries, for millennia, been made to suffer all manner of torment, persecution, and degradation for the alleged part of their forefathers in the trial and crucifixion of Jesus, when, in solemn truth, their forefathers took no part in them but did all that they possibly and humanly could to save Jesus . . . from his tragic end at the hands of the Roman oppressor. If there can be found a grain of consolation for this perversion of justice, it is in the words of Jesus himself: "Blessed are they which are persecuted for righteousness' sake: for theirs is the kingdom of heaven. Blessed are ye, when men shall revile you, and persecute you, and shall say all manner of evil against you falsely, for my sake. Rejoice, and be exceeding glad: for great is your reward in heaven" (Matt. 5:10–12).[27]

It is fitting that the work we have reviewed by a contemporary Israeli scholar should conclude with a citation from his fellow-countryman, the prophet of Nazareth, central figure in our drama. For thus is history's greatest perversion of justice sent to perdition, in a way that is at once authentically Jewish and authentically Christian.

[25] Cohn, *The Trial and Death of Jesus*, p. 329.
[26] Ibid., p. 320.
[27] Ibid., p. 331.

4

The Catholic Predicament

As late as 1961 Hans-Joachim Schoeps in *The Jewish–Christian Argument* could honor the twentieth century as the epoch in which "true dialogue" and genuine understanding between Christians and Jews had at last become possible.[1] Professor Schoeps was incapable of anticipating the two sentences of abortion that would be passed shortly thereafter upon the expected birth—the first in 1965 at Vatican Council II and the second in the summer of 1967.[2]

I

The drama of Vatican II began with an episode of hope; indeed, only through certain ostensibly sanguine preliminary

[1] Hans-Joachim Schoeps, *The Jewish–Christian Argument: A History of Theologies in Conflict* (New York: Holt, Rinehart and Winston, 1963), pp. 124ff.

[2] On the second of these developments, see chap. 10 of this book. Among the sources utilized in the ensuing section of the present chapter are: "A Vote Against Prejudice," *Time,* Oct. 22, 1965; "The Vatican's Dilemma," editorial, *The Christian Century,* 82:27 (July 7, 1965), 859–860; "The Anger of the Arabs," *Herder Correspondence,* 2:3 (March, 1965), 80–81; "Religion: Vatican Reaches a Consensus," *The New York Times,* Oct. 17, 1965; "The Papacy: Reluctant Revolutionary," *Time,* Sept. 24, 1965; "Final Approval of Text on Jews Given by Council," *The New York Times,* Oct. 16, 1965; endorsed text of the "Declaration on the Relationship of ·the Church to Non-Christian Religions," and "Decree Reflects Jews' Long Woes," *The New York Times,* Oct. 29, 1965.

events and pronouncements could the ensuing failure have become possible. Saintly Pope John XXIII conveyed the hope. In his view the Jewish people live at the very root of Christian salvation. And it was he who supported an initial brief, forthright text abrogating the ancient Christian charge of "deicide" against the Jews. Very soon, however, the venture deteriorated. The draft prepared for presentation to the Council's second session by Augustin Cardinal Bea, head of the Secretariat for the Promotion of Christian Unity, was withdrawn under pressure from the Vatican Secretariat of State and from bishops in Arab countries. Between the second and third sessions, conservative prelates brought forward an alternative draft which at once palliated the references to Judaism and set the Council on its fatal course. The section on the Jewish people was subsumed under a longer declaration recounting the church's attitude toward "non-Christian religions"—including, of course, Islam.

This draft was castigated bitterly by many liberal bishops. A later draft seemed to provide ground for optimism. It included the words "never should the Jewish people be represented as reprobate people, or cast out as guilty of deicide." Yet, decisively, even this new chapter lay confined within the larger framework of attitudes toward "non-Christian religions." On November 20, 1964, the chapter received an approving vote of 1,770 to 183. It was assumed at the time that the Declaration would go through the usual channels, be emended at minor points (in keeping with suggestions of those supporting it), be given final approval by the Secretariat for the Promotion of Christian Unity, and be voted routinely and without delaying debate at the fourth session. In point of fact, the process of dissolution already evident was carried even further. To the conservative minority any denial of the "deicide" charge meant an equal denial of the Gospel accounts of Jesus' passion.

In the meantime, Catholic and non-Catholic bishops in Arab countries gave moral support to Arab diplomats who were putting added pressure against the new Declaration on the grounds that it allegedly fostered propaganda for the State of Israel and thereby inspired anti-Christian reprisals by Muslim governments. The council of the Greek Orthodox community in Damascus issued a manifesto condemning "the decision taken by the Vatican Council to declare the Jews innocent of the blood of Christ, because it is contrary to the sacred Scriptures in which Christians have always believed." The Jacobite Patriarch Ignatius III Yacub, quoting the apostle Peter's words blaming the Jews for the death of Christ, expressed amazement that the one who identifies himself as Peter's successor could take an opposite position, and then concluded: "It is a dogma of the church that the guilt of the crucifixion of Christ must fall upon the Jewish people until the end of the world." Political officials, Arab Christians (Catholic and Orthodox), and state-controlled radio and press services joined the chorus, along with frequenters of Muslim mosques and bazaars. Hundreds of protesting telegrams were sent by Catholic faithful to the pope and to their bishops. A number of Christian communities in Jordan, at the urging of the Muslim mayor of Jerusalem, agreed to a ten-minute tolling of their church bells as a protest against the Council's anticipated endorsement of "the Jewish declaration."

In direct opposition to the wording overwhelmingly approved in 1964, Pope Paul intervened, just before the ensuing and final session began, in behalf of excising the "deicide" reference. *The New York Times* reported that the excision was a response to the claim of some that the church would be implying that it no longer believed in the divinity of Christ. Now, in place of the relevant words from the approved draft of 1964, was the statement that "the Jews should not be presented as rejected by God or accursed, as if this followed from the Holy Scriptures." A *Time* commentator dryly observed that "in compensation, the final draft included the first specific mention of anti-Semitism." (As a matter of fact, the draft of 1964 *deplored and condemned* "hatred and persecution against the Jews"; the replacement draft *decried* "hatred, persecutions, displays of anti-Semitism. . . .")

The final Declaration on "non-Christian religions" was approved October 15, 1965, by a vote of 1,763 to 250, and promulgated October 28, with a formal approving vote of 2,221 to 88. The Declaration states that "what happened [to Christ] in His Passion cannot be charged against all the Jews, without distinction, then alive, nor against the Jews of today." Yet, predictably enough, the final Declaration contends that "Jerusalem did not recognize the time of her visitation, nor did the Jews, in large number, accept the Gospel; indeed, not a few opposed its spreading." And allusion is made to "Jewish authorities" who, with their followers, pressed for Jesus' death. It is affirmed that "Christ underwent His Passion and death freely, because of the sins of men and out of infinite love," but immediately added are the words, "in order that all may reach salvation." In fact, at the very climax of the Declaration lies the claim that the cross of Christ is "the fountain from which every grace flows."

This fourth and final document is, of course, the one that constitutes the authoritative and official teaching of the Catholic Church.[3]

II

The bitter struggle extending over the entire life of the Council had issued in compromise. Compromise is, to be

[3] A curious distortion of the record of Vatican II has been circulating: the false claim that the Council retained the erstwhile denunciation of the charge of deicide. Two examples of this error include: Charles D. Ward's allusion to "the Council's disavowal of deicide" ["Anti-Semitism at College: Changes Since Vatican II," *Journal for the Scientific Study of Religion,* 12:1 (March, 1973), 88]. And, in an obituary of Jacques Maritain in *The New York Times* (April 29, 1973), the writer's reference to Maritain as a spokesman "for those who succeeded, at Vatican II, in exculpating the Jews from the age-old charge of deicide." For the actual and complete text of the Declaration on the Relationship of the Church to Non-Christian Religions (Nostra Aetate), see W. M. Abbott, ed., *The Documents of Vatican II* (New York: Guild Press—America Press—Association Press, 1966), pp. 660–668.

sure, not total defeat. Five years' effort could hardly repair the damage of nineteen centuries. Several important passages survived the campaign against Cardinal Bea and the liberal majority: The Council remembered "the bond that spiritually ties the people of the New Covenant to Abraham's stock," the church could not "forget that she draws sustenance from the root of that well-cultivated olive tree onto which have been grafted the wild shoots, the Gentiles," etc. Yet the truth remains that the compromise was an enforced one, a failure of nerve, a triumph of minority dictation. An appropriate, revealing judgment came from a Roman Catholic, John Cogley, who was at the time religion editor of *The New York Times*: The never-ending controversy over the Jewish statement in the Council served to blunt its intended effect. The statement was meant to foster love and friendship. But it soon became a source of bitterness and disappointment, "a reason for shame and anguish on the part of many Catholics and of suspicion and rancor on the part of many Jews."[4]

How could the Roman Catholic Church ever have maneuvered herself into this incredible state of affairs, ending up with a watered-down declaration which, despite an emphasis on the theological solidarity of the church and Israel, is—to cite Robert C. Doty—"less clear and urgent in its injunctions to Catholics to reject anti-Jewish attitudes grounded in religious themes, and . . . more hedged with theological qualifications"? How could it happen that despite their protracted and courageous fight for an unequivocal Declaration in the spirit of Pope John, the bishops and experts of the Secretariat for the Promotion of Christian Unity, custodians of the schema, had to yield to top-level pressure and resign themselves to the wording of the final draft?[5]

Answers to these questions can hardly avoid the whole painful history of the Catholic Church's attitudes and behavior toward Judaism and the Jewish people, and particularly the

[4] John Cogley, *The New York Times*, Oct. 16, 1965.
[5] Robert C. Doty, *The New York Times*, Oct. 13, 1965.

great ambivalence toward Jews that continues to pervade that Church (as well as the Christian church in its entirety). The antisemitic virus is a chronically nagging presence in the Christian corpus. The required answers must also give due weight to specific dilemmas of Christian dogma as these are considered throughout this book.

It is hard to have hope for Christianity when the most prominent body in all Christendom should trumpet forth to the world, through its Second Vatican Council, the unspeakable calumny that the "Jewish authorities and those who followed their lead pressed for the death of Christ. . . ." For this calumny, as Haim Cohn points out, not only preserves the fatal errors of past ages, but keeps intact "the emotional basis, and the pseudo-ethical and pseudo-theological justification for the traditional prejudice and animosity against the Jews. Two thousand years may have elapsed, but the Jews of today still are, and claim to be, descended from the murderers of Jesus, and what is worse, so many choose to identify themselves with their ancestors, in lieu of repudiating and disowning them for ther deeds. . . ."[6]

That the Roman Catholic Church cannot acknowledge the exclusive role of the imperial Roman overlords in the crucifixion of the Jew Jesus, as shown in modern scholarship, but must instead continue to preach the falsehood of Jewish culpability, reveals a kinship with the worst forms of Protestant and Orthodox fundamentalism.

III

At Vatican Council II the heavy burden of history was tied with Christian ambivalence to produce fateful resistance within the strategy of Christian renewal and to push off balance Christian moral and theological effort. Had the expressed theological solidarity with the original people of God been truly unqualified, the Council would never have com-

[6] Haim Cohn, *The Trial and Death of Jesus* (New York: Harper & Row, 1971), p. 323.

mitted its primary, specific offense: Political and quasipolitical interests would not have been allowed to gain a foothold.

In her stated wish to avoid the political issue (as emphasized again and again by the Secretariat for the Promotion of Christian Unity), the Church became the pawn of politics. An unavoidable note of dissimulation, redeemed only a tiny bit by wistfulness, is sounded in the words of the final text, "the Church, . . . moved not by political reasons but by the Gospel's spiritual love, decries hatred, persecutions, displays of anti-Semitism, directed against Jews at any time and by anyone." While the deploring of such evils obviously has to be motivated by the gospel rather than by politics, the stern truth is that political factors played a very large role in the formulation of the conciliar text on Judaism and the Jewish people. The original challenges to the Council were to acknowledge Christian crimes against the Jewish people in such a way that the admission would steadfastly refuse to be sidetracked or silenced by political or other "practical" considerations, and to repent of these crimes—as François Mauriac put it—"without a trace of tactful circumlocution." But the Council failed to stay with these challenges. It allowed the worldly interests and conflicts of men to color and weaken its doctrinal formulations. It ended up putting Caesar before Christ.

The claim was made that Christians living among Muslim majorities are threatened by oppression. H. A. Reinhold, in an article titled "The Reputation of the Council at Stake," responded to that claim with an all-too-obvious analogy: "Here we have a situation parallel to that of the nations under Hitler in the last war. Position after position was bargained away by Christians to save their decisive resistance for a later time. The slow undoing of the Jews in the Third Reich, step by step, permitted the churchmen to postpone their protests and countermeasures until it was too late for any kind of protest. As a result bishops can now be dismissed with contempt—*vide* the Hochhuth case."[7]

[7] H. A. Reinhold, "The Reputation of the Council at Stake," *Journal of Ecumenical Studies,* 1:4 (Fall, 1965), 474.

Acts of compromise are morally forbidden to the church whenever the obligation in question is confession of the sin of Christians. Are certain detractors of Christianity right after all in claiming that Christian faith and morality are finally shackled to political demands and worldly temptations? When ever Christian theology is invaded by political interests the sure result is corruption of doctrine. In the case of Vatican Council II the perverse logic was forthcoming that since the church holds to the divinity of Christ, the charge of "deicide" against the Jewish people is not to be denounced! The Council's primary offense of succumbing to political enticements at once contributed to and was made possible by a theological and moral offense. As George A. Lindbeck writes, "It is not . . . Jews who must prove that they continue to be the Chosen People, but rather the Gentiles who need to defend their claim to be fellow heirs of the promises, to be one with their Jewish brethren."[8] If Christians have been granted a "claim," this is the one. And yet Vatican II could fall into the absurdity of lumping the faith of Israel under the treatment of "non-Christian religions."

It was imagined by some that by the introduction of "other" non-Christian religions into the decree a purely religious intention for the statement could be demonstrated, and thus the political question could be avoided. In point of fact, this guileless understanding played directly into the hands of the conservative clerics, who with great guile could easily prostitute those universal values of brotherhood which everyone acknowledges, to the end of destroying the unique force and contribution of the schema *De Judaeis*. For the placing of the chapter on Judaism and the Jewish people within a Declaration on "non-Christian religions" was anything but a matter of Christian ethics. It was a case of pressure, of compromise, and ultimately of appeasement before hostile forces within and without the Church. A double irony was called forth: Defeat was administered to a dead pope and

---

[8] George A. Lindbeck, "The Jews, Renewal and Ecumenism," *Journal of Ecumenical Studies,* 1:4 (Fall, 1965), 472.

to an overwhelming majority of living bishops by a handful of cardinals who obtained the assent of a living pope in the furtherance of the dying cause of anti-Judaism; at the same time the surrender to minority dictation constituted a serious blow to vital theological trends and historical scholarship within the contemporary Church. Once more the children of this world were in their generation wiser than the children of light. In the end, the Council leaped from the frying pan of allegedly pro-Israeli sentiment into the fire of pro-Arab subjection.

To link the Christian–Jewish relation with other histories is irresponsible and ludicrous. The ambivalence of Christians toward Jews finds absolutely no counterpart in their relations with Muslims or anybody else. In all church history there is simply no parallel to the horrendous tale of Christian treatment of Jews. This is why the concession of shifting the schema on Jews to the larger context of interfaith and intergroup relations was wrong. The demanding purpose of *De Judaeis* was bargained away.

The final outcome had to be unbelievable: Arab and other pressures could capitalize on historic Christian burdens and continuing Christian ambivalence to ensure that the Council would not act to remove the charge of "deicide" against "the Jews"—a crime of which the latter had never been guilty! As NBC's Rome correspondent pointed out on the day of the pope's visit to the United Nations, the deletion of the "deicide" passage had to be construed as a weakening of the Council's position, simply because the passage had been conspicuously present in the draft overwhelmingly approved by the bishops in 1964. From this perspective, the pope was wrong to support excision of that passage. To remove the abrogation of the charge was to imply support of the charge. To be sure, the mouthing or publication of words boasts no ontological power in itself. But to retreat from words once promised is to serve evil.

The war at Vatican II made strange bedfellows: Anti-

Jewish Christian clerics from the Middle East and elsewhere were conjoined with non-Christian Arabs who could not care less religiously—they cared very much politically—about the how and why of Jesus' crucifixion.

In vain does one search the Declaration of Vatican II for the slightest positive sign of Christian penitence. Because none is present, an opportunity of the century was betrayed. The absolutely unique relationship of Christians and Jews lies all but buried within expressions of "unity and love among men," of sympathy for Hindu "contemplation," Buddhist "realization," and Muslim "adoration." The concrete moral demand haunting the entire Christian community is dissolved in the vapid praising of universal brotherhood. It was we Christians, not the Jewish people, who needed the absolution —for the sake of our souls. But we were not given it. The Roman Catholic Church could have risen to become our true *Stellvertreter,* it could have represented and interceded for us all. For once, it could have attained unto true catholicity. But it failed.

We must emphasize, however, that the Catholic failure simply reflects and complicates the entire church's failure. Although Vatican Council II is a *cause célèbre,* Protestant and Orthodox Christians can only find their own image in the unhappy events at Rome. Non-Catholics are ill suited to castigate the Catholic Church for the disaster at Vatican II. The Catholic predicament is shared in varying degrees by all the churches of Christ.[9]

IV

Some who welcomed the so-called Jewish Declaration of Vatican Council II have sought to justify their case by arguing that even if the statement is not ideal, its issuance will inspire independent efforts to transform the church's attitudes toward

[9] Rome, it is true, has qualified for, and hence been tormented by, more formidable publicity.

Judaism and help produce fruits of repentance among Christians. Although this argument has some force,[10] its limitations are severe. To gain perspective on this matter, let us turn to Augustin Cardinal Bea's book, *The Church and the Jewish People*,[11] which appeared a year after the Vatican Declaration. It is important to bear in mind that Vatican Council II merely exemplified, and did not produce, the Christian predicament.

The character of the Vatican Declaration as condescending to Jews is manifested with equal, and perhaps greater, force in the late Cardinal's study. Bea's commentary on the Vatican pronouncement comprises an apologetic carte blanche, an imprimatur for the entire conciliar schema, placed in the framework of all-too-familiar dogmatic presuppositions. Perhaps no different presentation could have been expected from a cardinal of Rome, but then too, no ecclesiastical law dictated that Bea's apologia had to be written, and certainly not by one who is known to have been disappointed by the final draft of the Declaration.[12] The informed reader has no choice but to wonder whether Cardinal Bea really believed what he wrote. Exactly one passage in the volume can possibly be read as a slight reservation upon testimony to the Declaration's general magnificence;[13] this makes for almost an air of unreality, as do the Cardinal's enthusiastic words of commendation, personal defense, and Church-defense.

We are early advised by Bea that "the painful phenomenon of anti-Semitism draws its sustenance neither principally nor exclusively from religious sources"; that his study "has no other purpose than to highlight the Church's teaching

[10] Cf. the "Guidelines for Catholic-Jewish Relations" issued in March, 1967 by the Subcommission for Catholic-Jewish Affairs of the U.S. Catholic Bishops' Commission for Ecumenical and Interreligious Affairs. The "Guidelines" are discussed in chap. 13 of this book.

[11] Augustin Cardinal Bea, *The Church and the Jewish People* (London: Geoffrey Chapman, 1966).

[12] See Joseph E. Cunneen, "The Vatican Council and American Catholicism," *Midstream*, 12:3 (March, 1966), 24.

[13] Bea, *The Church and the Jewish People*, p. 86n; cf. pp. 12, 131.

and reveal it in all its splendor"; and (most self-righteously of all) that "Christians are the first, perhaps, to speak in this way of our own defects and transgressions."[14] This last instance of pride wearing a mask of humility becomes a particular affront through its advocated support in Saint Paul. Any such claim cannot avoid an insinuation that the Hebrew Bible failed to inaugurate a confession of human sinfulness. Could it be possible that the Cardinal never read the Book of Psalms? Bea's tacit fundamentalism of the New Testament continually freezes confessional affirmations into assertions of reputedly objective fact.[15] As one would readily expect, he insists that all relevant New Testament passages are innocent of any taint of antisemitism.[16]

The truth that good theology can never be founded upon bad history ensures from the start that Cardinal Bea's well-meaning efforts must prove futile. We are told that the final conciliar text "begins by establishing the facts as they are reported in the New Testament and constantly read by Christians." Yet it is simply not the case that the New Testament reports are necessarily identical with the "facts." Bea's naïve and unhistorical hermeneutics (biblical interpretation) is epitomized in one part of his stated explanation of "the refusal of the majority [*sic*] of the Jewish people to accept the Gospel." His rationale is that of Paul, "namely, the idea which the Jews had formed of salvation. They claimed to work out their salvation themselves through their own works and the observance of the law, and not through faith in Jesus Christ, through whom salvation came as a gratuitous gift of God. To prove this, St. Paul takes his stand on the fact . . ."— which becomes Bea's opportunity to reproduce Romans 9:30ff.[17] Such resort to the "facts" could not be on more slippery and even reprehensible ground; the real *fact* is that Pauline interpretive polemics and the historical facts are

[14] Ibid., pp. 8–9, 18.
[15] See, e.g., ibid., pp. 105ff.
[16] Cf. ibid., pp. 14–15, 72ff.
[17] Ibid., p. 97.

scarcely identical. From a Jewish point of view, salvation through human works and the observance of the Law are a contradiction in terms. Salvation, including the revelation of Torah (teaching, truth), is a free divine gift.[18]

Cardinal Bea's Christian orientation can only issue in the charge of Jewish lack of faith and disobedience to divine demands and truth, a charge that he repeats again and again.[19] That the context of his allegations is often an attempted softening of absolute Jewish blameworthiness (through such contrasts as ignorance and knowledge, and forgiveness and punishment, together with stress upon the judgment of God upon Christian sin and the freedom of God to work for the "salvation of souls" beyond the church) does not annul the immorality of the above charge in and of itself. Even when Bea expounds the familiar Catholic doctrine of invincible ignorance he hedges, and then does more than that. He tries to capture available divine grace for the christological dispensation: While God "is not limited to the collaboration of the visible organization of the Church and to the means put at her disposal," the divine grace through which non-Christians "are effectively enabled to work for their own salvation by following the dictates of right conscience" must mean "the power of the redemptive death which our divine Saviour suffered for all mankind. . . ." Furthermore, "if it is true that God helps those who through no fault of their own are ignorant of Christ, it is also true that only in the Church can one find the fullness of the means of salvation of those enfeebled and wounded by original sin and surrounded by the temptations of the world through which they are exposed to the attacks of the princes of this world and the powers of darkness."[20]

Of course, within the Catholic dogmatic context, marked

---

[18] Cf. Schoeps, *The Jewish–Christian Argument,* pp. 163–165.
[19] Bea, *The Church and the Jewish People,* pp. 11, 70, 74–75, 78–79, 87, 93, 95, 96, 107, 165.
[20] Ibid., p. 39.

uncertainty obtains on whether "ignorance" among the Jewish people is culpable or inculpable. Although Cardinal Bea struggles manfully with the issues of responsibility for Jesus' death and for the "rejection" of Christ, and also with the dilemma of collective blameworthiness in contrast to individual blameworthiness in the reputed Jewish spurning of the Christian gospel, he only gets himself in deeper. True, he comes out categorically against the notion of Jewish culpability. But all through his exposition, any duality of collective guilt and individual guilt proves to be largely a distinction without a difference.

One section of Bea's analysis may suffice as an example: "The judgement which will smite Jerusalem." At the very place where the Cardinal emphasizes that "it is *not* the fact of belonging to the people of God which determines the judgement," he insists on two other points: the decisiveness of "the act of opposing God and his prophets and messengers, above all Jesus," and the judgment on Jerusalem as constituting "a type and symbol of the universal judgement on all evil and on the powers hostile to God." Obviously, much more than the fate of first-century Jerusalem is at stake here. The "judgement to come" will be visited upon all of those who are guilty of, among other things, a "revolt against truth."[21] We scarcely need to raise Pontius Pilate's question, "What is truth?" For Cardinal Bea's existential accounting makes any intellectual discussion unnecessary: "Christ directly offers the possibility of escaping the judgement visited on Jerusalem to those who have segregated themselves from the 'perverse generation' and submitted to his Gospel."[22] Here, as at other places, the warning to present-day Jews is hardly even veiled. Thus, precisely at the point where Bea opposes "presumed collective guilt," he is prepared to foster the age-old accusation of continuing Jewish culpability because of the "rejection" of the gospel. What, after all, is the moral difference

21 Ibid., pp. 81, 82.
22 Ibid., p. 85.

between the idea of collective guilt and the reputed "guilt" of unnumbered individual Jews? A final rebuke to the Jewish people is masked in the best of intentions: "Even after the condemnation of Jesus, God did not in any way reject the people he had chosen. On the contrary, he continued to offer them the Gospel of salvation."[23]

Could there be a more formidable instance than that recounted above of a constitutional incapacity among great numbers of Christians to achieve empathy with Jews? Even in these years after the Holocaust, few Christians seem able to grasp—even in intellectual terms, not to mention the spiritual–moral aspects—how all the church's preachments about the Christian gospel of salvation can only be an act of effrontery against the Jewish people. As J. Coert Rylaarsdam points out, the Christian world has never really overcome its assumption that the only "good Jews" are either dead ones or Christians. Apparently, God can only love Jews either "for the sake of the Fathers" (Vatican Declaration, following Saint Paul) or somehow "through the Son." The largest single body of the church—in company, of course, with many other Christian bodies—still dogmatically refuses to allow, in Professor Rylaarsdam's apt phrasing, "that God loves the Jew for what he is now," for *himself*.[24] This repudiation is among the most frightening evils in contemporary Christendom. Here is an inner spiritual disease that rots away current Christian endeavors to be brotherly. For we are confronted here with more than an attack upon humanity or even upon Jews. The ultimate sin is to circumscribe, and thereby to blaspheme against, the divine sovereignty.

[23] Ibid., p. 91.
[24] J. Coert Rylaarsdam, letter to editor of *The Christian Century*, 83:43 (Oct. 26, 1966), 1306.

5

The Protestant Predicament, Dutch Style[1]

The General Synod of the Nederlandse Hervormde Kerk (Reformed Church of Holland) recently adopted a statement entitled *Israel: People, Land and State*.[2] This pronouncement is a vivid expression of how Protestants share in the Christian predicament concerning the Jewish people and Judaism. We may, accordingly, apply an appraisal of the Dutch statement to our present purposes.

I

On the commendatory side, the Synod is committed to a uniquely Christian obligation toward Jews and the people

[1] The present chapter is considerably revised from a critique entitled "Commentary upon the Statement of the Hervormde Kerk, Holland" (mimeographed; copyright © 1971 by the Commission on Faith and Order of the National Council of the Churches of Christ in the U.S.A.). The critique was prepared by the author as a member of the Israel Study Group, under the joint collaboration of the above Commission and the Secretariat for Catholic-Jewish Relations of the Bishops' Committee on Ecumenical and Interreligious Affairs. The critique has been translated into Dutch by Coos Schoneveld, under the title "Commentaar op de Handreiking voor een Theologische Bezinning," and published in *In de Waagschaal* (Utrecht), No. 7 (2 juni, 1973), 17–21.

[2] The version of *Israel: People, Land and State* considered here is a mimeographed English translation made available in October, 1970 to the Department of Faith and Order, National Council of Churches. The statement was adopted by the Dutch Synod in June, 1970.

of Israel—this in contrast to Christian heretics and schismatics who have flouted such accountability. The Dutch churchmen emphasize that the Jewish people are the continuation of the elected nation of which the Bible speaks. Therefore, a special connection obtains between Christians and the Jews of today. It is clear, we are assured, that the discontinuity among the Jewish people, as affirmed by the New Testament, "takes place within the framework of the continuity of God's special acting with Israel." Because the divine election is grounded solely in God's faithfulness, the Jewish people remain the chosen ones, and their sonship and the divine promises to them are still valid—this despite their (reputed) alienation from God through the rejection of Jesus. Indeed, when we today encounter the Jewish people, "we are always dealing with God himself."[3] Furthermore, these Dutch Christians are prepared to accept, fully and responsibly, the political consequences of faith.

Israel: People, Land and State is fraught, nevertheless, with serious theological and moral problems. For one thing, the pronouncement reflects certain biblical confusions. The Synod endeavors to build its case upon the authority of the Bible, and particularly that of the New Testament. Inevitably, this gets its authors into difficulties. For neither Testament takes a singleminded view of our subject. The New Testament materials are, as we have earlier emphasized, greatly influenced by apologetic and polemical considerations. Fact and confession are never absolutely distinguished or distinguishable. In addition, postbiblical and extrabiblical notions have conditioned and often distorted successive renderings of the biblical record. The Dutch churchmen seem highly unaware of these complications. They are themselves affected by Christian polemics.

The Synod asserts, to give some examples, that Jesus "came into diametrical opposition to the 'pious' ones who

---

[3] *Israel: People, Land and State*, pars. 1–3, 19, 23, 32.

tried to ensure and maintain the continued existence of the chosen people by faithful observance of the law," and that Jesus "repudiated those who wanted to restore national independence and who in this way strove for the self-preservation of their people."[4] There is no objective warrant for either of these judgments. As a good Jew and a Pharisee, Jesus was surely dedicated to the honoring of the Law. And there is much evidence, as S. G. F. Brandon and others have shown, that Jesus sympathized with and actively supported the cause of independence for his people.[5] Again, how can the generalization possibly be put forward that "the Jewish people as a whole" rejected Christ?[6] True, some Jews—with very good reason—could not be persuaded that Jesus was the Christ. But most Jews of the time probably never even heard of Jesus. Further, the "rejection" or "acceptance" of one or another messianic claimant has never been the all-decisive factor within Judaism that it was early to become for Christianity.

It is simply incorrect to attest, without essential qualification, that in the New Testament picture of Jesus as the Christ is found "the continuation and fulfillment of the history" of the Jewish people, and that the Jews who accepted Jesus "attained in him the true nature of God's people."[7] The dominant messianic expectation of the Jewish people of the first century—an expectation made possible and nurtured by Israel's faith and the divine promises—involved the redemption of Israel through the overthrow of her oppressors,

---

[4] Ibid., par. 22.

[5] With respect to the goal of national independence, cf. S. G. F. Brandon, *Jesus and the Zealots* (New York: Scribner, 1967); also S. G. F. Brandon, *The Trial of Jesus of Nazareth* (London: B. T. Batsford, 1968). See in addition the important review-article by Walter Wink, "Jesus and Revolution: Reflections on S. G. F. Brandon's *Jesus and the Zealots,*" *Union Seminary Quarterly Review,* 25:1 (Fall, 1969), 37–59. Despite his very serious criticisms of Brandon's work, Professor Wink acknowledges that Brandon has succeeded "in reviving the prospect that Jesus' eschatological convictions were really fleshed out in the form of Jewish nationalistic longings" (p. 54).

[6] *Israel: People, Land and State,* par. 28.

[7] Ibid., pars. 21, 28.

an expectation that was totally contradicted in the actual fate of Jesus. As Reinhold Niebuhr showed in his Gifford Lectures of more than three decades ago, Jesus "disappointed" the biblical messianic expectations much more than he fulfilled them.[8] (The apostle Paul indirectly testifies to this state of affairs in his assertion that Christ crucified was a stumbling block to the Jews; I Cor. 1:23.)[9] To say of the Jewish people that Jesus is "their Messiah"[10] is as ludicrous as it is offensive. That Jesus Christ is "not yet recognized by Israel as a whole as the fulfillment of *its* destiny"[11] is triumphalist and worse than condescending. The time is long overdue for Christian churchmen to repudiate the falsehood that the (alleged) Jewish "rejection" of Jesus as Messiah[12] constitutes unfaithfulness rather than faithfulness.[13]

The Dutch Synod is inaccurate in certain of its own renderings of biblical materials. Where does Jesus ever speak of "expulsion from the land" as a judgment upon the Jewish people?[14] More fatefully, the Synod's conviction that the divine faithfulness preserves the elect status of the Jewish people[15] is arbitrary, from the very standpoint of the statement's general theological orientation. The authors' (regrettably) biblicist preconceptions ought to have kept them from ignoring such a passage as I Thessalonians 2:14–16.

The Synod also typifies the contemporary and familiar idealization and misrepresentation of Romans 9–11 that is widespread on the European continent. I refer to the alleged Pauline denial of the view that "after the rejection" of Jesus,

---

[8] Reinhold Niebuhr, *The Nature and Destiny of Man,* vol. 2 (New York: Scribner, 1943), chaps. 1, 2.

[9] Cf. also Paul's tantalizing caveat, "No one can say 'Jesus is Lord' except by the Holy Spirit" (I Cor. 12:3).

[10] *Israel: People, Land and State,* pars. 20, 30, etc.

[11] Ibid., par. 55.

[12] Ibid., par. 22, etc.

[13] This emphasis is developed further in chap. 6.

[14] *Israel: People, Land and State,* par. 25.

[15] Cf. ibid., par. 31.

the Jewish people "would no longer be defined by their vocation to be God's special people."[16] This reading of Paul is one-sided. For the apostle, Israel's place *in the present dispensation* has been taken by the church. Original Israel's (sacred) history is ended. Israel has effectively betrayed and lost its vocation. We would do better to concede that the apostle was in error on this matter—as I believe—than to try to make him say the opposite of what he in truth says. It is no good to cite the assurances that "all Israel will be saved" and that "God's choice stands" (Rom. 11:26, 28). Such assurances are wholly eschatological. For Paul, in the present epoch, original Israel lacks any positive theological identification or dignity. The election of Israel is *now* a nonfunctioning election. Any attempt to utilize Paul as authority for a declaration of positive historical blessings for Israel (e.g., the retention of Eretz Yisrael, the land of Israel, in realization of the divine promises, the *Landesverheissungen*) is indefensible. Paul's expressed position is that in "rejecting" the Christ, Israel enters upon a period of spiritual occultation from which it will reappear only at the end time.[17]

The Dutch authors would have been infinitely more consistent with their (insufferable) triumphalist attitude had they come right out with the obsolescence of Jewish faith to which their version of Christian messianism actually forces them to subscribe. To protest that God must still somehow cling to the Jewish people even though they have "rejected" him in Christ is to fall into the device of a *deus ex machina*. The idea that the elect status of the Jewish people is not annulled even for the present dispensation may be entirely valid, as I believe it is. But to try to sustain that conviction while seeking to preserve the New Testament as one's final authority is poor scholarship and worse biblical theology.

---

[16] Ibid., par. 23.
[17] A. Roy Eckardt, *Elder and Younger Brothers: The Encounter of Jews and Christians* (New York: Scribner, 1967), pp. 55–58.

II

In places, the Dutch statement merely restates the classical anti-Judaic pronouncements of Christendom, with all the links to antisemitism that these allegations invariably sustain. Thus, we are advised that it is "but a small step from loyalty towards God's commandments to legalism. Because of their zeal for the law the Jews have rejected Jesus." And we are apprised of "the moralism and legalism into which the observance of the law has often degenerated among the Jews."[18]

Much more reprehensibly, we are told that the very Jewish act of taking refuge from death through a return to Eretz Yisrael is to be linked to alienation[19]—this from authorized spokesmen for the Christian church, which helped to ensure the extermination of the Jews of Europe.

Even the praiseworthy motivations of Christians today often cannot deliver them from traditional Christian immorality toward the Jewish people and Judaism. Why is this? Many powerful historical causes are involved. In the case of the Reformed Synod and comparable groups, one formidable answer is that they are held captive by their biblicism. The biblicist theologizing of the political order[20] is hard put to escape immorality. This biblicist temptation invariably means the attempted religionizing of the Jewish people.

The evils of biblicism are exemplified in the constant demands of the Dutch churchmen upon Jews. The churchmen identify the Jewish people as a completely "historical reality," but then they renege on this whole idea by ruling that alone among the nations, Israel must walk according to a peculiar righteousness. We have to object that if Israel is indeed a historical reality, its rights, achievements, and shortcomings

[18] *Israel: People, Land and State,* pars. 35, 39.
[19] Ibid., par. 36.
[20] Strictly, the theologizing of politics (the subjecting of politics to the demands of faith) differs from the politicizing of theology (the subjecting of faith to the demands of politics). The former has its source in theological endeavor, the latter in political endeavor. Yet the integrity of theology and of politics is lost in both cases.

are to be apprehended and dealt with in ways that strictly parallel the disposition of other historical entities (ancient Rome, ancient Babylon, modern Egypt, modern Syria, et al.). We note the Synod's refusal in one place to extend the integrity of original Israel's land to its right to an independent state and even to the City of Jerusalem—a refusal that reappears later in their effort to apply God's promise to "the lasting tie of people and land, but not in the same way to the tie of people and state."[21] This curious disjunction between residency and sovereignty must only play into the hands of those who would have the Jews remain a tolerated or nontolerated minority devoid of independent political existence and defense.

It is true that the Dutch authors concede "the relative necessity" of a Jewish state. But what is the possible moral justification for being so restrictive here, when the restrictiveness is nowhere applied to other nations? And despite their relative sanctioning of the Israeli state, the authors continue to "wonder" whether "the special place of the Jewish people" does not make questionable "the right of existence" of the State of Israel. We are told that "the land was the place allotted to this people in order that they might realize their vocation as God's people to form a holy society."[22] There is an all-too-evident insinuation here that decisive Jewish irresponsibility in respect to such a society would justify punitive or other expulsion from the land. The immorality of this kind of understanding is demonstrated in the fact that we never take such a stance respecting Egypt, Syria, or Jordan— or the United States. In this context, it must be stressed that a responsible politico-moral comparison is *not* Israel and "Christian states"[23] but Israel and the states that now surround her.

That some of the foregoing emphases of the Synod ap-

[21] *Israel: People, Land and State,* pars. 13, 43.
[22] Ibid., pars. 44, 11.
[23] Cf. ibid., par. 48.

pear under the heading "The Jewish People in the Old Testament" does not exempt these churchmen from our criticisms. One may ask: What moral service or function is performed by the Synod's concentration upon the biblical record? In this connection, no point in the Dutch pronouncement is more ominous or revealing than the Synod's implicitly affirmative response to the question of whether things said of Israel in the "Old Testament" are "still valid for the Jewish people today."[24]

All through Christian history theological pronouncements upon the subject of the Jews have infected the political domain and prevented the same moral standards being applied to the Jews that are applied to all men on the sole basis of their common humanity. For Christians to expect from Jews "more than we expect from any other people" is not only horrendous; in light of the evil history of Christian treatment of Jews, the Synod's demand that the State of Israel be "exemplary"[25] constitutes in and of itself a wholly illicit act. Christian concern becomes, in effect and quite unwittingly, a contributor to harrassment—even a form of cruelty.

The only available way to keep from applying such a double standard to Israel and other states is to stop employing the Jewish tie with Eretz Yisrael that is based upon the divine promise[26] as a vehicle for moving into the political domain. We must concentrate instead upon the historical, jurisprudential, and moral rights that Jews have to the land (not, to be sure, in replacement of Palestinian Arab rights). For the Synod's theological imperialism against the human, political domain is as unfortunate when it is supporting Israel as when it is criticizing her. In the world of today we simply cannot try to justify the Jewish people's right to Eretz Yisrael through theological argumentation.[27] To do so means unwarranted

---

[24] Ibid., par. 19.
[25] Ibid., pars. 52, 47.
[26] Cf. ibid., par. 52.
[27] Cf. ibid., par. 24. This contention is developed further in chap. 9.

special pleading for the Israeli cause—another form of the double standard and an equally regrettable one.

We are further advised by these churchmen of the Netherlands that the sign of God's faithfulness "is primarily seen in the fact that they [the Jews] still exist; the Jewish people cannot be done away with."[28] Here the Synod becomes Pollyanna in a way that must impress many Jews as almost obscene. With six million European Jews dead, three million Russian Jews under oppression, and the contingency of a new Holocaust in the Middle East, we are assailed by (false) prophets who promise that the Jewish people will not be destroyed. God will take care of them. (As he did in Auschwitz?) Then, almost as though it cannot stand a total abrogation of the traditional Christian assurance that, after all, the Jews must "have it coming" to them, the Synod does not totally dissociate itself from the finding, so cherished among anti-Israelists, that "the Jewish people now, as in the time of Jesus, are in danger of falling victim" to "nationalistic self-assertion."[29]

Spokesmen within Jewry may succeed in propagating or opposing the doctrine of the election of Israel. That is their business and their privilege. But when Christian representatives seek to intervene in that doctrine (other than perhaps in nonsupersessionist application of the doctrine to the church), they seem unable to surmount the historical and ideological corruptions of Christendom. More specifically, whenever there appears a Christian declaration that the Jews are "unlike" all other peoples, we have to be on special guard against conclusions that are not only theologically suspect but morally harmful. The way the Dutch Synod intrudes the doctrine of election into the historical life of Israel is a perfect illustration. Expressed differently, the framers appear incapable of comprehending the difference and the tension between the sacred and profane spheres. Their document is most defec-

28 Ibid., par. 34.
29 Ibid., par. 39.

tive at the points of connection between Israel as the elect people of God and Israel as a historical entity. These Dutch Christians are doubtless reacting against the terrible separation of theology from politics in the 1930s and 1940s. Therefore, we must be charitable toward them. Yet the fact remains that their statement fails to relate and to distinguish responsibly biblical–convenantal obligations and today's politico-moral situation. At least, the authors' simplistic, repeated summons to "Old Testament" covenantal norms makes that failure inevitable.

III

I think that one of the special enjoyments among the evil powers of this world is to mete out theological–moral chastisements as the appropriate historical sequel to human agony. That in this day after Auschwitz a Christian body should dare to stress again and again the alienation of the Jewish people from God[30] is not merely an instance of human callousness, but also a proof that the voice of the church is sometimes a satanic voice. Have we totally forgotten the truth that suffering, especially the suffering of innocent people, is the very opposite of alienation from God? Hypocritically, we have readily granted this truth for almost any Christian martyr. But with respect to Jews, even the Jews of Auschwitz, we cast about for other "explanations" that will harmonize with our preconceived notion of Jewish "alienation."

In claiming that Jews are alienated from God—an alienation that reputedly arises from the denial of special peoplehood in behalf of other peoples[31]—while at the same time accusing Jews of retaining an alienated peoplehood that rejects Christ, the Dutch Synod damns the Jewish people whichever way they turn. Just what are the Jews supposed to do? The Synod's possible effort to extricate itself from this

---

[30] Ibid., pars. 30, 31, etc.
[31] Ibid., par. 33.

entrapment of the Jews by adding that they "are still the chosen people" and, as such, are "a sign of God's faithfulness"[32] is empty consolation indeed. Furthermore, to summon Jews to accede to Christian ideas of redemption when in truth the world remains unredeemed, and especially when in her treatment of Jews the church has greatly compounded the world's unredeemedness, is to mock Jewish dignity and Jewish self-understanding.[33]

A most ironic lesson of *Israel: People, Land and State* is that the identical stereotypes and falsehoods that have perpetuated antisemitism for centuries should be disseminated by an official Christian body devoted to the generous sharing of the Christian gospel and wholesomely committed to high humanitarian ideals. The very Christian world that has brought incalculable harm to Jews continues to spawn well-meaning, extremely moral representatives who nevertheless level the same old accusations against Jews and make the same old demands upon them. This is most diabolical. It serves to remind us that man's highest moral and spiritual attainments can become peculiarly effective instruments of sin. One way to fight such a state of affairs, in the present context, is for the Christian church to stop lecturing Israel and the Jewish people as though church spokesmen were biblical prophets. Such lecturing transforms theology into an instrument of human oppression. Moral outrages against Jews will persist until the church extricates itself from the politics of moralistic biblicism.[34]

[32] Ibid., par. 34.
[33] The question of redeemedness and unredeemedness is pursued further in chap. 15.
[34] Additional commentary upon the Dutch Synod's position on the State of Israel is found in chap. 9.

6

The Mutual Plight
of the Churches

Protestantism, Catholicism, and Orthodox Christianity share the one predicament respecting the Jewish people and Judaism. As used in this book, the phrase "the Christian predicament" refers, comprehensively speaking, to Christendom's failure to reconcile three domains: historical fact, theological claim, and ethical behavior. The predicament is perpetuated by the struggle between "truth" and morality. Specifically: Where is the law of love in the treatment of Jews through most of Christian history?

I

The pathos of the Jewish–Christian meeting in our time is that the norm of equality, to which both sides must pay homage in principle, is undermined by the ongoing Christian threat to the integrity and self-identity of Jews. For example, I recently heard a Jew identify Christian missionary efforts among Jews as a "religious Holocaust" possessed of the same potential consequences as the Nazi crematoria: the extinction of the Jewish people. From this point of view, it would be immoral for the Jew to consider a Christian his equal until it is made clear that the Christian fully accepts the Jew in terms of the latter's own self-understanding (which, when applied to both parties, is what we mean by authentic dialogue). Jews do not seek to destroy Christians or Christianity. In the Jewish view, Christians have always been eligible for membership in the righteous of the world: "Heaven and earth I call to witness that whether it be Gentile or Jew, man or woman, slave or handmaid, according to the deeds one does, will the holy spirit rest on him."[1]

The pathos referred to above is embodied in a so-called dialogue between a Christian, Jean Daniélou, and a Jew, André Chouraqui, entitled *The Jews: Views and Counterviews.*[2] For Daniélou's entire aim is to marshal support for "the truth." Thus the question of Pontius Pilate again presents itself: "What is truth?" Daniélou contends that Jesus "*fully* realized in himself *all* the messianic hopes of Israel." The Christian's mission is to proclaim Jesus Christ "to every man, as St. Paul said, whether he be pagan or Jew." Daniélou announces bluntly: "We cannot give up trying to convert you."[3]

So absolutist a position naturally carries absolutist consequences. One result is a coercing of the biblical data into a single fold. Our Christian protagonist offers the customary and wearisome either—or: Jesus either blasphemed or he was "truly the one foretold by the prophets of the Old Testament" and right in his claim to be equal to God. It was "certainly" Jesus' hope that "the Jews as a whole would acknowledge him." Daniélou contends, in addition, that the Gospels "prove in an absolute manner" Jesus' claim to have the right to forgive sins and to possess a dignity equal to Yahweh.[4] But the Gospels prove nothing of the kind; they are secondary sources

---

[1] Yalkut on Judges 4:1, as cited in Ben Zion Bokser, *Judaism and the Christian Predicament* (New York: Knopf, 1967), p. 139.

[2] Jean Daniélou and André Chouraqui, *The Jews: Views and Counterviews* (Westminster, Md.: Newman Press, 1967).

[3] Ibid., pp. 69, 70 (italics added).

[4] Ibid., pp. 25, 31, 32.

put forward by men who were *confessing* such things in the name of Christ. Yes, let us indeed pursue the *truth!*

We should have hoped that Daniélou would at least *refer* to the long-recognized consideration that the authenticity of Jesus' alleged claims respecting his own person are very seriously in doubt. Daniélou's allegation that Jesus separated himself from Judaism[5] is absolutely contradicted by the fact that Jesus lived and died a faithful Jew. The fault here would not be so ironic or serious were Professor Daniélou not himself a historian of early Christianity. Polemic is a hazardous enough enterprise, but when it is compounded by historical error among those who try to lead us to "the truth," the device becomes ludicrous.

Another result of Daniélou's absolutism is his failure either to allow or to account for the persistence and permanence of Israel. The familiar effort is made to reduce Jewish existence to a strictly sociological phenomenon. We are advised that Israel rightly retains an ethnic and cultural dimension. Daniélou seems at a few points to go beyond this by including within the peculiarity of Jewry its testimony to the living God. But then he retracts: "Israel has its place in the universal Church of Jesus Christ, and I hope that one day it will find it." Thus, any integral, theological existence for original Israel is annulled through a subjection to the Christian dispensation. All that is left is the "right to be a people among other peoples."[6] A final consequence, as we would fully anticipate, is Daniélou's effort to capture the "dialogue" for Christian presuppositions. He insists that the meeting must center upon the question of "the fulfillment of Israel's hope." Since [*sic*] Jesus was "not simply a great prophet, but the irruption into the world of the eschatological event," it follows that the "fundamental dialogue is situated around this interpretation given to the person of Jesus."[7]

[5] Ibid., pp. 32–33.
[6] Ibid., pp. 44, 45, 70; cf. also pp. 13, 15–17, 22, 40, 46, 55.
[7] Ibid., pp. 23, 24.

What could Dr. Chouraqui have been thinking all this time, as a man and as a Jew? The strength of his rejoinder lies in his existential and moral rendering of truth. If Professor Daniélou must concentrate upon the reality of crucifixion, let him not forget that millions of Jews have been crucified "in order to bear witness to a certain honor in man." We cannot ignore, as Daniélou does, "the permanence of the Jews in spite of everything and everyone, even in spite of us Jews. . . . The Jew who is furthest away from the Word of God, by the simple fact that he exists as a Jew, remains faithful, although sometimes involuntarily and unconsciously, to the covenant of Abraham and to its permanence." In addition, Chouraqui calls for historical perspective: "We shall advance the more in our dialogue the better we avoid projecting into the past the realities of today. When you say that the Jew is well adapted for conversion to Christianity, . . . [you speak as a man of today who] forgets the arsenal of war forged by the Church to efface the Jew." If the Christian apologist is tempted to excuse one historical period by recourse to the "standards" of the times, the Jew must concentrate upon the condition of his people as a whole. The antisemite is "defined by his opposition to the Jew" in *any* time, and this is what counts.[8]

While Daniélou then grants some Christian culpability for antisemitism, his admission is compromised by self-defensiveness in behalf of the church. He protests that antisemitism preceded Christianity, that Christians "certainly are not more wicked than other men," that "we cannot transpose to the fourth century our conceptions of religious freedom," and that historic antisemitism was more often a popular movement than the responsibility of the religious and political powers.[9] Chouraqui replies that antisemitism was systematically encouraged and increased by theologians and saints, that "only an iniquitous state" could sanction and practice injustice

[8] Ibid., pp. 35, 39, 46, 50, 61.
[9] Ibid., pp. 57–60.

against the "outsider," and that Muslim treatment of Jews was infinitely more moral than that of Christendom with its unconscionable hatreds.[10] However, Chouraqui remains too much the gentleman, when he ought to tell the protagonist to go to hell: "I am grateful to you for having said these things with so much frankness."[11] Professor Daniélou's careful insistence that "you will not find a single Christian persecutor of the Jews until the time of Theodosius"[12] is, in this time after the death camps, conducive to emesis.

Chouraqui has fallen into the other's trap by acknowledging that Christians have a right to try to convert Jews, as part of a universal aspiration that ought not discriminate against the Jewish people.[13] That Daniélou's very next comment should be, "we must not minimize the question of truth," reveals the futility and self-defeating consequence of Chouraqui's kindliness, and it points up the necessity for Jews to expose as evil the Christian missionizing position. For that posture and the posture of dialogue are totally incommensurate. If the Christian community must insist upon missionizing, and hence upon extinguishing, the Jewish people, it ought to be honest enough to abandon the duplicity of claiming to foster friendship and understanding.[14] Chouraqui goes on to say that he has known "well-meaning young Jews to consider Jesus not as he really was but as the leader of a social group whose vocation, whose mission, was to desire and organize the extermination of the Jews."[15] Chouraqui ought to have added that the protagonist before him is a witting member of that very group. Yes, Professor Daniélou,

---

[10] Ibid., pp. 62–64.

[11] Ibid., p. 71.

[12] Ibid., p. 52. One needs no great knowledge of the history of antisemitism to recognize the absurdity of Daniélou's assertion that this malady "has nothing to do with the religious problem" but "is simply a human one" (p. 67).

[13] Ibid., p. 72.

[14] We return to the issue of the Christian missionizing viewpoint in chap. 15.

[15] Ibid., p. 75.

you are right: Dialogue "is not a question of being pleasant; it is a question of being first of all true."[16] The sword of truth has two edges.

On the other hand, Chouraqui is evidently alert to the unjust attempt to destroy the Jew's partnership in the dialogue via the device of christocentrism. He emphasizes that the Jewish–Christian confrontation belongs "on the teleological plane of historic finalities, rather than on the theological plane of the knowledge of God," and that the dialogue must start out *in spite of* the Christian claim and the Jewish nonacceptance of that claim. In theological terms, the Jew cannot possibly believe that God would be false to his word and his promise to his people. The true choice for Jews has been a quite different Calvary from that surrounding the person of Jesus; it has been "that of exile, which at least preserved the existence of Israel and safeguarded the chances of a redemption that would fulfill the Promise."[17]

II

Dr. Chouraqui's reference to the word of God in the context of truth points us to a fateful consideration. Christian ambivalence toward the Jews and Judaism has been preserved and aggravated by the presence within church dogma of certain historical–theological contradictions. These contradictions have helped keep the relationship between the church and original Israel among the most critical problems in all Christian theology. They are nowhere more evident than in the matter of scriptural authority, or, more generally, in the entire question of the nature of divine revelation and its human response.

I refer to the problem of the "Old Testament" and the "New Testament." That problem would never have arisen had the church followed the Marcionites and cast off the

16 Ibid., p. 71.
17 Ibid., pp. 29, 33, 42.

"Old Testament." But the church chose a quite different course: it insisted upon the divine authenticity of the "Old Testament." And when this insistence was combined with the affirmations of New Testament faith, the church was forced into an impossible position in regard to the "Old Testament," and the Jewish people and Judaism. Christianity has never found a way to reconcile its view (inspired by the church's own origin from within Judaism) that the Hebrew Torah contains the Word of God with the allegation that "the Jews" have said "No" to their salvation and repudiated their inheritance by "rejecting" Jesus as Messiah.

Christian thought has been driven almost to distraction by the effort to affirm the divine authority of one constituent part of its canon in face of the truth that its Lord, the acclaimed guarantor of its own election, cannot be readily fitted into the canonical promises. The *Tanach* ("Old Testament") supports neither the church's supersessionist claim for itself nor the church's denials of Judaism. The only way the Christian claim could be "proved" via the "Old Testament" was by distorting the materials there.[18]

For illustrative purposes we may return to Augustin Cardinal Bea's study, *The Church and the Jewish People.* What does it mean to attest, as the Cardinal does, that Scripture is "inspired by God" and is accordingly "the Word of God"? What does it mean to speak of "God's revelation handed down to us by the Jewish people in the writings of the Old Testament"?[19] At this point, Bea turns to the Vatican Council's Dogmatic Constitution on Divine Revelation. The

[18] See Bokser, *Judaism and the Christian Predicament,* chaps. 11, 13. Not only conservatives and fundamentalists are guilty of reading Christian doctrine into the Hebrew Bible; the practice is found among many Christian ecumenical leaders today (ibid., p. 323). The conflict here is not exclusively Jewish versus Christian. More and more Christian scholars are insisting that the church cannot justify on any ground, doctrinal or moral, her traditional subjection of Jewish Scripture to Christian alteration (cf. ibid., pp. 326, 328).

[19] Augustin Cardinal Bea, *The Church and the Jewish People* (London: Geoffrey Chapman, 1966), pp. 11, 121.

effect can only be disastrous, simply because that Constitution also tries to have things both ways: namely, to vindicate revelationally and yet to transcend christologically the so-called Old Testament. The disaster is assured by the traditional Christian tour de force that seeks refuge in propaedeutics, the notion of the "Old Testament" as purely preliminary and preparatory. As the Dogmatic Constitution has it, "the principal purpose to which the plan of the Old Covenant was directed was to prepare for the coming both of Christ, the universal Redeemer, and of the messianic kingdom. . . ."[20] Apart from the oblique insult to the integrity of the divine Covenant with Israel and to the sacred Scripture of the Jewish people, we are met here by a flagrant denial of major dimensions of that Scripture, a flouting of biblical authority, and a refutation of the Constitution's testimony elsewhere that "the books of both the Old and New Testament in their entirety . . . have God as their author" and are "without error."[21] By subjecting the so-called Old Testament to christocentrism, Cardinal Bea violates the revelational–historical integrity of that literature.[22]

To exemplify how identical the Catholic and Protestant predicaments are, we may refer to the United Presbyterian "Confession of 1967." On the one hand, the Confession states that the Christian church "has received the books of the Old and New Testaments as prophetic and apostolic testimony in which it hears the Word of God. . . ." Yet on the other hand, the Confession emphasizes that Jesus' "complete obedience led him into conflict with his people. His life and teaching judged their goodness, religious aspirations, and national hopes. . . . The Old Testament bears witness to God's faithfulness in his covenant with Israel and points the way to the fulfillment of his purpose in Christ. . . . The Old Testa-

[20] Dogmatic Constitution on Divine Revelation (Dei Verbum), *The Documents of Vatican II,* p. 122.

[21] Ibid., pp. 118–119.

[22] Bea, *The Church and the Jewish People,* see especially pp. 10, 34–35, 56, 59, 60–61, 128.

ment is indispensable to understanding the New, and is not itself fully understood without the New."[23]

In this Confession there is no sympathy with the anti-Judaism that compounds antisemitism. Yet we are met once again with Christian confusion over the nature of scriptural "testimony." We say that we hear God's voice through the "Old Testament," but we are unable to authenticate our central proclamations in a manner consistent with that Testament: here is the heart of the Christian problem. There is just no way to speak of God's "fulfillment of his purpose in Christ" without implying that this means "fulfillment" for Jews. But the centuries-old obstacle remains that the Hebrew Bible, *Holy* Scripture, gives no unequivocal support to the contention that Jesus was the consummation of Israelite hopes.[24]

III

Christendom has always assigned blame to the Jewish people for their attitude toward Jesus when, if anything, it ought to have been acclaiming them for their loyalty to the divine revelation to Israel. Were the church truly to honor the "Old Testament" as the Word of God it would know and proclaim that the Israel which lives on Torah not only bears no moral liability for the rejection of Jesus but is, in its very nonacceptance of the messiahship or lordship of Jesus, achieving fealty to the divine promises. It is to be praised for its objective obedience to the Word of God in an unredeemed world.[25]

[23] Edward A. Dowey, Jr., *A Commentary on the Confession of 1967 and An Introduction to "The Book of Confessions"* (Philadelphia: The Westminster Press, 1968), pp. 14, 18.

[24] A. Roy Eckardt, "Can There Be a Jewish–Christian Relationship?" *The Journal of Bible and Religion*, 2 (April, 1965), 128; "The Jewish–Christian Dialogue," 12.

[25] For additional discussion of the problem of biblical authority see A. Roy Eckardt, *Elder and Younger Brothers* (New York: Scribner, 1967), pp. 120–140.

As practiced dialecticians, we Christians could perhaps talk our way out of the above difficulties were not a deeper question at stake. It is a question that drives us to the very rim of sacrilege—only to snatch us away from that condition: *Is God true to his word? Could he have misled original Israel?* But how can we, without falling into the Marcionite heresy, ever believe that the Lord of truth and justice would nurture the messianic consciousness of his people in several directions—including, preeminently, Israel's "national hopes"—only to count Israel blameworthy for not following one of these rather than another?

For Christians committed to the essential authenticity of the biblical witness, the one alternative to such demonizing of God is to attest that it has not been God's revealed will or purpose to bring the greater part of original Israel to acclaim Jesus as the Christ. Israel's persistence in faith, its allegiance to Torah and Covenant, is accepted and supported within the providence of God, in entire independence of the Christian faith.[26] As a pastor from the Netherlands has said, "The Lord goes his own way with his own people."

[26] Eckardt, *Elder and Younger Brothers,* pp. 135–136.

7

Enter the Devil

How are we to account for the horror of antisemitism that has afflicted the Christian church throughout its life and that endures to this day? How is the evil to be rooted out or at least reduced? The one question is as baffling as the other. A lifetime of study may uncover a few clues, though probably no demonstrable certainties.

I

Edward H. Flannery, a prominent Catholic historian and leader in the reconciliation of Christians and Jews, has expressed pessimism toward the future of Christian–Jewish relations, chiefly because of the Christian failure to comprehend the historical plight of the Jewish people.[1] Father Flannery's pessimism is sustained by the persistence of Christian ideology: the notion that Jews are somehow special in a negative sense. The prevalence of this attitude among Christians helps to explain how antisemitism so often goes hand in hand with Christian religiousness. Revealingly, no less than 80 percent of all American Southern Baptists and 70 percent of Missouri

[1] Edward H. Flannery, as cited in *The Jewish News* (Detroit), June 16, 1972.

Synod Lutherans queried in the Glock–Stark study, *Christian Beliefs and Anti-Semitism,* agreed with the statement, "The Jews can never be forgiven for what they did to ' Jesus until they accept Him as the True Saviour."² Toward no other people does Christendom take the position it assumes toward Jews. Reputedly, Jews have, in a singular way, "rejected their Lord," and they continue to do so. They must be missionized, restored to their own spiritual destiny, converted to the "true faith." And if and when they resist the "truth," this must reflect their characteristic stubbornness and hardheartedness. (The pervasiveness of the above interpretation among Christians shows how impossible it is to treat the Jewish–Christian problem in the same ways that Christian relations with other groups or religions are to be treated.)

The historian and theologian must be faithful to the objective record of centuries of maltreatment of Jews within Christendom. Opposition to Jews is the one constant of Christian history. On the other hand, the analyst must be aware of the question of the measure in which Christendom's behavior and teaching hostile to Jews are anti-Christian rather than Christian. In different terms, to utilize a phrase of Professor Bernard Blumenkranz, how can there be "a gospel without love"? Or, in still different terms, could antisemitism embody the peculiar work of satanic forces?

For some time I have sought to till soil that is shared by depth psychology, theology, and ethics. The more I have reflected upon the dreadful tale of antisemitism, the more I have found confirmed a certain hypothesis that I came to a number of years ago: Generically speaking, the war against the Jews is a war of pagans against the God of Abraham, Isaac, and Jacob, whom Jews represent. More delimitedly, antisemitism is the war we Christians wage against Jesus the Jew; it is the symbolic reenactment of the crucifixion of Jesus, who

² Charles Y. Glock and Rodney Stark, *Christian Beliefs and Anti-Semitism* (New York: Harper & Row, 1966), p. 62. Among Roman Catholics, by contrast, the percentage was 14. For all Protestants it was 33.

confronts Christians with God; the rejection of the Jew Jesus, turned against his own people. There is a coincidence which is not a coincidence: the Jewishness of Jesus and Christendom's endemic death wish for Jews. How can it be a mere coincidence that in all our history we have accused only the people of Jesus of a world conspiracy against humankind? We have fought for almost two thousand years to get Jesus off our backs. We cannot put our hands on him directly, but we can easily put our hands on his people. A more qualified scapegoat is simply unimaginable. When we Christians accuse "the Jews" of spurning and crucifying the Christ, the charge represents our own below-conscious wish to kill Christ and to dispose of him once and for all. As a matter of fact, God himself is not exactly innocent in this whole affair. Why did he have to reveal himself and his will in a Jew? We shall see about that! And so antisemitism becomes a compulsive re-enactment of the murder of God.[3] Through our persecution of Jews, we Christians can try to manage our guilt for defaulting before gospel demands. "The Jews" are, after all, the real culprits. They are the ones who *really* reject the Christ. In sum, the ineluctable tie between Christianity and antisemitism derives from a primordial fact: Jesus was a Jew.

The above (somewhat eclectic) interpretation is not to be discarded. But we may appropriately ask whether God and man are the only protagonists in this revolting drama, or whether the devil is not also a member of the cast. For one way to comprehend the historic Christian charge of Jewish devilishness is to discern its inspiration within the devil himself. The continuing Christian war against the Jewish people then becomes explicable, not by a mere delineation of exclusively historical pressures and counterpressures, but rather by grasping the primordial conspiracy of Christendom with the

[3] A. Roy Eckardt, *Elder and Younger Brothers* (New York: Scribner, 1967), pp. 22–25. For a full discussion of my views on the nature of antisemitism, see chaps. 1 and 2, and *passim*, of that study; also, my *Christianity and the Children of Israel* (New York: King's Crown, 1948), chap. 1.

demonic powers. Minimally speaking, it is hard to face up to the reality of Christian antisemitism, which encompasses hostility to Judaism and to the State of Israel,[4] apart from the recognition of devilishness.

I hypothesize that a major field of operations for Satan is our collective unconscious. In Christian antisemitism certain eruptions of the collective unconscious are taken captive by pathology. The pathology assumes a unique form. We are beset by a reality quite different from ordinary racial, ethnic, or political prejudice. The utilization of the Christian pulpit to defame Blacks or Germans or even Communists has, indeed, become quite unfashionable. Yet we shall continue to stand up to read the "Word of God" in, for example, the Gospel of John—and no one had better call the Anti-Defamation League. Who would wish to be charged with undermining "religious freedom"?

II

If it is true that one of the devil's continuing tasks is to make people believe he is dead, then that helps us understand two things. The first is the deceiving effort among antisemites to show that there is really no such thing as antisemitism. There are only evil Jews, against whom moral men naturally and praiseworthily react. Or if anyone is to blame for antisemitism, surely they—those wrongly accused of antisemitism —are not guilty.

In point of truth, we must be very much on guard when the protest is forthcoming that antisemitism is rare or is dying out, or that the word "antisemitism" is to be used very sparingly or with great caution, lest name-calling afflict us. True, not everyone who believes that antisemitism is diminishing is an antisemite. Yet the fact remains that the antisemitic world has a vested interest in seeking to convince other men of the

---

[4] The second of these considerations is analyzed in Part Two of this volume.

nonreality of antisemitism. We must not hesitate to apply the terms "antisemitism" and "antisemite" whenever and wherever the truth warrants.

The second thing we are helped to understand is why the Christian world does not, for the most part, tolerate the admission of Auschwitz into its own responsible psyche. The failure is manifest in acts of cowardice; cowardice is invariably present when repentance is absent. An example is the fate of the original draft of a postconciliar document from the Vatican Secretariat for the Promotion of Christian Unity urging Catholics to acknowledge the importance to Jews of the link to the Land of Israel. The Vatican bowed to Arab pressures and expunged this counsel.[5]

Seymour M. Lipset lists certain criteria for discerning the presence of antisemitism. Two that have the most direct relevance for our particular analysis are the drawing upon age-old hostility to Jews in order to strengthen a political position, and the charge "that Jews are guilty of some primal evil."[6] It is here adjudged that hostility to Jews is actualized through the accusation that Jews are themselves hostile people. Classical Christian enmity toward Jews concentrates upon the hostilities that Jews reputedly manifest toward God or the church or the human race, or all of these together. I should not want this latter judgment to obscure the truth that antisemitism is possessed of a profound life of its own that is quite independent of the presence or behavior of Jews. Antisemitism lives in the mind of the devil, the antisemite. This explains why it is that changes in Jewish behavior are of no decisive consequence in the presence of antisemitism. Only antisemitism simultaneously demands that certain human beings behave as angels yet insists they are devils. Just as the reality of the devil is to be unreal, so antisemitism is

---

[5] *Jewish Chronicle* (London), April 3, 1970.
[6] Seymour M. Lipset, " 'The Socialism of Fools'—The New Left calls it 'Anti-Zionism,' but it's no different from the Anti-Semitism of the Old Right," *The New York Times Magazine,* Jan. 3, 1971, p. 6.

immured from reality. Thus, anti-Israeli Christians need have little if any connection with or knowledge of Jews or the real Israel. They fabricate their own Israel: militant, aggressive, inflexible, vengeful, irreligious, alienated.[7]

What is the relation between the attack upon Man, upon the dignity of humankind, and Christendom's attack upon the Jew? Is antisemitism simply one more of the devil's unnumbered stratagems, just another species within the genus of prejudice-persecution-annihilation? Or is it of the very essence of the devil, the special malignancy that suffuses and destroys the entire divine-human creation? The assertion is sometimes dared that the very imperium of the societal libido is, at least in the West, somehow relatable to antisemitism. To David Polish, for example, "the truth of every cause is validated or found fraudulent in the way in which it confronts the Jewish people."[8]

III

It may be, then, that one means for achieving discrete and substantive understanding of the devilishness of antisemitism is to concentrate upon its uniqueness, its peculiarities. By way of further orientation to this viewpoint, I call attention to the achievements and the limitations of Friedrich Heer's powerful work *God's First Love*. Heer is a Catholic Christian who teaches the history of ideas at the University of Vienna. His contribution is particularly salient in his application of social–theological psychoanalysis to the history of Christian antisemitism, and in his search, within the same scientific domain, for ways of salvation from this malady.[9]

[7] In chap. 5 we referred to the Dutch Synod's associating of Israel and the Jews with alienation and irreligiousness. With respect to the other allegations against Israel listed, see chap. 11.

[8] David Polish, "The Tasks of Israel and Galut," *Judaism*, 18:1 (Winter, 1969), 10.

[9] The German edition of *God's First Love* received a Martin Buber–Franz Rosenzweig medal. Purely literary merit could hardly have been the primary criterion for the award. The work is afflicted with vexing discursive-

We have raised the question of whether antisemitism is just one more of the devil's many enterprises or an absolutely peculiar malignancy. A both–and judgment upon this question is not impossible. However, by his inconclusiveness, Professor Heer falls short of even this option. Often he construes antisemitic outbreaks as, essentially, dependent variables born of externally sovereign forces. Thus, "the collapse of the European 'balance of power' for which England had struggled for centuries . . . was basically responsible for the Jewish tragedy culminating in 1945. . . . The masses did not ask for antisemitism; they merely wanted to hate." A corollary of such reasoning is that the problems of the Jewish people entail, as in Karl Marx, the same exigencies that all humanity faces.[10] On the other hand, Heer sometimes appears to opt for the all-decisive power and peculiarity of antisemitism. Antisemitism has its own offspring: racialism, anti-Communism, clericalism, and anticlericalism. Heer also supports a finding in psychopathology that the antisemite is simply describing and living out his own disturbed condition.[11] Essentially, according to this argument, antisemitism lives within the col-

---

ness, excessive citation, a tendency to proof-by-quotation, opaque style, repetitiveness, an aptitude for guilt-by-historical-association (cf. pp. 150, 343, 352), serious imbalances in the assignment and utilization of space, and a largely useless index limited to names. Heer writes in impulsive, stream-of-consciousness fashion. He is only partially restrained by demands of either chronology or subject matter. The exact aim of his study is not readily apparent. The title, in German as in English, is not of great help. A student of mine suggested that the title seemed condescending; young men know that first loves fade all too quickly. Although Heer attests that the divine Covenant with Israel is everlasting, he provides anything but a systematic or concerted analysis of that election, and he wanders far from the promise of his subtitle, *Jews and Christians over two thousand years.* Yet once all these things are said, *God's First Love* (New York: Weybright & Talley, 1970) remains a significant work that cannot be ignored. While Heer's historical findings are hardly original, and some of his allegations are questionable (for example, he attempts to limit church resistance against Hitler to a defense "of the clergy's rights in their narrowest sense"; p. 322), his study is notable, not only as a mine of information, but for its prophetic strictures and passion.

10 Heer, *God's First Love,* pp. 148, 191, 253.
11 Cf. ibid., pp. 116, 169, 220, 350, 351–352, 443.

lective psyche of Jew-haters. Thus, Christians who accuse Jews of torturing the sacred host merely reveal their own doubts and secret desires.[12] The presence/absence and behavior/nonbehavior of Jews are, in a decisive sense, irrelevant. The disease requires only imagined Jews, in contrast to ordinary prejudice, for which real Blacks, Slavs, et al. are needed. Adolf Hitler was entirely right: were there no Jews, we should have to invent them.

The trouble is that whenever Friedrich Heer appears ready to support a declaration that antisemitism is at once sui generis and *the* key to the decline and fall of Western humanity, he draws back. In the very moment that he numbers among the causes "of a specifically Christian sense of outrage" the Jew Jesus as a stumbling block in the presence of much older faiths, and the many centuries in which "Christendom has shown itself to be the people guilty of God's murder" through the murder of the people of God, Heer retreats, curiously, into the indiscriminate truism that "every murder of a man is deicide." "For 'Jewish' any other hate object can be substituted at will."[13]

Again, Heer writes: "Christendom today stands close to the abyss of self-destruction through nuclear weapons. This suicide follows in historical terms logically from the practice, stretching over fifteen hundred years, of killing the blood relations of the Jew Jesus, the son of the Jewess Miriam, Mary. It is being prepared at deeply concealed levels of the subconscious. This subconscious is aware that Christendom has failed in its attempts to liquidate the Jews and to conquer the world." But once more Heer draws back. He goes on to intimate that antisemitism is simply a species of the wish to destroy and to die.[14] It is almost as though in the death camps we merely gave ourselves practice in the most up-to-date techniques of *self*-destruction. Here is a decisive failure

[12] Ibid., p. 137.
[13] Ibid., pp. 395–396, 509.
[14] Ibid., p. 392; cf. pp. 393–394.

to point out that in the gas ovens and crematoria *we* disposed of *them*. Rather than reducing our destruction of Jews to an undertaking that provides inspirational help and incentive toward our future self-annihilation, Heer could have moved, *on the basis of his own reasoning,* to the conclusion that nuclear suicide would comprise Christendom's specific revenge upon itself, as upon a bungling world, for the one unforgivable sin against the Holy Ghost: the failure to dispose of the Jews once and for all.

A most severe lapse is Heer's categorical judgment that "the disregard of the fate of the Jews between 1918 and 1945 can only be understood as part of a general disregard for Man and the world."[15] Heer's own chronicle of the unending, universal horror of Christian antisemitism ought to have suggested the very opposite judgment: that the disregard of the fate of Man between 1918 and 1945 (as in other periods) is to be understood in terms of the disregard of Jews. As Heer puts it elsewhere, "the Jew Jesus was to blame. The Jew Jesus has to be repressed."[16] The blame and the repression were visited upon the Jews, and then only derivatively upon other men. It is not that our self-destructiveness accounts for antisemitism; rather, antisemitism accounts for our self-destructiveness. Antisemitism is the special way we murder God. Thus, we have, in a sense, already destroyed the world.

Finally, Professor Heer ignores the obvious. Men almost unanimously deplore and fear nuclear destruction. This was anything but the case with the destruction of six million Jews. In point of fact, the Nazis were as greatly surprised by the world's silent admiration of them as they were by the absence of any serious resistance to the "final solution."[17] But Heer's own obsessive fear of the coming nuclear end of mankind acts to obfuscate in his own thinking the truth that in Christian antisemitism the works of the devil very "carefully"

[15] Ibid., p. 401.
[16] Ibid., p. 424.
[17] Ibid., p. 336.

and "responsibly" usurp the works of God.[18] On the ground of this latter truth, a universal nuclear death becomes, morally speaking, a comparative triviality, which may, in fact, be stumbled into rather than—as was the case with the destruction of European Jewry—be reasoned out as the "will" of God executed by Jesus Christ's avengers.

IV

Although Friedrich Heer fails to establish a final position on the crucial question I have introduced, the data he amasses surely point to the uniqueness (*Einzigartigkeit*) of antisemitism, whether we concentrate upon the antisemite as such or upon the Christian antisemite. Christianity has not taught that there are bad Jews along with bad Huns, Vandals, Arabs, Indians, or Japanese; instead, it has taught that "the Jews" killed God. To *be* a Jew is to deserve punishment. In historic Christian thought there is agreement that the devil and the Jew are one. Thus, as Professor Heer points out, it was "historically consistent" that at the Second Vatican Council no fundamental declaration could be produced that acknowledged Christian guilt.[19] Christians are not guilty; Jews are.

The reign of the Lord extends to all men, yet he chooses his own people. The dominion of the devil is also universalistic—his kingdom is indiscriminate—yet he too has his chosen ones. These are the antisemites. He does not leave himself without special witnesses. Through the centuries and in all places his faithful persist. The universality transcends the particularity, yet it is realized *through* the particularity. Jews are hated without limitations of date or boundaries of place.

[18] At one decisive juncture Heer fails to provide a necessary, relative moral judgment between crimes against Jews and modern warfare (ibid., pp. 359–360). His fixation upon the latter's destructiveness ought to keep him from choosing between the contemporary causes of Egypt and Israel, even though elsewhere he demands precisely such a choice.

[19] Ibid., p. 247.

The proof of the incomparability of antisemitism is its pervasiveness in time and space. The devil is universal yet very particular. As Friedrich Heer puts it, the Christian theologians proved Jewish guilt a thousand times. And we noted how the Johannine Jesus decrees that "the Jews" are not God's children, but children of the devil. It takes the devil to know the devil.

Men who are entirely separated by different periods of history and by totally different locales, and who indeed are often enemies of one another, are nevertheless friends at one fundamental point: they may always share in *Judenfeindschaft,* enmity toward Jews. Thus, one compelling basis for discerning a unique link between the devil and antisemitism is the manifesting of antisemitic depravity in so diverse and persisting an assembly of sources. Consider these recent examples taken more or less at random: the assurance by Michel Chartrand, a Canadian labor leader, that Israel is engaged in the mass murder of Palestinian Arabs;[20] the murder in Toulouse of a fifteen-year-old boy by several older boys, reportedly because he was Jewish; the sale in Dijon of Nazi-type caricature dolls labeled "Jew"; anti-Zionist and antisemitic statements by Orthodox churchmen in Greece; the appearance of a new edition of the *Protocols of the Elders of Zion* in the bookshops of Rome; and an antisemitic campaign in the Argentine by a right-wing politician, Walter Beveraggi Allende. Nor is the devil's program restricted to the Christian domain. As these words are written, antisemitism has attained renewed heights in the Soviet Union. In Morocco, violently antisemitic leaflets, threatening Jews with "reprisals" once the King is gone, have been circulating. And, in Cairo, *Al-Akhbar* declares that "many European Jews, obeying a secret Talmudic injunction, have returned to the tradition of human sacrifice, choosing Christian children as their victims, as taught by their elders. Incidents of kidnapping

[20] *The Gazette* (Montreal), Aug. 30, 1972.

have been discovered in a number of European cities. The children's bodies gave evidence of having been butchered in a special way and their blood sucked."[21]

For the Communist, the Jew lies behind capitalism and imperialism; for the capitalist, the Jew lies behind Communism. And the antisemite "knows" that both accusers are right. The antisemite does not comprehend Jewishness as a mere instance of human evil; he comprehends human evil as the incarnation of Jewishness. As one Hungarian antisemite deduced, since the Jews refuse to face "the truth" about themselves as revealed by the continuing persecutions of them, they are even the cause of antisemitism.[22] There is nothing for which they are not to blame. Russians and Americans may have their conflicts, and so may Frenchmen and Germans, Serbs and Croats, Egyptians and Syrians, Vietnamese and Chinese. But these and other peoples can always achieve a measure of unity through common opposition to Jews. As we shall emphasize in succeeding chapters, anti-Zionism and anti-Israelism, the most telling forms of contemporary antisemitism, are in no way limited to the Western world.

When contrasted with antisemitism, other forms of prejudice reveal themselves as, very largely, instances of historical transience. They appear and then they are gone. (I do not mean to underestimate the continuities that antisemitism shares with prejudice. William Stringfellow has referred to the genocidal foundation of white American religion, wherein the central reality of the cultus is "the idolatry of death" as the ultimate moral power.[23] Yet the basic discontinuity and ontological peculiarity of Christian antisemitism cannot be gainsaid: Jesus was a Jew.) The identifying of the Jews, *only* the Jews, with the devil is the devil's unique work, for only

---

[21] The foregoing examples are reported—and lamented—in "Newsnotes," *sidic (service international de documentation judéo-chrétienne,* Rome), 5:2 (1972), 39–40. The date of the *Al-Akhbar* item is Jan. 28, 1972.

[22] Heer, *God's First Love,* p. 339.

[23] William Stringfellow, "Harlem, Rebellion, and Resurrection," *The Christian Century,* 88:45 (Nov. 11, 1970), 1347.

the devil himself could uncover the devil in the Jews. Only the devil can fabricate and deliver devilish accusations. Morally as well as psychologically speaking, the charge of Jewish devilishness reveals the satanic conquest of the Christian soul. The Christian is the "Jew" he despises. And the Jew is the "Christian": Jewish ideals and behavior are the polar opposite of Christendom's accusations. The Jewish world conspiracy is the invention of demon-ridden Christian and other conspirators against Jews.

Strictly historical reasoning is transcended but then paradoxically reinstated with the aid of psychohistorical analysis such as that just offered.

8

Nemesis

The way we construe the nature and meaning of antisemitism will not only influence our reading of its centuries-old record; it will also determine, fatefully, our choice of weapons in waging the warfare to which Friedrich Heer and others call us.

I

If antisemitism is a truly incomparable wrong possessed of incomparably demonic power, our strategies against it must be radically different from those we should utilize were we to identify antisemitism as merely one wrong among others. Although in his work, *God's First Love,* Professor Heer concentrates upon the Christian contribution to the abiding, collective insanity, he believes—or at least he hopes— that Christianity can yet redeem itself. His study culminates in one of the first applications of a "theology of hope" to Christian–Jewish relations. Even if Christianity is itself the *fons et origo* of Christian and Western antisemitism, Heer maintains doggedly that in Christian faith itself, *once its Jewish foundation is restored,* lies the only real deliverance from antisemitism. The secular basis and counterpart of his reasoning is the social–Freudian claim that the one way to the future is through a "positive dissolution" and rehabilitation of the past.[1] Through a massive act of self-analysis Christendom may yet purge itself of its sins.

According to Professor Heer, everything depends upon whether Christendom will surmount its Augustinian (and Pauline) contempt for the world, entailing as this does an exclusivist negation of true messianic hope. Religion has made "the barbarian peoples from the fourth to the twentieth centuries" even more barbaric: their exclusive Christ–God is "a dreadful weapon of self-assertion directed both outwards and inwards. . . ." We must "return to the Old Testament roots of Christ's own piety and to even older roots—to the original faith in which man felt himself to be both God's creature and his responsible partner." Christianity must again "reestablish its roots in the ancient soil of its Jewish fatherland." Were Christianity to recognize and condemn its own repetition of the murder of its Christ through the murders of his brothers and sisters, it would be, in that very moment, set free to return to where it belongs: to the Jew Jesus. "By rooting itself in its true soil, Christianity would achieve the great acceptance of the world—the acceptance of 'earthly' love. Only Eros can dissolve the neuroses and pathological self-isolation of Christianity in relation to the Jew Jesus, to Man's history and to itself. . . . A Christendom enriched by Israel and Jewish piety would recognize that the so-called eternal values are only true and genuine when they are made incarnate, when they become flesh in history and when they are realized in the society of Man."[2]

To a limited extent, Heer's demand upon the church is already being taken seriously. Within Christian scholarship and theology there is increasing affirmation of the Jewishness of Jesus and of the Jewish dimensions of Christian faith. Again, the struggle against asceticism now sweeping the

---

[1] Heer, *God's First Love*, p. 417.
[2] Ibid., pp. 30, 401, 415–416, 417, 426.

Christian world must be noted on Heer's side. For it is possible to discern in antisemitism an inevitable product of celibate, ascetic monks and priests with their natural (or unnatural) fantasies of Jewish "carnality" and "materialism."[3] This would seem to suggest that, other things being equal— though they never are—the abolishment of a celibate clergy would comprise, hopefully, a greater blow against antisemitism than a thousand educational programs. However, Heer does not really dispose of the obvious rejoinder that Protestantism, which is in more than one respect the antithesis of Catholic Augustinianism, is no less blameworthy than Catholicism in respect to antisemitism—and in some instances, displays a worse record.[4] On the other hand, Heer does attest that the preservation within Calvinism of Christianity's Jewish roots has kept Calvinist countries from bloody persecutions of Jews.[5]

II

I believe that the very psychological considerations to which Professor Heer rightly draws our attention compound our problem more than they help to resolve it. The identification of antisemitism with the devil does nothing to make the devil go away. He may simply thrive on the publicity. The denial of Christian Jewishness has, it is true, opened the way to antisemitic diabolism. Yet it is most doubtful that we can any longer expect the contrary result by virtue of any attestation of Christian Jewishness. The affirmation that Christianity is Jewish at its roots may simply make for a metastasizing of antisemitism. We are advised by Heer that for seventeen centuries "the Christians' murderous hatred of the Jew was, at bottom, directed against the Jew Jesus, of whom Christians despaired, whom they hated and blamed . . . for the

---

[3] Cf. ibid., pp. 37–39, 89, 128, 290–291, 402.
[4] Cf. ibid., pp. 129–134.
[5] Ibid., p. 410.

heavy burden of history."[6] This seems to suggest that a genuine acceptance of Jesus will mean the acceptance of his people. But is the Christian acceptance of Jesus (other than by individuals here and there) any longer a possibility? Has not the entrenched union of Christian sin with the faits accompli of history cut off any real eventuality of this form of social regeneration? Is it not now much more probable that any self-identified Jewishness on the part of the church will simply intensify its adherents' hatred of Jews and, thereby, of Jesus? We live after, not before, Auschwitz.

There is the agonizing question of whether a full disclosure of historic Christian sins against Jews will have good consequences or bad ones. After all, the truth that the Nazis only brought to fulfillment historic Christian teaching can be readily utilized by enemies of Jews.[7] Indeed, to suggest to Christians that they are antisemitic is quite likely to make them more antisemitic. Were it not for the Jew—they may secretly tell themselves—no one could ever go around making the insufferable charge of antisemitism against them. In the opening chapter of the present study it is intimated that the very raising of the issue of Christian guilt may prove counterproductive. Alan T. Davies points out that even minor Christian guilt feelings over Auschwitz

produce a curious reaction: one is tempted to conclude that it comes almost as a relief to [Christians] to discover that Jews, like Christians, are capable of wrongdoing. The frequent journalistic comparisons between Zionist militarism and nazi militarism are instructive at this point. To find Israel in a morally ambiguous situation releases the Christian from thinking too much about Auschwitz and his own vicarious participation in one of the darkest moments of Western history. It is as if the Christian conscience whispers: "See, we aren't that bad after all—look at what the Jews are doing now!" Such an attitude, conscious or unconscious, is doubly bad. It is bad because it makes the Christian vulnerable to anti-Semitism as well as to anti-Zionism, and it is bad

[6] Ibid., p. 425.
[7] Cf. ibid., p. 388.

because it deflects the church from its own sins by concentrating on the sins of others.[8]

The insinuation to Christians that they and their religion have been invaded by demonic forces may—no matter how diplomatically or psychotherapeutically the judgment is tendered—merely erect more formidable obstacles to redemption. To reidentify Judaism as the religion of the father, with Christianity as the religion of the son,[9] or even to offer the symbology of elder and younger brothers, as I myself have done, may be to call up angry and destructive impulses. The most horrifying eventuality of all is that the new Christian testimony that the Jewish people are not cast away by God, but remain the people of his Covenant, will only drive us deeper into the hell of antisemitism by arousing as yet unconquered hostilities within the Christian soul. Friedrich Heer's testimony that in the Jews there lurks "the hidden God, who unmasks the living lie in every human being"[10] grasps us with its truthfulness. Yet it also brings the dread promise of further suffering for Jews. Heer himself wonders whether Christendom, which has for ages considered itself mortally wronged, can now bear the insult of being exposed as the real criminal.[11] If Christianity is in fact hell, who has ever found a human path up from hell? It is very hard to believe that the way out is through some kind of social–psychological, theological, or even moral reform.

That Vienna, home of Sigmund Freud, should be the place from which Professor Heer writes epitomizes at one and the same time much of the appeal and much of the irony of his work. Massive societal–religious entities simply do not respond along the personal–redemptive lines he proposes. The presumption that social–psychoanalytic therapy can somehow

---

[8] Alan T. Davies, "Anti-Zionism, Anti-Semitism, and the Christian Mind," *The Christian Century,* 87:33 (Aug. 19, 1970), 989.

[9] Cf. Heer, *God's First Love,* p. 350.

[10] Ibid., p. 444.

[11] Ibid., p. 396.

salvage a centuries-old institutional structure is infinitely more tenuous than the claim for the psychoanalytic salvation of the individual. The latter claim itself remains highly debatable. Lamentably, diagnosis, however compelling, is not in itself a cure.

However, Friedrich Heer is in this very connection so honest and perceptive that he senses a pursuit by failure. The word "only," which he repeatedly uses, signifies not alone a uniquely qualified remedy but also, I submit, the probable impossibility of realizing so high an ideal as his: *Only* the remorseless self-analysis that wholly uncovers our past, that "takes us into and through the hell of Christian hatred of the Jew," can make a neurotic Christianity whole again; yet any such process remains "as perilous as the psychoanalysis of a single person." *Only* a few have thus far attained the requisite mental and spiritual maturity. "Within the deeply sick community of Man dwell deeply sick churches, and they form the centers of pathological processes constantly leading to new explosions." Revealingly, Heer questions whether it "would be possible to find within a Christianity very largely composed of wounded, outraged, and sick souls and minds, personalities strong enough to take on" the arduous journey through hell which is self-analysis.[12] Heer is himself forced to retreat from the macrocosm of social redemption to the microcosm of a small elite. And, pitiably, for the entire Holocaust period he can uncover only three Christian theologians prepared for the journey. One of these is Dietrich Bonhoeffer, who (although Heer fails to point it out) held a position vis-à-vis the Jewish people that remains highly problematic.[13] Heer calls out for heroes, but he must also concede that most

[12] Ibid., pp. 396, 398, 411, 415, 426.
[13] Cf. Dietrich Bonhoeffer, *No Rusty Swords* (New York: Harper & Row, 1965), pp. 221–242. For a totally different and fresh interpretation of Bonhoeffer and his final martyrdom, see William Jay Peck, "From Cain to the Death Camps: An Essay on Bonhoeffer and Judaism," *Union Seminary Quarterly Review,* 28:2 (Winter, 1973), 158–176.

of us barbarians are neither ready nor willing nor able to serve.

III

No concept is more relevant to the morphology and life of Christian antisemitism and anti-Judaism than "nemesis." Nemesis involves an act of retribution. Throughout her history, the church has sought to justify her anti-Jewishness through association with some kind of rightful or meritorious punitiveness. But "nemesis" is also linked to fate: it signifies a condition that resists the restoration of goodness and justice. There is, however, a grave moral danger that the amassing of prophetic judgments against the Christian community may combine with our terrible knowledge of erstwhile Christianity's fate to make us abandon the war against Christian antisemitism. It is a blessing that we know so little of the battles that rage in heaven. We are ignorant of the exact intentions God has for the devil. Consequently, we can see ourselves as free. We are responsible men. We have to fight against our own nemesis, lest sin gain the one victory it yet must covet: our final consent.

To adjudge that Friedrich Heer's "only" solution is sadly utopian need not in itself rule out hope, though it does demand the total transformation of our thinking in commitment to an alternative "only": the death of erstwhile Christianity itself. Death, after all, acts to overcome the past at least as tellingly and valuably as does psychoanalysis, and probably more so.

The final nemesis remains that any contemporary program of salvation from Christian antisemitism may have come too late. The church that collaborated in the Nazi "final solution" dealt herself mortal blows. From that Jewish crucifixion and Christian self-crucifixion there could and did come a Jewish resurrection—the State of Israel—but not a Christian resurrection. Does the church have anywhere to go now? She is as Cain, a fugitive upon the face of the earth. The all-decisive consideration is that the church of the "final solution" was living out to the ultimate fulfillment her own historical fate. For Christian antisemitism was born at the moment of God's first death. How, then, is antisemitism to die unless there is a new resurrection, a fresh birth of God?

In *God's First Love,* Friedrich Heer implies the following conclusion, though he does not ever express it (perhaps he cannot stand the terrifying consequence of so many of his own words): Because we took the wonderful goodness of Christianity and changed it into God's misdeed, because we have transubstantiated that faith into a cancer for humanity, we can now only commit ourselves to the demise of whatever remains of Christianity—lest worse crimes be done. We can now only deny God for his sake, that is, for the sake of other human beings of his. Perhaps the only chance left is for God to die in this way. Perhaps then he may live once more, not because of us, but because he is "the coming God: a God of the present and of the future, in which he will submerge the brutal past."[14]

[14] Heer, *God's First Love,* p. 444.

Part Two
CHRISTIANS, ISRAEL, AND THE MIDDLE EAST CONFLICT

9

Christian Perspectives on Israel

As we give intensive consideration now to the question of Israel and the Middle East, we shall first review major Christian positions on the subject of Israel. The topic is essential in and of itself; it is taken up at this point partly for orientation purposes.

Writing in general terms, Alice L. Eckardt says: "Israel as a nation is treated much the same as the Jewish people have been treated throughout history."[1] This reminds us that those contemporary Christian attitudes toward Israel which are hostile must be understood in continuity with the long tradition of Christendom's antipathy toward Jews and persecution of Jews. On the other hand, we must not ignore Edward H. Flannery's point that many views of Israel can hardly be considered Christian, even if they come from Christians, and some of them are positively un-Christian.[2]

Among Christian spokesmen, the points of view on Israel as a Jewish state run the gamut from total rejection to acceptance and celebration, with various attitudes and images falling between the two poles.

[1] Alice L. Eckardt, "The Enigma of Christian Hostility to Israel," *Women's League Outlook*, 42:3 (Spring, 1972), 25.
[2] Edward H. Flannery, *A Christian View of Israel*, pamphlet published by Seton Hall University, South Orange, N.J., May, 1970, p. 2.

101

I

Within Eastern and Western Christendom, antisemitism has traditionally been carried forward by means of anti-Judaism and by denigration and persecution of Jews bereft of political protection. However, for some years these weapons have been supplemented and refined by means of anti-Zionism and/or anti-Israelism, the chief instrumentalities of contemporary Christian antisemitism. The question persists, nevertheless, of whether anti-Zionism and anti-Israelism are *necessarily* representative of antisemitism.

To Seymour M. Lipset, "one may oppose Israeli policy, resist Zionism or criticize worldwide Jewish support of Israel" without being antisemitic.[3] On the other hand, the presence of the State of Israel as, allegedly, an aggravator of the world's woes, together with the permissiveness and even the favor accorded anti-Zionism and anti-Israelism, can certainly be used to excellent advantage by antisemites. Lipset himself points out that in New Left and Black antisemitism the word "Zionist" is "simply a code word for Jew, just as it has become in Eastern Europe."[4]

Alan T. Davies contends that the most fashionable contemporary guise for antisemitism *is* anti-Zionism. As Davies expresses it, antisemitic convictions "can be transposed without much difficulty into the new language of anti-Zionism, as meanwhile the reality of a Jewish nation-state offers a tangible scapegoat." It would almost seem here that the antisemites involved "have it made": they can emphatically protest their "innocence" of any hostility to Jews as Jews. Davies quite properly emphasizes that it is out of the question to exempt the State of Israel from the same moral criteria to which any nation-state is subject. The real issue is "the context into which criticism of Israel ought to be placed. It is one thing to judge Israel on the grounds that—as with all

[3] Seymour M. Lipset, " 'The Socialism of Fools'. . . ," *The New York Times Magazine,* Jan. 3, 1971, p. 6.
[4] Ibid., p. 26.

nation-states—the reality of power is the end of innocence. But clearly it is quite another thing to attack Israel because of its Jewish—and specifically its Zionist—foundations."[5]

Insofar as anti-Zionists manifest hostility to Jews— particularly to the Jews of Israel—there is little moral or scientific choice but to characterize them as antisemites. Professor Lipset reports that recent attacks in France upon Jews, Judaism, and Israel spread from the student New Left to different Catholic groups that "deny the historic claims of the Jews to Israel on the theological grounds that the church, rather than contemporary Jewry, is the true heir of ancient Israel."[6] This suggests a criterion for the correct identifying of anti-Israelism as a newer form of antisemitism. One measure of the presence or absence of antisemitism lies in answers to the question: Is the integrity of the State of Israel being honored?

In 1970 an international conference of Christians meeting in Beirut, Lebanon demanded the total "disappearance of Zionist structures."[7] Was this an embodiment of antisemitism? The phrase used by the group is nothing but a euphemism for the destruction of Israel. Before 1948 it might have been possible for someone to question the practical wisdom or feasibility of the reestablishing of a sovereign Jewish state at a given time in Palestine without being charged with antisemitism. We live a generation later. The assertion today that Jewry has no right to Eretz Yisrael and therefore, by implication, that the State of Israel ought to be abolished is an instance of antisemitism. For there is no way to call for the

---

[5] Alan T. Davies, *Anti-Semitism and the Christian Mind* (New York: Herder & Herder, 1969), p. 182; "Anti-Zionism, Anti-Semitism, and the Christian Mind," *The Christian Century*, 87:33 (Aug. 19, 1970), p. 989; letter to editor of *The Christian Century*, 89:27 (July 19, 1972), 777. In the final citation here Davies is referring to the anti-Israeli position of the United Church of Canada *Observer*.

[6] Lipset, " 'The Socialism of Fools'. . . ," *The New York Times Magazine*, Jan. 3, 1971, p. 26.

[7] As cited in Alice and Roy Eckardt, *Encounter with Israel: A Challenge to Conscience* (New York: Association Press, 1970), p. 257.

destruction of Israel without supporting a new Holocaust, the suffering and death of as many as two and one half million Jews. (I do not in any way suggest that the fait accompli of the State of Israel constitutes a legitimate argument for her sovereignty.)

We must, in addition, address ourselves to the advocated distinction between unconscious and conscious hostility. Edward H. Flannery provides a penetrating analysis in the *Journal of Ecumenical Studies*. Although he does not equate anti-Zionism or anti-Israelism with antisemitism, Father Flannery nevertheless shows the marked affinities among these phenomena, especially at unconscious levels. While stressing a need for caution and tentativeness, he argues that the similarity of reaction in Christendom to the Holocaust and to the emergence of the State of Israel is symptomatic of "determinative unconscious forces, specifically, of an unrecognized antipathy [to] the Jewish people." The Holocaust and the State of Israel are at opposite poles in the existence of Jews. "One is its nadir; the other, its zenith: Israel prostrate and Israel triumphant." Yet even though the stimuli are poles apart, the response to them is identical: apathy–hostility. Such an inappropriate outcome could hardly come from rational sources. The very multiplicity of the indictments of Zionism by Christians conceals unrecognized motivations. "A certain vague uneasiness attends the idea of Jews restored to Palestine, and to Jerusalem in particular. This uneasiness *may* serve as the subliminal foundation for a Christian anti-Zionism and as the dynamics [behind] the various 'reasons' supplied for disfavoring the State of Israel, its policies, and its activities."[8] The Christian death wish for Jews has gained a contemporary incarnation.

A ready illustration is today's *Christianity and Crisis,* which—as we are reminded in another source—has, "except for occasional showpieces," become "consistently hostile to

[8] Edward H. Flannery, "Anti-Zionism and the Christian Psyche," *Journal of Ecumenical Studies,* 6:2 (Spring, 1969), 174, 178, 179, 181.

the redemption of the Jewish people in Israel."[9] A familiar device is utilized by this journal: the double standard. When space is provided for contributions sympathetic to Israel or critical of antisemitism, careful provision is made for hostile rebuttals. But attacks upon Israel and the Jewish people are not treated in a corresponding way. Most often, the final word is given to the anti-Israeli, anti-Jewish side.[10] It was to be expected that Mrs. Reinhold Niebuhr and her son Christopher should recently insist that because of the journal's anti-Israeli animus, the late Reinhold Niebuhr's name as founding editor be removed from the masthead of *Christianity and Crisis.*[11]

II

In certain cases anti-Zionism and anti-Israelism among Christians reflect more than merely unconscious anti-Jewish attitudes. They comprise overt, conscious embodiments of out-and-out antisemitism. Among differing Christian perspectives on Israel, this position is located, obviously, far to the rejective end of the spectrum. An example is John Nicholls Booth, a Unitarian-Universalist pastor. I refer to his article, "American Freedom Versus Zionist Power," in a recent number of *The Cross and the Flag,* official organ of Gerald L. K. Smith's Christian Nationalist Crusade. Booth finds in Zionism a terrible crime and conspiracy against humanity. Zionism is the enemy of human dignity, the supressor of human freedom. One widespread stratagem among contemporary antisemites —represented, for example, in and by the Soviet Union—is

[9] *CCI notebook,* Christians Concerned for Israel, no. 9 (May, 1972), 4.

[10] For three recent examples of this, see *Christianity and Crisis,* 32:7 (May 1, 1972), 111; 32:9 (May 29, 1972), 129; 32:10 (June 12, 1972), 151. The second example is especially clever; it seeks to utilize the late Reinhold Niebuhr's name in behalf of the journal's new brand of "evenhandedness." See Eugene Rothman, "The Evolution of a Christian Perspective," *Midstream,* 17:2 (February, 1971), 3–12.

[11] See *The New York Times,* May 8, 1972; *The Jewish News* (Detroit), May 12, 1972.

carefully to avoid the word "Jews" and to substitute the word "Zionist" and sometimes the words "Israel" and "Israelis." At times Booth adheres to this practice, as when he writes that "Zionists have been able to establish a climate of deceptive impressions, international tensions and domestic political decisions that undermine the foundation principles of our republic," and when he states that the "corrupting influence of gutter Zionism on American life is only beginning to surface." However, Booth also resorts to another widespread technique among antisemites—namely, the accusation that a major weapon in the Jewish world conspiracy is the blackmail charge of antisemitism and, indeed, the Jewish fabrication of antisemitism where antisemitism is, in fact, absent. Furthermore, in places Booth does not bother with the semantic trick I have mentioned. Thus, Zionism is a "coordination of Jewish skills, loyalties and money"; American Jews, rather than Israel, are the real directors of "the global aims of Zionism"; and "the Jewish establishment" is spending millions "to spread suspicion and hate, as well as shut down those who would educate the public in what is occurring." In these ways Booth's approach reflects a return to a more traditional practice in Christendom: the explicit identification of the enemy of humankind as the Jew. The Jews are tribalists who oppose "universal, humanitarian man." Here Booth is completely at one with Gerald L. K. Smith's introductory commendation of him for revealing "the stubborn dogmatic tyrannical, world-wide institution known as Jew-Zionism."[12]

Almost identical sentiments are offered by Booth in a subsequent piece called "How Zionists Manipulate Your News," in the United Church of Canada's *Observer,* a publication edited by Canada's most notorious Christian antisemite, the Rev. A. C. Forrest.[13] The United Church of

---

[12] John Nicholls Booth, "American Freedom Versus Zionist Power," *The Cross and the Flag,* 30:11 (February, 1972), 8–13.

[13] See three analyses, "Antisemitism and the United Church of Canada," *CCI notebook,* no. 7 (March, 1972), 1–2; "More on Antisemi-

Canada is the country's largest Protestant denomination. In the latter article, Booth asserts that the Zionists have "crushed into silence" innumerable voices of conscience. "Israeli intelligence, through B'nai B'rith's [Anti-Defamation League], Zionist organizations, temples and rabbis, penetrates every part of our nation. . . ."[14] Thus, what Booth in fact wishes to tell us is: "How Jews Manipulate Your News." Booth's efforts in these publications, in *The American Mercury,* and in public addresses carry forward the goals of *The Protocols of the Elders of Zion,* the infamous forgery that "portrays" an unending Jewish program of world conspiracy, intimidation, control, and conquest. One effect of Booth's work, together with A. C. Forrest's, will be, I should imagine, an upsurge of credence for *The Protocols.* After all, these men boast the social qualifications of liberal Christian clergymen.

A comment in the *CCI notebook* suggests that there is no sharp division between conscious and unconscious hostility: "Editor Forrest's basic problem is in fact no different from that of any of us who have grown up in a Christendom that has lied about the Jews for centuries. Of course, as he protests, he is not an antisemite in the intentional sense: he is an unwitting *Kulturantisemit,* like most of the baptized. . . . Between the common malaise of cultural antisemitism and the horrible outbreaks of political antisemitism there is a very narrow corridor, and the instincts of the victims or prospective victims are much sounder in spotting the danger than those of any of us among the Gentiles."[15]

Christian anti-Israelism and antisemitism are associated,

---

tism in the United Church of Canada," *CCI notebook,* no. 9 (May, 1972), 3; "A Wicked Book," *CCI notebook,* no. 13 (June, 1973), 5–6. In an open letter to A. C. Forrest, President Douglas Young of the American Institute of Holy Land Studies, Jerusalem writes: "I accuse you of falling into bloody hands and allowing your own to become stained with that blood . . ." (Aug. 1, 1969).

[14] John Nicholls Booth, "How Zionists Manipulate Your News," *The United Church Observer* (Toronto), 34:9 (March, 1972), 24, 25.

[15] *CCI notebook,* no. 7 (March, 1972), 1, 2 (slightly emended).

of course, with the biblicist and theological right within the churches. Is it the case that Christians who cast off central dogmas that have traditionally and historically nurtured anti-semitism and anti-Judaism will thereby develop more positive and sympathetic attitudes toward Jews? This has happened. But it does not necessarily happen. Orthodox Christian par-ticularists often criticize Jews for their universalism. But Christian universalists fault Jews for their particularism. The campaign of John Nicholls Booth is but one instance of anti-Israelism and antisemitism in today's theological left. The condemnation of Jewish particularity, including most de-cisively in our time the denial of a right to political independ-ence, remains pervasive within "liberal" Christianity.[16]

I introduce the case of Fred Gladstone Bratton, another Unitarian-Universalist. (There is no insinuation here that Unitarian-Universalists must be anti-Zionist; we think of such great sympathizers for Israel as John Haynes Holmes and Carl Hermann Voss.) In a volume titled *The Crime of Chris-tendom*,[17] Professor Bratton strives to dissolve the Jewish particularist–universalist symbiosis into what he calls "the Jewish dilemma." Bratton's Marcionite Protestant, "liberal"–universalist ideology forces him to censure Jewish particularity. He insists that Jews must not "represent a nation or a race" but only "a cultural and religious community." Perhaps most revealingly of all, Bratton contends that "ethnic and cultural anti-Semitism . . . was originally provoked and continuously nourished by the orthodox Jewish dogma of uniqueness." Bratton's demand upon Jews to give proper allegiance to essential, American norms points to the deep kinship between

[16] Quotation marks are placed around the word "liberal," because the point of view involved here is not true liberalism. Genuine liberalism is grounded, as Arthur J. Lelyveld points out, upon two basic presuppositions: "a concern for people and for humane values," and "an insistence on free-dom to think through every problem without prior ideological constraints" ["In Defense of Liberalism," *Congress bi-weekly*, 39:3 (Feb. 11, 1972), 4].

[17] Fred Gladstone Bratton, *The Crime of Christendom: The Theo-logical Sources of Christian Anti-Semitism* (Boston: Beacon Press, 1969).

"liberal"–universalist nationalism and the primitivistic homogeneity of fascism. Bratton's ideal is the "liberal Jew" who is "no longer obsessed with the idea of uniqueness." Jews are to "emphasize broad principles of living rather than particularistic beliefs." We are reminded here of the Napoleonic demand that "emancipated" Jews be "good" individual Frenchmen at the expense of their communal integrity. Not strangely, Bratton's attack upon Jewishness climaxes in an attack upon Zionism and Israel: The "fanatical leaders of political Zionism have forced upon Jews everywhere the idea that they are a part of an ethnic, racial, and political entity. . . ." In sum, Professor Bratton epitomizes the ongoing "liberal" Christian, imperialist refusal to honor Jewish particularity, the right of the Jewish people to be themselves. Anti-Israelism is the inevitable fruit of Bratton's moral and theological presuppositions.[18]

III

Anti-Israelism within circles that are, religiously speaking, relatively more conservative than the foregoing viewpoint often entails a negative theologizing of the political domain of erstwhile Palestine. By this I mean a resort to Christian religious judgments and scriptural passages in order to question and even to deny Zionist and Israeli claims. A perfect illustration of this is a pronouncement by sixty-odd missionaries and churchmen resident in Beirut:

Isn't it too simple to assume that [the military action of Israel] is a manifestation of God's grace? . . . [We] must challenge the assumption that the Israeli occupation of Jerusalem, and indeed of large portions of Palestine, represents the fulfillment of Old Testament prophecy. The Old Testament does speak of the return of Israel to the promised land, but Christians should remember three

---

[18] The foregoing paragraph is adapted from my review of Bratton's *The Crime of Christendom* in *Journal of Church and State*, 14:1 (Winter, 1972), 128–131.

things: (1) the great prophetic voices in the Old Testament . . . constantly warned Israel that a gracious God would judge severely any injustice his chosen people committed; (2) by the end of the Old Testament period such promises of return were understood as part of the action of *God* at the very end of history rather than of *men* within history; and (3) the New Testament understands the whole Old Testament experience as having been transposed into a new key by the coming of Jesus Christ: so that the Church is the new "Israel of God" (Gal. 6:16). If Jesus made it clear that God is to be worshiped neither on Mt. Gerizim nor in Jerusalem (John 4:21),[19] can Christians believe that God's promise is fulfilled by the occupation of Palestine by the modern political state of Israel? What do we mean when we sing, "Noel, Noel, born is the King of Israel"? [20]

The contention of the Beirut group was given renewed voice in a recent Palm Sunday sermon by Edward L. R. Elson, Chaplain of the United States Senate. In seeking to rebuke Christians who allegedly find a fulfillment of prophecy in the Israeli administration of Jerusalem, Elson told his local congregation that the Christian church is "the new Israel of God."[21]

Here are spokesmen who insinuate theological supersessionism into the political sphere. The Christian traditionalist–negativist stance toward the Jewish people is reapplied to the State of Israel. Jews are not treated as human beings; they are subjected to a triumphalist religion called Christianity. That the church, the "new Israel," has taken the place, reputedly, of the "old Israel," the Jewish people, becomes the ground for political opposition to Israel and Jews. But there is much more here than meets the eye. The surface insistence

[19] This is a misquotation. Jesus is actually reported by John as saying, "the hour is coming when neither on this mountain nor in Jerusalem will you worship the Father."

[20] "An Open Letter to Christians of the West," carrying a date of Spring, 1968. The signatures of the group are on file at the University Christian Center, Box 235, Beirut, Lebanon.

[21] Edward L. R. Elson, as cited in *Near East Report,* 16:13 (March 29, 1972), 51.

that theology is to judge politics is a cloak for other and ulterior purposes. Among anti-Israeli Christians today, no propaganda stratagem is more widespread than the utilization of Scripture to make weighty demands upon Israel and, in truth, to deny her right to exist. Professedly Christian reasoning becomes, in fact, an ideology to justify and advance a specific political program: the forcible transfer of the land to the foes of Israel. Let there be no doubt that this is the hidden but real intention of the Beirut churchmen; consider a later pronouncement by substantially the same group charging that "the Zionists have driven the Arabs into the desert" and that the Palestinian Arab homeland has been seized "by an alien Western political movement," and referring to "armed struggle" as probably the only way to restore justice. The solution is the "dezionization" of Israel—in alternative phrasing, politicide.[22] As for Edward L. R. Elson, he is a long-time pro-Arab apologist, the former head of the anti-Israeli organization, American Friends of the Middle East.[23]

These spokesmen make Christian theology subservient to political interest while claiming that they are fighting this practice. What is verbalized as independence for the Christian gospel is, in truth, a threat to that independence.

If Israel and the Jewish people are assailed by both the Christian right and the Christian left, the most formidable menaces must arise, logically, from ideologies that combine these two dimensions, since the inspiration is then compounded. The French group, "Christians for Palestine," closely linked to the publication *Témoignage Chrétien,* is a contemporary case in point. It joins together a New Left, politico-ideological condemnation of Zionism and Israel with tradi-

[22] As cited in Eckardt and Eckardt, *Encounter With Israel,* p. 257.
[23] Elson's sermon was criticized by a number of Protestant and Catholic leaders, as were the anti-Israeli sermons delivered in Washington, D.C. on the very same Palm Sunday, 1972 by Francis B. Sayre of the Episcopal Cathedral and Bishop Papken Varjabedian of St. Mary's Armenian Apostolic Church [*The Jewish News* (Detroit), April 7, 1972].

tional supersessionist theology, according to which, once again, the church is the fresh, spiritual "new Israel" replacing the outmoded, evil "old Israel."

A theologizing of the political order is not only found in Christian viewpoints hostile to Israel and the Jewish people. It is further exemplified among Christians who manifest very great sympathy for Israel and Jews. Along this latter line I refer once more to the Statement put forward by the General Synod of the Reformed Church of Holland, as considered in Chapter 5. We spoke of that body's attempted disjunction between Jewish residency in the land of Israel and Jewish sovereignty in that place, and to the aid and comfort that this dichotomy has to give to the enemies of Israel.[24] Again, the Synod's concern that the Jews may make their dwelling place "into a nationalistic state in which the only thing that counts is military power"[25] is, in the presence of foes committed to the obliteration of Israel, little short of a moral outrage. If these Dutch churchmen are really so worried about Israeli militarism, they had better address themselves to the parties responsible for this condition: the Arab states, the Soviet Union, and the terrorists. I have maintained that Christian moral transgressions against Jews will continue to occur until the church is redeemed from the politics of moralistic biblicism. This consideration explains why some of us must have great reservations about such subjects of study as "Biblical Interpretation and the Middle East," subjects that keep popping up in circles of the World Council of Churches.

An additional question presents itself: No theological problem is more vexing than that of whether contemporary events of time and place can be determinative for faith,

---

[24] We must also wonder about the sources of the Dutch Synod's "information" that non-Jews in Israel are treated as second-class citizens (*Israel: People, Land and State,* par. 50).

[25] Ibid., par. 48; see also par. 51.

which is allied to the issue of what meanings, if any, may be assigned to specific historical occurrences. In attempting to find meaning in the return of Jews to Eretz Yisrael, the Dutch Synod says: "Precisely in its concrete visibility, this return points us to the special significance of this people in the midst of the nations, and to the saving faithfulness of God; it is a sign for us that it is God's will to be on earth together with man." Such a peril as future expulsion "cannot prevent us from understanding the return positively as a confirmation of God's lasting purpose with his people."[26] In truth, the reestablishment of Israel provides no such sign or confirmation. It is highly questionable whether the identities and eventualities of history can ever vindicate faith, any more than they can finally refute faith. The necessity for our denial here is made obvious by recourse to the obverse of the Synod's proposition: Israel's annihilation tomorrow would presumably have to signify the nonfaithfulness of God.

IV

Let us move to the other side. Christian positions supportive of Israel are, taken overall, both polemical and affirmational. My own evaluative comments down to this point have illustrated some of the polemical elements. Those elements comprise a Christian moral reaction against antisemitism and against the denigration of Israel within and beyond the Christian world. Insofar as anti-Israelism is an instrument of antisemitism, hostility to Israel is meliorated to the extent that antisemitism goes—*if* it goes. Very great obstacles to the abolition of antisemitism persist. None of these is more stubborn than self-righteousness and self-defensiveness among Christians. Again I cite Alice Eckardt: The vehemence with which many Christians deny the need for a Jewish state due

---

[26] Ibid., pars. 41, 42.

to antisemitism (not the main foundation of Israel, to be sure) "reflects a refusal to admit the moral indictment of Christian civilization that is thereby implied."[27]

Among the interpretations of Christian faith that appear to undergird the integrity of the State of Israel is one we may identify as evangelical literalism. This outlook is widespread, numerically speaking, in the United States and elsewhere, within conservative, non-Roman Catholic circles. At the Jerusalem Conference on Biblical Prophecy in June, 1971, the cochairman, Carl F. H. Henry, declared: "We live already in the last days because of the Resurrection of the Crucified One. The dramatic and unmistakable message of the New Testament is that the very last of those days is soon to break upon us."[28] Evangelical literalists endeavor to summon attention to certain momentous happenings and overarching world developments: nuclear warfare, the population explosion, ecological disasters (present and future)—and the reemergence of the State of Israel. As the time of the end "draws near," the rebirth of Israel is at once a dramatic sign and an instrumentality of a divinely blessed event. Israel is possessed of a crucial historical role in "the final days" before the return of Christ. This is not to imply that evangelicals are of one mind in respect to the exact nature of Israel's role. For some, Christ will not come back until the regathered Jews have converted to the Christian faith. However, the conversionist position, while popular among many fundamentalists, is not universally agreed upon.

I do not know that an intensive consideration of this point of view is required. Presumably, one either subscribes to it or he does not. The hazards and attractions of timetable Christianity have been long debated. Perhaps we could begin to take religious literalists with some seriousness were they not at such violent odds with one another over the character of the single, literal truth. What may happen to the attitudes

[27] Alice Eckardt, "The Enigma . . . ," p. 7.
[28] Carl F. H. Henry, as quoted in *Newsweek*, June 28, 1971, p. 62.

of conversionists when, as seems certain, the Jews of Israel do not abide conversion is not happy to contemplate. What will happen to the evangelicals and their claims as the years pass and pass, and Jesus fails to "show," is a portentous question with respect to Christian attitudes toward the State of Israel. Of course, if Jesus did "show," the problem would ostensibly be resolved, at least so long as he fixed his radar in allowable directions.

V

In the forefront of Christian moral and theological support for Israel are certain Roman Catholic expositors. At the beginning of a recent essay, Father Edward H. Flannery writes: "There can no longer be any question but that the vast majority of Jews have identified with the State of Israel, whether they see it merely as a refuge from anti-Semitism, a source of Jewish identity, or a messianic fulfillment. Israel has always been central to Jewish belief and to the Jewish soul, and in times of exile, an object of aspiration and prayer. The latest return to the land has revived the sense of this centrality in Jews everywhere."[29]

We are immediately impressed here by an attitude radically different from the other views so far described. As against a subjecting of Israel to external demands and to extrinsic forms of understanding, the Jewish people are approached as though from within, on the foundation of their own concerns, hopes, and interests. This orientation is carried forward in Father Flannery's rejoinder to the dualism that seeks to divorce Judaism as a religion from Zionism as a modern political movement. He answers: Judaism is in its essence Zionist. From its very inception it entailed a trinity of people, Torah, and land, and it has always retained the idea of possession of or return to Zion. Flannery continues: "The over-

[29] Flannery, *A Christian View of Israel*, p. 1.

whelming majority of Jews today are Zionist or pro-Zionist. This cannot be contradicted without appeal to exceptions or mavericks in the Jewish community. It is particularly in-delicate of Christians to seek out Jewish anti-Zionists in order to bolster criticisms of Israel or espouse Arab interests."[30]

To allege that the Jewish people are devoid of rights to sovereignty, and may exist only as a religious or ethnic com-munity within someone else's sovereignty, is inseparable from antisemitism. Such harsh judgment is required, for, otherwise, we are imposing upon Jews other men's notions of Jewish identity, rather than accepting Jews on their own terms. How-ever, unless the State of Israel is possessed of a right-to-be that duplicates the very same right among other nations, testimony in behalf of Israeli sovereignty becomes special pleading and is morally dubious.[31] Here is a fundamental reason why we must stress that the Jewish commitment to Zionism and Israel infinitely transcends group self-interest, ideology, or a fait accompli—and even, in a sense, transcends religious affirmation. The commitment is grounded in objec-tive historical, moral, and juridical considerations. Here are primary elements in the support for Israel that is increasingly affirmed and shared by Catholics, Protestants, and others, as exemplified in the group Christians Concerned for Israel. Thus, a common front is present. Christians unite with those who speak from the standpoint of secular-ethical authentica-tion and of international law.

Few people have as compelling a right to their soil as Israel pos-sesses. . . . "no nation has a historical claim to the land of Israel that can even be compared with that of modern Israel."

The right of the Jewish people to Palestine antedates by hundreds of years that of any surviving people. As James Parkes expresses the matter, the real title deeds to the land are an endur-ing, continuous Jewish community. Ever since biblical times, in-cluding the period after 70 C.E. and well before Arab and Islamic times, Palestine has had a Jewish population. That population "has

[30] Ibid., p. 3.
[31] Eckardt and Eckardt, *Encounter With Israel,* pp. 229, 231.

always been as large as could find the humblest means of existence" in the land. Any reductions in the size of the community came only as a result of wars, deportations, persecutions, or economic difficulties. Unlike other nations that have passed into obscurity with the loss of political and communal structures, the Jewish people in dispersion retained their identity. They never surrendered the claim to their ancestral home, and they never ceased to look upon it as Eretz Hemdah, the land for which one yearns. They continued to sustain the Yishuv (the indigenous Jewish community) by immigration and contributions. Significantly, the Jewish people never attempted to take or claim another land for themselves, in contrast to other displaced or migrating peoples.

This unique set of circumstances—continuity of residence and claim, immigration, and fidelity to the nation's past as well as to its anticipated future in the one land—is the essence of the Jewish people's case for their historical rights in Eretz Yisrael.[32]

To all of this must be added legal and moral right, with particular reference to our century: the purchase of land; the creation of responsible, self-governing bodies; the world community's recognition through the League of Nations and the United Nations; the Zionist revolution against colonialism and human exploitation; the furtherance of social and economic justice for Arabs as well as Jews; the great human costs paid by the Jewish people in suffering and sacrifice; Israel's stewardship of the soil and of natural resources; her educational, cultural, scientific, and technological development; her achievements in democratic institutions; her extraordinary aid to other developing nations.[33]

VI

We cannot avoid a question that is as obvious as it is contentious: Within positions supportive of Israel, what provision is there for distinctively religious affirmation? Our present topic, after all, is "Christian Perspectives on Israel."

[32] Ibid., pp. 231–232.
[33] See ibid., pp. 232–235.

Current Christian scholarship and reflection are in a condition of massive uncertainty and debate on this matter. I call attention to two, not unrelated, efforts to cope with the question.

The one viewpoint is not prepared to forego a theological apologetic. I use the term "theological apologetic" in its strict meaning: a speaking in defense of theological interpretation. Some Christian thinkers today declare, or at least compellingly raise the question of, a divinely grounded rationale for the reemergence of Israel. A primary incentive for their doing so is experiential. The power and persuasiveness of the apologetic are linked to certain singular events of our time. Father Flannery observes: "The creation within fifty years of a strong, vibrant, and viable nation and state in the face of insuperable difficulties places a strain on the powers of rational explanation; and many will see this extraordinary development in frankly supernatural terms."[34] In this position, concurrence is found with the Dutch Reformed Synod's attestation of a special religious link between Christians and Jews, but in a way that, unlike the Synod, supports unequivocally the integrity and sovereignty of Israel as a state. In *A Statement of Conscience,* Father Flannery joins Monsignor Oesterreicher in testifying that "as Christians" they must say: "The people of Israel not only have a right to live—they have a vocation to live for the Lord." And the hope is expressed that it will be granted these people "to bear witness to the God of Abraham, Isaac, and Jacob on His favored land, as never before."[35] Elsewhere Flannery poses a most germane question: "Is not the refusal to allow a theological consideration of Israel a residue of the deicidal myth, which included the idea that Israel could never return to its homeland or temple, or again of that old theology of rejection which consigned Israel to

[34] Flannery, "Anti-Zionism and the Christian Psyche," p. 176.

· [35] John M. Oesterreicher and Edward H. Flannery, *A Statement of Conscience* (leaflet) (South Orange, N.J.: The Institute of Judaeo-Christian Studies, Seton Hall University, Nov. 17, 1967).

obsoleteness in the Christian dispensation?" "Further, if we must believe with St. Paul that Judaism still has the covenants and promises (Rom. 9:4–5), and these originally involved the land, on what ground must the land be excluded from them in post-Biblical times? The ancient prophecies always spoke in terms of a divine pattern or sequence, involving sin, exile from the land, repentance and return to the land. Whereupon would Israel's latest return elude these prophecies?"[36]

I refer also to an exposition by Charlotte Klein of London entitled "The Theological Dimensions of the State of Israel." With respect to any attempt to found the political integrity of Israel upon the *Landesverheissungen,* the divine promises of the Land, Dr. Klein insists that the empirical–historical fortunes of the State of Israel do not, taken alone, boast messianic significance. And she is uncomfortable with any implication that Jewish self-understanding, including religious self-understanding, is in and of itself capable of authenticating a geopolitical claim. Nevertheless, Dr. Klein contends that the establishment of the State of Israel "seems the required sign of the God-willed perpetuity of Jews and Judaism," even were the State, heaven forbid, to cease to exist.[37]

From the standpoint of this form of theological apologetic, the political and juridical integrity of Israel can be in no way invalidated or questioned by theology. Of equal importance, that integrity is not forced to wait upon some kind of special theological authentication. Here, I submit, is a most salient contribution from within this view. But at least two problems remain. First, reference has been made to a blessed readiness to approach the Jewish people as though from within. Yet the truth is that many Jews, and especially Israeli Jews, maintain a secular rather than a religious stance toward Israel. To interject that, traditionally, Judaism allows of no

---

[36] Edward H. Flannery, "A Christian View of Israel," *United Synagogue Review* (Fall, 1971), 11, 30.

[37] Charlotte Klein, "The Theological Dimensions of the State of Israel" (unpublished).

essential separation between the secular and the sacred domains does not meet the issue. For the fact remains that Christians who remand Zionism and Israel to religious understanding thereby take sides with one segment of the Jewish community in contrast to another segment. It is one thing for Jews to subject Israel to a religious viewpoint in this way, but something quite different for Christians to do it, for that appears to echo the centuries of conceiving of Jews in Christian religious terms.

The second problem that confronts a theological apologetic in behalf of the State of Israel has also been alluded to earlier; it is the question of assigning theological meaning to discrete historical occurrences. Can the contingencies of time and place ever perform a positive theological function? What does it mean to identify an event or a congeries of events as a "sign"? How could we ever call upon faith for the business of historical explanation? Christians and Jews are possessed of infinite and unending obligations to the secular–historical realm. Yet I do not see that we are able to make reference to that realm in behalf of a theological apologetic. To marshal theological justifications for the State of Israel is either to fall into a double standard that places the State of Israel above other political entities, or to threaten the foundation of the State should Jewish covenantal requirements ever be finally impugned.

VII

We are brought to the very opposite end of the spectrum from where we began. There is a nonapologetic viewpoint that is fully supportive of Israel, a confessional viewpoint, an existentialist–theological outlook that makes no claims for itself, or at least tries desperately to avoid them. "While the justification of Israel for what she shares with other nations must be strictly historical and moral, the spiritual affirmation of the *laos* [the peopleness] of Israel means honoring her in and for her uniqueness."[38] The theme of this last viewpoint is celebration, thanksgiving for a gift. Celebration succeeds all apologetics, in either our brethren's behalf or ours, or even God's. Christians may participate in the celebration because their Jesus Christ was and remains a Jew, and because of what Franklin H. Littell calls "the essential Jewishness of Christianity." This is why we have to assert that Christian anti-semitism—and therefore Christian anti-Zionism and anti-Israelism—is the Christian world's vengeance upon itself, an act of self-hatred and of self-destruction.

This last point of view is developed more extensively in Chapter 12.

[38] Eckardt and Eckardt, *Encounter with Israel,* pp. 243–244.

10

Christian Silence
and Christian "Neutralism":
A Predictable Response[1]

The events of May–June, 1967 and their sequel are fatefully
pertinent to our subject. The entire contemporary relationship of Jews and Christians was tellingly affected. The behavior of the Christian community in conjunction with the
Six Day War and its aftermath produced a grave crisis, the
effects of which are still very much with us. The Christian
response cast great doubt upon the genuineness and depth
of any reputed change of heart among Christians toward
Jews. However, on the basis of what we already know of
attitudes toward Jews within Christendom, the Christian
silence and the Christian "neutralism" in the face of Israel's
extermination were anything but unpredictable.

---

[1] This chapter is based upon revisions and updating of several articles: A. Roy Eckardt and Alice L. Eckardt, "Again, Silence in the Churches,"
The Christian Century, 84:30 (July 26, 1967), 970–973; 84:31 (Aug. 2, 1967),
992–995; A. Roy Eckardt, "The Reaction of the Churches," *The Anatomy
of Peace in the Middle East*, Proceedings of the 1969 Annual Conference
of the American Academic Association for Peace in the Middle East (New
York: AAAPME, 1969), pp. 69–89; and A. Roy Eckardt, "Die gegenwärtige
Situation der christlich-jüdischen Begegnung in Nord Amerika," part II,
trans. H. D. Leuner, *Emuna* (Cologne), 3:2 (June, 1968), 121–128. The
articles listed contain much fuller documentation for the argument in this
chapter than can be provided here.

I

No Christian body took the initiative in calling public attention to the immorality of the annihilationist campaign against Israel. In the hours when that campaign was reaching its full height, no influential church group declared the right of Israel to defend herself. The few voices that were raised only helped to make the general stillness louder, and the scattered exceptions only included Christian leaders speaking as individuals. To our knowledge, in this country only one published series of articles appeared from the Christian side[2] condemning the general silence in the churches before, during, and immediately after the hostilities. With the cease-fire, many anti-Israeli pronouncements were made, demanding that Israel "give back the Arab territory," opposing the so-called conquest of East Jerusalem—even calling for the "internationalization" of all Jerusalem, and expressing Christian "distress" over the "unjust plight" of Arab refugees, not alone those of a first generation but now those of a second. Many Christians apparently succumbed to the falsehood that Israel cruelly expelled the Palestinian refugees in 1948, and then refused to do anything to meliorate their suffering. A similar mythology was quickly fabricated twenty years later: Israel was assigned blame for the new refugees. (The first of these allegations and, by prevenience, the later one were alike refuted long ago by a high Arab official. With complete honesty, he said: "That there are these refugees is the direct consequence of the unanimous action of the Arab States in opposing partition and the Jewish State"; Emil Ghoury, Secretary of the Palestine Arab Higher Executive, September 6, 1948.)

In 1967 a number of spokesmen for Christianity, whose views were reproduced in religious and secular media, displayed extreme sympathy for the Arab side, and many were most denunciatory of the Israeli cause. From among innumerable instances, we may adduce selected examples.

[2] Eckardt and Eckardt, "Again, Silence in the Churches."

Writing in *The New York Times,* Henry P. Van Dusen, former president of the Union Theological Seminary, New York, compared the Jews of Israel with the Nazis. He said that he was "aghast at Israel's onslaught, the most violent, ruthless (and successful) aggression since Hitler's Blitzkrieg . . . in the summer of 1940, aiming not at victory but at annihilation." He spoke of Israel's "callous indifference to the more than a million displaced Arabs" who have been "subjugated or driven into exile."[3] Van Dusen typified those Christian leaders who called black "white," who labeled as "aggressors" the victims of aggression, who identified as "annihilationists" those who barely escaped being annihilated by a foe pledged to turn them into corpses. Perhaps we will next be advised that the death camps were actually protective measures generously furnished by the Nazis to ensure that Germans would be kept from extermination by Jews. That many Nazis *did* believe this to be the purpose of the death camps offers a frightening clue as to how Van Dusen could label Israel an annihilationist aggressor.

The most influential Christian periodical in the United States, *The Christian Century,* reacted to a rabbi's proposal that interfaith discussions be contingent upon support by Christian leadership of the territorial and political integrity of Israel this way: "If interfaith dialogue must cease until all Christians become Zionists, then, of course, there will be no dialogue"—as if the rabbi were proposing that Christians become Zionists! In addition, the editors found "appalling," "unfortunate," "tragic," and "false" the criticisms that had been made of the Christian community for its neutral position in the Arab–Israeli conflict.[4] We may add here that Israelis found especially repellent the repeated demands from Christian spokesmen (and from other sources, including the

[3] Henry P. Van Dusen, letter to editor of *The New York Times,* July 7, 1967.
[4] "Israel and the Christian Dilemma," editorial, *The Christian Century,* 84:29 (July 19, 1967), 884.

editors of *The New York Times*) that Israel ought to be magnanimous to her Arab foes. Thus, *The Christian Century* dared to insist that the new burden and "advantage" of Israel "should be handled without arrogance [*sic*] and with great restraint and wisdom."⁵ (The wholly unsupported assumption here is that if Israel will only behave as others ask or demand, her detractors will become reasonable and want to be friends.) In general, *The Christian Century* has been, through the years, most ambivalent toward Israel. Time and again, it has sought to *do* something with her, to refashion her. In one editorial, curiously titled "To Zionists, with Love," the editors counseled wariness of "uncritical combinations of religious faith and political loyalty," the kind of combination to be found among "some of you Zionists." After protesting their support of Israel's existence, the editors went on to allege that Israel had a role in igniting the June War, and spoke of her repeated defiance of and scorn for the U.N., and of the ascendancy of hawks in the Israeli body politic.⁶

In *Theology Today,* E. G. Homrighausen charged that "Christians have been chided and criticized" by Jews "for not enthusiastically supporting the swift and brilliant Israeli victory over Arab threats to their national existence."⁷ Homrighausen's charge is a falsification. Where did there appear a single statement warranting any such accusation against Jews? The issue was not at all one of applauding the Israeli victory; it was one of concern over the very real possibility of Israel's

⁵ Ibid., p. 883.
⁶ "To Zionists, with Love," editorial, *The Christian Century,* 85:41 (Oct. 9, 1968), 1263–1264. At the time of the original crisis in May–June, 1967, the *Century* editors acknowledged that "Arab recalcitrance and belligerence" tilted their "sympathies sharply toward Israel." But they also contended that Jewish criticisms "erroneously assume that Christian commitment to Judaism and to Israel requires hostility to Arabs" ("Israel and the Christian Dilemma," pp. 883, 884). No documentation was offered to support this incredible charge. In addition, *The Christian Century* saw fit to describe as "war booty" the accession of East Jerusalem ["Israel Annexes Old Jerusalem," editorial, 84:29 (July 19, 1967), 884].
⁷ E. G. Homrighausen, "Christianity and the Arab World," *Theology Today,* 24:3 (Oct., 1967), 375.

extermination. The confusing here of the "before" and "after" of the crisis does not seem accidental. It was *before* the fighting ever started that Jewish dismay became evident—during the terrible three weeks between May 14 and June 5. This response from *Theology Today* almost seems to be saying that Israel's real offense was her refusal to die. When a Christian clergyman of avowedly Arab sympathies was asked whether the Israelis ought to have lain down to be slaughtered, his reply was, "Israel should never have been established in the first place." Presumably, for him, the nation's execution would have rectified the error. His attitude was not untypical of Christian representatives who condemned Israel for her "crimes" against the Arabs.

That Israel succeeded in turning the threat to her existence into a military victory was viewed in some quarters as somehow a vindication of the Christian "neutralists." Yet it was fraudulent to employ Israel's triumph as a device to protest ex post facto one's earlier "innocence" amidst a threat that "proved" to be "not really serious" after all. The situation in the Middle East remains as forbidding as ever, and the root question in the conflict—the rightness or wrongness of the State of Israel's reality and claims—is still in the forefront.[8]

A "special issue" of the United Church of Canada *Observer* bore the title, "Aftermath in the Middle East." It gave primary attention to the refugees—but only Arab refugees. Its accusations against Israel were among the most malignant to appear in any Christian source. These charges were prepared and the writing was done by the magazine's editor, A. C. Forrest, whom we encountered in the previous chapter. One page heading read in huge type "INJUSTICE," and the subhead stated, "In her present policies Israel stands con-

---

[8] The underdog–topdog shift as between Israel and the Arab nations in June, 1967, insofar as it can be talked about at all, did not appear to have been a very significant factor in altering varying expressions of Christian opinion.

demned before the world." The text included these allegations: Israel "will continue to flout the UN and world opinion
on anything that she feels is not in her national interest."
" 'The Israelis are very good at frightening people they want to
leave,' a nurse [among the refugees] said." Israel follows "intolerable racist policies." We condemn "the treatment of the
Arab people in occupied territory in the weeks that followed
the war and the harsh, inhumane treatment of the refugees
now, and the 19-year old record of inhumanity to Palestinian
refugees." "Israel, who refuses to be generous, should be
pressured to be just." "For another 200,000 homeless—and if
Israeli policies remain the same they are going to stay homeless—the future seems grim again in the Holy Land." "Arab
nations are suffering under a greater sense of injustice than
ever—accentuated by humiliation and frustrated by incredibly
bad leadership, and have evidence to confirm their greatest
fears of Zionist expansionism." The inclusion of certain grudg-
ing concessions (e.g., Israel's right to exist—a point invariably
included in such sources, in a way rather reminiscent of the
white racist's protestation that *of course* Blacks have a "right
to exist") does not change the fact that horrendous anti-
Israeli and anti-Jewish propaganda was here put forward
within the pages of an official publication of a large Christian
denomination, propaganda that doubtless achieved much of
its effectiveness by being cloaked in the guise of humanitarian
concerns. Many photographs were included.[9] Through a syn-
dicated arrangement, the *Observer's* "report" was reproduced,
with varying degrees of editing, in a number of the largest
denominational publications in the United States, including
*Church and Home, The Episcopalian, The Lutheran, Presby-
terian Life, Presbyterian Survey, Together,* and the *United
Church Herald.*[10]

[9] "Aftermath in the Middle East," *The United Church Observer*
(Toronto), special issue, 29:13 (Oct. 1, 1967), 9ff.
[10] In *Together,* for example, much of the anti-Israeli slander was
edited out. Still, no comments were appended concerning Jewish refugees.
It seems hard to believe that the *United Church Herald* editor was not

II

When, at the beginning of the crisis in the Middle East, Protestant and Catholic organizations were asked by the American Jewish community to call upon the U.S. government to stand by Israel, there was no institutional response. The U.S. Conference of Catholic Bishops gave no word and the National Council of the Churches of Christ in the U.S.A. was content to urge "compassion and concern for all the people of the Middle East" and the formulating of a solution by the United Nations. Some Christians even found an element of presumptuousness in the Jewish request; they claimed it did not allow them to reach a moral judgment of their own. But the fact is that church groups either remained silent or hastened to produce "neutralist" manifestoes that were, in actuality, partisan in character. There was, of course, a great deal of sympathy for Israel among "ordinary" Christians and in the American public in general. But this is not the main issue. All in all, the prevailing popular support for Israel came not through the inspiration of church leadership, but, for the most part, despite that leadership's dominant, expressed attitudes.

At the height of the crisis a forty-member "Emergency Middle East Task Force" was appointed by the National Council of Churches. It issued a statement asserting that the N.C.C. "is neither pro-Arab nor pro-Israeli." R. H. Edwin Espy, General Secretary of the Council, maintained in an address prepared for delivery during the very week the War was waging that the N.C.C., together with the World Council of Churches, could not take sides. For these organizations, Espy said, neutrality is "the only just and wise position."

---

joking when he introduced the materials with the comment that they represented "a breakthrough in church journalism," a "fully professional job of objective reporting overseas" (issue of Oct., 1967). In *Presbyterian Life* (Nov. 15, 1967) there were vigorous protests against the Forrest "report"— in letters from laymen, not from clergymen.

Indicative of the ambivalence toward Jews that has been regnant in American Christian leadership was the "Resolution on the Crisis in the Middle East" adopted by the Executive Committee of the N.C.C. Most significantly, this declaration was not put forward until July 7, 1967, more than two months after the threat to Israel had come to a climax and she, totally alone, had managed to survive. This fact makes quite hollow the framers' admission that for a generation "Christians have said little and done little to seek assurance for Israel that extermination would not be her fate."

A visitor from another planet could read this lengthy Resolution from end to end and never find out that the Arab world had anything whatsoever to do with bringing about the Six Day War. Church documents are as revealing for what they omit as for what they say. The declaration followed the familiar and tiresome line of charging Isreal with basic responsibility for the plight of Arab refugees. (The greatest calumniation of Israel among Protestant spokesmen—in some contrast to Catholic spokesmen—has involved commitment to one side in the refugee question.) Nowhere did the Resolution acknowledge who the primary culprits were; on the contrary, it asserted that "among the few who have heard" the cries of the refugees "have been Arab leaders, outraged at the establishment of Israel in the first place and fearful of her future expansion." The statement called upon "Israel, together with the Arab states and other members of the international community, [to] share responsibility for solving this refugee problem." To speak in the same breath here of Israel and the Arab states represents, at the very least, a form of moral blindness. By the time this N.C.C. statement was issued, Israel had already initiated major efforts in behalf of the welfare of Arab refugees, now that she was at last enabled (in part) to do so, in contrast to the long years when most Arab nations had refused to do anything. Revealingly, the N.C.C. Resolution was totally silent in respect to the hundreds of thousands of Jewish refugees from Arab countries as well as the frightening condition and persecutions of Jews still left in those lands.[11]

Further, while the statement conceded that "indispensable to peace in the Middle East is acceptance by the entire international community of the State of Israel," it insisted that "the National Council of Churches cannot condone by silence territorial expansion by armed force" on the part of Israel. The Council made no attempt to relate the territorial integrity of Israel to her chronic need for defensible borders and to her navigation rights, nor did the Resolution anywhere refer to the role of the Soviet Union in fomenting Arab aggression. The churchmen appeared to imply that somehow Israel ought to be criticized for making plain that she would defend herself against attack.

We were told, in addition, that the Council could not approve "Israel's unilateral annexation of the Jordanian portions of Jerusalem. This historic city is sacred not only to Judaism but also to Christianity and Islam." Beyond the evident incapacity of the fabricators of this document to offer the discriminate moral judgments that are so vitally necessary respecting the "sacredness" of Jerusalem (including especially that fact that Israel moved quickly to implement freedom of religion in the relevant area, while Jordan had always refused this), the statement was wholly silent on several decisive historical truths: Had the Arab world agreed, as did the Jewish leadership, to the United Nations Partition of Palestine in 1947, Jerusalem in its entirety would have become an internationalized city. Transjordan repudiated that

---

[11] A subsequent N.C.C. document on the refugees was even more one-sided and pro-Arab. Incredible as it may sound, the reader, studying a lengthy 1968 report of an N.C.C. deputation to the Middle East, was given no indication at all of the Arab world's dedication to destroying Israel or of the existence of Jewish refugees—this in a study devoted to the refugee question and describing itself as endeavoring "to maintain objectivity throughout" (*Report of Deputation to the Middle East*, July 19–31, 1968, National Council of Churches, mimeographed). Yet the General Board received the Report and transmitted it for study to the National Council's thirty-three member churches.

decision by the world community and waged war upon Israel, conquering and annexing, among other territories, the eastern part of Jerusalem. Even today, East Jerusalem would be in Jordan's hands had that government honored Israel's guarantee of nonbelligerency in 1967 and refrained from hostilities. Instead, Jordan shelled West Jerusalem, and the sequel is before us. The truth is that Jerusalem has never been the national capital of any people save the Jews. It is deceiving to suggest that East Jerusalem is "Arab Jerusalem." In point of fact, until the late nineteenth century Jerusalem meant essentially the Old City. For longer than the century that culminated in the rebirth of the State of Israel, Jews were the largest single population in Jerusalem, and particularly the Old City. When the Transjordanians seized East Jerusalem they destroyed the Jewish quarter and evicted its people, killing many of them. In sum, those who have criticized Israel for her reunification of Jerusalem but who (as in the case of the National Council of Churches) remained silent concerning the Transjordanian and Jordanian invasion, conquest, and acts of destruction are guilty of dissimulation.[12]

Where were the Christian voices when the Arabs were desecrating synagogues and Jewish graves?[13] Where were the Christian lamenters in the years when thousands of souls were being used as mere pawns in the refugee diplomacy practiced by the Arab leadership to the end of exterminating Jews?

Finally, the N.C.C. Resolution called for a United Nations' presence (for example, in the monitoring and control

[12] Alice Eckardt and Roy Eckardt, *Encounter with Israel* (New York: Association Press, 1970), pp. 215–216.

[13] "When the Jordanians held the Old City, they closed the border so that no Israeli Jew or Arab could visit any of his holy places; they destroyed 35 out of 36 synagogues; they used tombstones from the ancient Jewish cemetery on the Mount of Olives to pave the footpaths and latrines of the Arab Legion camp in Bethany. To cede the Old City to Jordan would be for Israelis to participate in those acts of impiety." [John M. Oesterreicher and Edward H. Flannery, *A Statement of Conscience* (leaflet) (South Orange, N.J.: The Institute of Judaeo–Christian Studies, Seton Hall University, 1967).]

of arms), counsel that in light of bitter Israeli experience at the hands of that hopelessly partisan body could only bring added offense to Israel and the Jewish people.

Meanwhile, back at the Holy See, matters were also taking a predictable turn. Silence with respect to the justified cause of Israel is bad enough; positive demand and reprimand against the Israelis are much worse, especially when inseparable from self-interest. Any presumption of Vatican neutrality in the Middle East conflict is refuted by the example of the Catholic Church's opposition to the reunification of Jerusalem. As long as Jordan held the Old City, permitting Christians to come to the holy places but forbidding Israeli Jews and Israeli Arabs to do so (in flagrant violation of the 1949 armistice guarantees), the Vatican showed no perturbation. It seemed content to condone religious discrimination in the Holy City. But when this discrimination was abolished by Israel, the Church authorities suddenly remembered their traditional call for the internationalization of the entire city. *Unbelievably, the Vatican demanded that Israel cede territory she possessed before the Arab states attempted to commit politicide against her.* On June 23, 1967 the permanent observer of the Holy See at the United Nations distributed a note calling for a *corpus separatum* (separate territory) for *all* Jerusalem, under an international regime. This demand by a Christian body for the surrender of the erstwhile territory of a nation that had just been subjected to wanton aggression was not only immoral, it also—coming as it did from a religious entity that is at the same time a secular state—constituted illicit intervention in the affairs of another sovereign state. The demand would have come with somewhat more grace, though still without any legitimacy, were the Vatican prepared to grant full recognition to the State of Israel. The Catholic Church's deficiency here makes it a very poor candidate for arbitration, for giving political advice, or for making political demands. In view of the historic Christian persecutions of Jews and the representative character of the Vatican before the world, that state ought to have been among the very first to offer diplomatic recognition and sustenance to Israel.

III

Great was the shock and the disillusionment within the Jewish community. A New York rabbi's sermon topic epitomized the realities of the situation: "Preparing for a Second Holocaust: The Christian Response to the Middle East Crisis." The Synagogue Council of America, national coordinating agency for the three wings of American Jewry, issued a restrained statement that nevertheless recorded with sadness and regret "the tolerance of some Western opinion" toward the Arab threat and its attempt to commit genocide against Israel, "a tolerance which inevitably serves to abet the possibility of mass murder."[14] An editorial in the *Jewish Spectator* observed that it was the very proponents of Christian–Jewish ecumenical dialogue who had remained silent. With very few exceptions, these parties "were either 'neutral' or maliciously defamatory during and after Israel's victory in self-defense." The journal went on to affirm that this kind of Christian behavior, "not unlike that of the Holocaust years, has served effective notice on Jewish proponents of interfaith dialogues that they have been chasing an illusion"—the illusion that the church had somehow moved from its traditional hostility to the Jewish people.[15] Rabbi Balfour Brickner, Director of the Commission of Interfaith Activities of the Union of American Hebrew Congregations, spoke of "the spectacle of nearly total absence of support for the State of Israel during her hour of need by *at least* the establishment of organized American Christianity."[16] Rabbi Marc H. Tanenbaum, Direc-

[14] "The Crisis in the Middle East," a statement by the Synagogue Council of America, October, 1967.

[15] "When 'Dialogue' Died," *Jewish Spectator*, editorial, 32:9 (Nov., 1967), 2.

[16] Balfour Brickner, "Needed: Candor in Interreligious Relationships," *Jewish Spectator*, 32:7 (Sept., 1967), 21.

tor of the Interreligious Affairs Department, the American Jewish Committee, sought to provide a balanced view. He emphasized that for the most part the substantial numbers of American citizens who supported and sympathized with the Israeli cause were, after all, Christians; and, further, that significant numbers of prominent and influential Catholic, Protestant, and Orthodox Christian leaders and journals of opinion spoke out for Israel's right to live as a sovereign state in freedom from Arab belligerency. Dr. Tanenbaum's own disclaimers became, accordingly, that much more important:

Jewish leaders directed their most valid, serious and justifiable criticism at the "establishment" institutions of the Catholic and Protestant churches. . . . When the U.S. Conference of Catholic Bishops [finally issued a statement on June 8, 1967], it asked for "a crusade of prayer for peace." . . . In the face of what appeared to most Jews as the imminent prospect of another Auschwitz, [such] rhetoric, with its echo of the . . . flight into pietism by Christian leaders in Nazi Germany, contributed to a pervading sense of gloom in American Jewry.

Nor were the statements of the National Council of Churches . . . [a] reinforcement for Jews or for Israel. In [a telegram to the President, Council officials] appeared to equate Israel's right to exist with the need to resolve the Arab refugee problem. In their July 7 resolution, the National Council of Churches contributed to the moral confusion of cause and effect by labeling Israel's retaliation to Arab provocations "aggression" and "expansionism."[17]

Jews had been divided on the subject of relations with Christians. Although this was the case for a long time before the Six Day War, the division was noticeably aggravated by that event. Not strangely, a number of Jewish spokesmen ex-

[17] Marc H. Tanenbaum, "Israel's Hour of Need and the Jewish-Christian Dialogue," *Conservative Judaism,* 22:2 (Winter, 1968), 7–8. The last reference is to the "Resolution on the Crisis in the Middle East" issued by the Executive Committee of the National Council of Churches, July 7, 1967. See also two research analyses by Judith H. Banki: *Christian Reactions to the Middle East Crisis* (New York: The American Jewish Committee, 1967); "Emerging Issues in Jewish–Christian Relations," *The Dialogue* (published by the National Conference of Christians and Jews), Oct., 1968, pp. 1–9.

pressed serious reservations about continuing the "dialogue" with Christians. Some of these representatives turned against "dialogue" completely.[18] Leaders of the Rabbinical Council of America, representing Orthodox Jews, called for a cessation of interfaith discussions until such time as the churches' leadership should come to recognize and to support the territorial and political integrity of the State of Israel. Parallel views were expressed in Conservative and Reform Jewish circles.[19]

Jews cannot forget, and they ought not, that in the forefront of "neutralists" and detractors of Israel during the recent and continuing crisis have been representatives of Christianity, in contrast to many nonreligious groups who have shown sympathy for Israel's right to live.

IV

Why has there been such great opposition to Israel in the Christian world? Why does that opposition continue? We are not dealing with past history. As this volume was being readied for publication, a noted scholar who was engaged in research at the World Council of Churches headquarters in Geneva reported that he had encountered a total of exactly one Christian working or visiting there who did not condemn everything that is related to Israel. "You know my 'philo-gentilism' of many years," the scholar wrote, "but my faith in those dialogue partners is now totally crushed."

[18] Jacob Neusner, an exponent until the summer of 1967 of dialogue with Christians, reversed his position: "The silence of most, though not all, leaders of American Christianity in the face of . . . well planned genocide against the people of the State of Israel cannot be ignored. . . . Religious and theological conversation has, I think, been closed by the massive indifference and, I think, craven silence of those from whom some of us hoped for better things" ["Reconsiderations," *Judaism*, 16:3 (Summer, 1967), 363]. See also David Polish, "Why American Jews Are Disillusioned," *The Christian Century*, 84:30 (July 26, 1967), 965–967.

[19] *The New York Times*, June 27, 1967; see also statement by Marc H. Tanenbaum in the *Daily News Bulletin*, Jewish Telegraphic Agency, Oct. 3, 1967; and article by Balfour Brickner, "Needed: Candor . . . ," p. 22.

Let us refer first to certain specific interpretations that are intended either to provide an empirical accounting of the situation or, in some cases, to legitimate the behavior or inaction of the Christian community.

A first and obvious influence is that of propaganda from abroad directed at the American people. Huge funds are expended for this purpose by oil-rich Arab countries. Rabbi Tanenbaum of the American Jewish Committee recently warned of a covert, unprecedented, and highly skillful campaign by Arabs to penetrate the "institutional systems of the American Catholic and Protestant churches with propaganda that is not only blatantly anti-Israel and anti-Zionist but also, in many cases, virulently anti-Semitic." One example is a leaflet providing a Muslim version of the medieval blood libel charge and a revival of the *Protocols of the Elders of Zion*. A primary resource center for the campaign is Lebanon, where many Christian groups and leaders are collaborating in the effort.[20] Yet the question still pursues us: Why are these Christians so involved?

It is true that a measure of uncertainty is to be found in the Christian communities of different lands. Some Christians and their leaders have not known what to say or do. Evidently, some churchmen have simply not believed that the enemies of Israel could or would move actually to destroy her.

Many parties point to the enormous complexity of the conflict in the Middle East, and maintain that the question of Israel as such cannot be separated from this complex state of affairs. They emphasize that not only the rights and interests of the Israelis are at stake but also those of the Arabs, most specifically the Palestinian Arabs. However, there is no principle in Christian ethics which insists that Christians are to refrain from moral evaluations or commitments because of

[20] Marc H. Tanenbaum, statement before the New York chapter, American Jewish Committee, Jan. 12, 1969 (mimeographed). For an account of Arab and pro-Arab propaganda on the American campus see Irwin Suall, "The Propaganda War Against Israel," *ADL Bulletin*, 30:4 (April, 1973), 4–5.

great complexity or controversy. Morally speaking, the recent conflict in Southeast Asia was infinitely complex and debatable. Yet numerous church bodies and spokesmen made unequivocal moral judgments on the issue and put forth all kinds of controversial political demands on American policy. And if some churchmen have avoided making decisions upon the Middle East conflict on the ground that it is essentially a power issue, the truth remains that institutional bodies are never forced to temporize or to avoid commitments within the power-political sphere. The World Council of Churches is providing funds for liberation movements in Africa. The General Board of the National Council of Churches twice deplored the Soviet invasion of Czechoslovakia, despite a different view among some churchmen in East European countries. All in all, the silence of the churches before the threat to Israel can neither be fully explained nor substantially justified by arguing that the situation is too complex or controversial or "political" to permit a decision.

There is, further, a persisting hope that the Christian community may somehow fill a conciliatory role between Arab and Jew, a role that would presumably be annulled once sides were taken. This hope must impress many of us as sentimentalist, but the moral intent behind it has to be acknowledged.

The concern for peace is of undoubted import, if one is to take seriously a great many petitions and pronouncements. Great fear has been expressed of renewed warfare and, indeed, of a world conflagration. Yet it is surely unwarranted to imply that those churchmen who plead for Israeli rights are insensitive to the explosive state of affairs in the Middle East. Many such churchmen emphasize that a sure guarantee of war is the harassment and nonacceptance of Israel. Curiously, many Christian bodies have shown little concern over the threat to world peace in the abiding Arab plan to destroy Israel.

It seems plausible to suggest that some potentially pro-

Israeli voices were muted by the severe opposition in the churches to United States' participation in the war in Vietnam, as well as by recent isolationist influences in our country. There is also the persisting pacifist tradition within Protestant- ism, an ideal that appears to some to be flouted by Israel. On the other hand, Christian pacifists can hardly be enthusiastic about the actions and policies of such Arab countries as Egypt and Libya.

The influence of church interests and ties in the Middle East is undeniable. This is readily conceded by such a pro- Arab spokesman as Willard G. Oxtoby, who says about his own denomination: Presbyterians "have for a century invested in the educational resources of Syria, Lebanon and Egypt; the good will built up over a century can vanish overnight if Americans close their ears to the Arab side."[21] Foreign church bodies have many stakes—financial, psychological, and "spiritual"—in missionary and other institutions in Arab lands. Almost all Christians in the Middle East are Arabs, in contrast to the infinitesimal number of non-Arab Israeli Chris- tians (toward whom gentile Christians have uncertain feelings anyway). The response to the 1967 crisis of the Standing Con- ference of Orthodox Bishops in the Americas was to seek to ensure that "the traditional and inalienable rights of the Greek Orthodox Patriarchate of Jerusalem" be defended and pre- served, that "the shrines of all faiths in the Holy Land be given an internationally guaranteed status," and that the tragedy of the Arab refugees be alleviated.[22]

Some four million Christians are to be found in today's Middle East.[23] Many Arab Christians and some non-Chris-

---

[21] Willard G. Oxtoby, as cited in Solomon S. Bernards, "The Arab— Israel Crisis and the American Christian Response," *The Lutheran Quar- terly,* 20:3 (August, 1968), 271–272.

[22] June 24, 1967, as reported in *Newsletter,* Committee on the Church and the Jewish People, World Council of Churches, Dec., 1967, p. 9.

[23] In Israel today, Christians, mainly Arabs, number about 77,500; of these, more than 11,000 live in Jerusalem. The principal groups include

tians have been trained in schools and colleges founded and supported by American missionary enterprise. A number have been aided greatly by clinics, hospitals, and philanthropic institutions. Apprehension is often expressed over the future of the Christian church in the Middle East.[24] There is a marked tendency within Arab nations to identify their Christian minorities with alien Western interests. Hostility to Americans among Arabs is numbered among the serious obstacles to the Christian cause. Fears are expressed over the welfare and security of Christians in the Arab states. (This may be more of an admission than some realize. Applied to Christians within Israel, such fears would be quite ludicrous.) *The New York Times* has pointed out that the substantial numbers of Catholic institutions in Arab countries make the Vatican peculiarly subject to diplomatic pressure—but not necessarily American Catholic leadership.[25]

V

In seeking to comprehend the motivations underlying the words and deeds of the Christian community, we face a dilemma: Seemingly plausible explanations, those on the surface, somehow do not seem capable of bringing us to the heart of the matter; yet the deeper the interpretation, the more difficult and perhaps even impossible is its verification.

The factors considered in the previous section of this chapter—to which can be added the contention that Christians simply do not understand the depth of Jewish feeling for Israel and of the nature of Jewish peoplehood—hardly offer a convincing or complete explanation. While it may be

---

Greek Catholics (25,000), Greek Orthodox (22,000), Latins (16,000), Maronites (3,500), and Protestants (2,500) [*Facts About Israel 1973* (Jerusalem: Ministry for Foreign Affairs, Information Division, 1973), p. 76].

[24] At their 1967 Convention, American Southern Baptists voiced much more concern for their missionaries in Arab lands than they did for the fate of Israel (*Newsweek,* July 3, 1967, p. 73).

[25] "Review of the Week," *The New York Times,* Jan. 5, 1969.

that the "plausible" interpretations we have listed help to account for Christian uncertainty and even silence—and perhaps some Christian fears as well—they scarcely account for all the partisanship,[26] the hostility, the bitterness. They do not explain the marked ambivalence toward Israel that pervades the churches.

What are we to make of the double standard so evident within the Christian community? Why have so many churchmen focused so much more upon Israeli sins than upon Arab sins? Such a practice is, to say the least, incapable of truthful vindication. Critical judgments upon specific Israeli policies or phases of Israeli life are one thing, and are as justified and essential as corresponding assessments of other peoples. Israel is and will remain far from perfect. But why is it that the Christian world has challenged no other nation's right to exist in the way it has that of Israel? Of what other people is that right called into question and even ridiculed? In effect, we have told Israel, "If you are good to the refugees, we just may be nice to you." When has this ever been said to the Arab world? Why do outside churchmen constantly lecture Israel, only Israel, on how she is to behave? Sometimes the lecturing would be comic were it not so fateful: it extends even to the building plans the country is to be permitted to have![27] Why have so many Christian spokesmen condemned Israel for her alleged territorial expansion, and not arraigned the Arab nations for producing that "expansion" by seeking to obliterate Israel? Why have Protestant, Catholic, and

[26] The late William Foxwell Albright, the celebrated archaeologist, was a staunch defender and advocate of the renewed nation of Israel. But "he was one of only a handful of [Christian] biblical scholars in this country who adopted this position and found himself at variance with the great majority which included a number of his former students" [David Noel Freedman, "William Foxwell Albright: In Memoriam," *Bulletin of the American Schools of Oriental Research*, no. 205 (February, 1972), 8]. Why should this have been? One might suppose that the proportion would be fifty–fifty, or at least thirty–seventy.

[27] Cf. Stephen Whittle, "Jerusalem Longs for a Prophet," *This Month*, World Council of Churches (April, 1972), 6.

Orthodox representatives castigated the Israelis for reunifying Jerusalem, yet found no sin in Jordan for her conquest of the Old City and for her persecutions of the Jews there? Why is it that Christian leaders—Catholic, Protestant, and Orthodox—have so often denounced Israel for her responses to terrorist attacks, but failed to denounce the terrorists?[28] How could it be that, in June of 1972, three reputedly Christian nations, the United Kingdom, France, and Belgium, sponsored a resolution in the U.N. Security Council condemning Israel for reprisals against terrorist positions in Lebanon while not only omitting any mention of the attacks upon Israeli civilians that incited the raids, but putting the resolution through in the immediate aftermath of the Lod Airport Massacre that killed twenty-six persons and injured more than seventy? For the Security Council, it was as though the mass murder at Lod never happened. But it was one thing for the Security Council (some Christian nations, some not) to ignore the massacre and something else, something really diabolical, for Christian nations to initiate turning the sequel of the massacre into a condemnation of Israel in the world body.[29] (The

---

[28] For example, Christian leaders, including Pope Paul, condemned Israel for her raid on the Beirut Airport in 1968—an act that carefully avoided taking any life—after having said nothing of the terrorist attack in Athens that led to the raid, or of other acts of violence and terror that destroyed Jewish lives. Officials of the National Council of Churches went out of their way to commend the American government for joining in the rebuke of Israel in the United Nations Security Council for the Beirut raid. Cf. Rabbi Jacob P. Rudin, "On World Reaction to Developments in the Middle East: A Statement," *The Christian Century,* 86:4 (Jan. 22, 1969), 110; Arthur J. Lelyveld, "Christian Morality and Arab Terrorism: An American Jewish Congress Statement," *Congress bi-Weekly,* 36:1 (Jan. 13, 1969), 2. On January 28, 1969 the Pope did deplore the public hangings in Baghdad of fourteen Iraqi "spies," nine of whom were Jews. James Feron surmised that this appeal and a subsequent one to the Jordanian authorities seeking clemency for two Christian Arabs were perhaps connected with the bitter criticism of the Pope by Israeli leaders following upon the Beirut raid in December, 1968 (*The New York Times,* Feb. 1, 1969).

[29] The reprisals against terrorist positions in Lebanon took place after the ambush of an Israeli tourist bus by Palestinian terrorists, who killed two civilians. See *Near East Report,* 16:23 (June 7, 1972), 93–94; 16:26 (June 28, 1972), 117, 120.

depravity of the Security Council was narrowly kept from further official expression in September, 1972 by a U.S. veto of a near-unanimous resolution demanding an end to military operations in the Middle East—meaning Israel's assaulting of terrorist bases—while totally ignoring a prime and immediate cause: the Arab terrorist massacre in Munich of eleven members of the Israeli Olympic team. Once again Israel was, in effect, condemned for having been attacked. For the Security Council now—as at the time of the Lod Massacre—it was as though the Munich murders had never taken place.)

One might answer questions such as those listed above by maintaining that Christian behavior simply mirrors or repeats the rest of the world's behavior, and the world as a whole is hostile to Israel. Christians are part of the world. But this reply is not very convincing. It only raises other questions: Why is the world so hostile? Need churchmen always follow the world? Has the church no independent standing ground? At the very least, resort to a double standard among Christians comprises an essential refutation of their claim to be pursuing a morally equitable or evenhanded course in the matter before us. The claim is a deceit.

Again, has the church been imitating the world, or has the world been learning more and more to be *der Stellvertreter,* the representative of historic Christendom? Indeed, the disease has spread to some exotic places. Two illustrations of the global metastasizing of antisemitism may be adduced from among many available ones. Idi Amin, Muslim President of Uganda, recently avowed that Adolf Hitler was completely right in burning and gassing more than six million Jews. For the Israelis "are not people who are working in the interest of the people of the world."[30] (The ironic fact will be recalled that early in our century a Jewish settlement in Africa was seriously proposed, in an area that included

[30] *The New York Times,* Sept. 13, 1972.

the highlands of Uganda.) A second example is that of the People's Republic of China:

There is something ludicrous as well as hideous in [Communist] China's intrusion into the Israeli-Arab complex. It represents the consummation of "one world" callousness. . . . There is a famous passage in one of [Charles] Lamb's essays which runs somewhat as follows: "Suppose you could by merely willing it bring about the death of someone in China, so that you would inherit his wealth, would you do it?" Lamb chose a Chinese as the ultimate symbol of human remoteness, someone whose obscure disappearance was not worth mentioning. Israel is surely just as remote from the concern of the Chinese leaders. . . . [Yet the] obliteration of the State of Israel is one of the favorable moves contemplated by the Chinese leadership. The extinction of a nation, a people and a culture would seem to the masters of the greatest emergent world power something like the musing in the mind of the inoffensive English essayist—with the difference that while he had not the slightest power to influence the event, Chinese guns in the hands of Arab guerrillas and Chinese encouragement of Arab genocidal plans are bitter realities.[31]

VI

As is suggested in Edward H. Flannery's essay, "Anti-Zionism and the Christian Psyche," there is more to Christian anti-Israelism than meets the eye. It would appear that the Christian world is conditioned by impulses that lie beneath the surface, impulses abetted by certain ideological influences.

The entire movement to reestablish the sovereignty of the Jewish people in their own homeland, culminating in the reconstituting of the State of Israel in 1948, has been a traumatic experience for the collective Christian psyche, which has never really recovered from the events. This condition is revealed, on the one hand, in the inability of many representatives of the churches to find any theological lessons

[31] Maurice Samuel, "Israel and I Today: A Personal Memoir," *Midstream*, 18:6 (June/July, 1972), 8, 9. Part of this citation comprises most of the very last full paragraph written by this great Jewish writer just before his death.

in the drama, together with their attempted reduction of Israel to a purely profane phenomenon, and, on the other hand, in the contention of many that something has gone awry religiously. The preponderant Christian failure to acknowledge and support the peoplehood of Jews cannot be dissociated from persisting Christian commitment and doctrine. This is no new thing.

Central to Christian teaching and deep within the Christian psyche is the assurance that the Jewish people were cast out of the land because of their transgressions, and most crucially for rejecting "their" Messiah. Jules Isaac, the distinguished historian, has shown how "the dispersion of the Jews" from their homeland as "divine punishment for the Crucifixion" (a dispersion that in plain fact never took place *in toto*) became a foundation pillar in the Christian "teaching of contempt" for Jews and Judaism.[32] "The Jews" are barred from Zion unless and until they repent of their evil and receive the Christ. Now God could not very well have made a historical–theological miscalculation by sanctioning the "return" of the Jews before the proper time. So therefore the whole Zionist and Israeli operation must be the work either of the devil or of human idolatry, or both. How presumptuous of Israel to be "reborn" in plain violation of Christian eschatology!

To comprehend the strength of Christian opposition to Jewish existence we must further bear in mind the historic disjunction in Christendom between the sacred and the profane. The church has never really won through to a genuine reconciliation with secularity. The notion among many religionists that a given international conflict is merely a "power struggle" warranting a plague upon both or all houses is often traceable to a dualistic worldview. The church's mind has been severely conditioned by a dualism of "spirit" and "matter," an impossible dichotomy in the prevailing Jewish

---

[32] Jules Isaac, *The Teaching of Contempt: Christian Roots of Anti-Semitism* (New York: Holt, Rinehart & Winston, n.d.), pp. 39–73.

view and one that stands in sharp contrast to the Hebraic insistence upon the sacred unity of all life. For the vast majority of Jews, Jewishness means not just a faith but a people. By contrast, the Christian dualist protests: Is there not something radically wrong with Israel *spiritually?* Are not the Israelis, with Jews everywhere, a crowd of materialists? Is not Israel itself a case of nationalist, even tribalist, regression?

All through the modern period the church has been afflicted by an idealistic universalism that is inherently distrustful of life's particularities. The church is caught between an *advocacy of religiousness* (though of course a religiousness inseparable from anti-Judaism) and an *apolitical universalism* (in implicit opposition to Israel as a secular state). On both these grounds, the religious and the universalistic, we encounter a failure or refusal to take seriously the Jewish people in their Israeli dimension, to accept them on their own terms.

We Christians strive manfully to reduce Jewishness to a religion called "Judaism." Then when the existence of Jews as a people is threatened, we can dissociate ourselves from all the anxiety. What obligations could we have to all those worldly Zionists? The consequence of Christian dualism is the driving of a wedge between Christians and Jews. We become estranged from the Jews as human beings.

The kind of ideological edifice that is under observation here is connected directly with many practical issues, including the fabrication that the "Holy Land" and the "holy places" are somehow "above" or "beyond" politics, beyond the sovereignty of the people of Israel, including even the *capital* of the nation. Here is suggested much of the hidden motivation behind recurring, chronic demands from within the Christian community for the "internationalizing" of Jerusalem. That demand is symptomatic of the imperialism of Christian universalism. For who would ever dare to apply the notion of internationalization to Damascus, Rome, Geneva, or Washington? We have earlier referred to the fact that, to this day, the Vatican has refused to recognize the State of Israel. There is no such place as "Israel," apparently; there is only the "Holy Land" or "Palestine"! In the final analysis—we Christians are presuming—Israel is not in fact the property of Israel.

Spokesmen for the World Council of Churches and other non-Catholic bodies did not react with warmth to the Vatican demand that Jerusalem be entirely taken from Israel. But subject as they themselves are to the Christian dualism referred to above, not to mention other conscious and unconscious motivations, they have not been able to furnish any positive theological rationale for this disagreement. They could only say that the question of Jerusalem was strictly "political" and that religious interests could not be discussed until a political settlement had been reached.

If, as is stated elsewhere in these pages, the events of history do not prove (or disprove) faith, we are not thereby released from the duty to apply theological understanding to the secular domain. The lengths to which various Christian apologists have been driven in order to rule out any divine undergirding of the reestablishment of Israel as a state are indicative not only of an insistence that Jewish history be subjected to christocentric history, but also of a Christian deficiency in relating life's transcendent dimensions to the political order. We Christians tend to vacillate between the theologizing of politics and the heresy of setting God above politics. For the Jew there is a divine link between faith and life, between doctrine and action, between the sacred and the secular. That link is righteousness (*zedakah*). The perennial Christian temptation is that of a lovely mystical universalism exempt from the duty to fight human oppression.

If Christian silence before the plight of Israel is the silence of the Christian deity, he is better off dead. Woe unto Israel had she waited for the God of neutralism and apolitical "love" to deliver her. Instead, she refused to die, and thus—

with lesser or greater faith, with "worldly" or "unworldly" aspirations, with "atheist" or "believing" assumptions—she was enabled to celebrate the living Lord of creation and the God of righteousness. Christians, with other residual pagans, may not wish to be disturbed by this God of justice, who earns his living in wholly worldly ways.

Perhaps the Christian community could never endure the tension of bringing together doctrine and politics. For once it were to acknowledge and confirm theologically the unqualified right of Israel to live, it would be confronted not alone with a fateful ideological crisis, but with the moral necessity to cast its lot publicly with Israel, in opposition to the exterminationism of her enemies. Where there is no *zedakah* the people fall silent—or perish.

Though one hopeful sign in the current theological temper may be the affirmation of a "secular Christianity," and though this may, in some measure, be construed as a yearning in the church for a return to its Hebraic roots, the fresh outlook has not as yet, unfortunately, produced a uniquely Christian rationale for the State of Israel as a temporal fulfillment of the Covenant—a rationale that would correspond to the Jewish understanding of Israel as a decisive step in the creative normalization of Jewry.

VII

The obstinacy and the pervasiveness of Christian anti-semitism require that we probe deeper. Is there not a link between that horror and the contemporary international campaign against the Jews of Israel? The one bond that unites the Arab peoples—the *only* substantive or operative one—is their conviction that Israel deserves to die. But this very conviction finds a deep hold within the Christian psyche as well. In earlier pages we have stressed the centuries-long Christian indoctrination in the identical idea: Jews have no integral or ultimate right to exist as Jews. (It has been estimated that less than 20 percent of the Jews were able to survive as Jews in Christian Europe from the fourth to the twentieth centuries.)[33] In Chapter 2 we alluded to the traditional and entrenched European Christian stand respecting the Jews. The church said to them: You may convert, or leave, or die. The eternal war against the Jew makes strange bedfellows—or are they really all that strange? We must not underestimate the place and the power of extra-Christian antisemitism, and particularly the indigenous forms of Arab and Muslim antisemitism.[34] But we must also adjudge that the nations of the world and especially the Arab collaborators have received the Christian mantle; they have become the latter-day executors of Christendom's conspiracy to destroy the Jewish people. True, Muslim Arab defamers would never suffer Jews to convert to their faith. Yet a related demand is very much present: the conversion to statelessness. And the defamers do stand unambiguously for the other two choices—departure or death. Israeli and other Jews may either leave "our land"— they may go to Germany, for example, "back where they came from"—or they may stay to fight and die.[35]

The silence and "neutralism" of the churches are preeminently matters of human perversity, in combination with pathological impulses that live within the collective unconscious of the Christian world. Whenever original Israel is assailed, certain repressed, macabre elements in the Christian soul are stirred to sympathy with the assailants, the murderers. It is most difficult to account in any other way for the vehemence and the mendacity of the Christian attacks upon a harassed Israel. "In earlier, more 'religious' times, Christians would resort to Jesus Christ as their major weapon against 'the unbelieving Jews.' Today a different weapon

[33] Arthur Gilbert, *The Vatican Council and the Jews* (Cleveland– New York: World, 1968), p. 19.

[34] See Professor Y. Harkabi's definitive study, *Arab Attitudes to Israel* (Jerusalem: Israel Universities Press, 1971), espec. chap. 5.

[35] Eckardt and Eckardt, *Encounter with Israel*, p. 224.

seems more fitting and effective: Christians invent a 'militant, aggressive' Israel that 'threatens world peace' and harms 'innocent' Arabs. The weapon has changed; the campaign of vilification is the same."[36] In such a figure as Henry P. Van Dusen, who makes the Israelis into the equivalent of Nazis, the pathological–satanic unconscious of Christendom boldly comes to the surface. There could be no more obscene or devilish parallel than one that lowers the Israeli defense forces to the very same level as the Nazi hordes who were pledged to destroy Jews. Van Dusen is telling us, in effect: "The Jews are *the* enemy. The more they *appear* to be helpless victims, the more they are *in reality* conspiring as the devil's own agents of destruction. Before the Antichrist succeeds in destroying the world, let us expose him for what he is."

Had there been no war in 1967, the void within the Christian soul that refuses any authenticity to Israel—on any other than strictly Christian terms—would still have been present as a formidable barrier to Christian sympathy for Jewish existence. The cancer of antisemitism lies just below the surface waiting to be spread, with the help of varying historical circumstances. Just as in the 1930s unnumbered people in the churches were never really convinced that the Nazis with their "final solution" were not the unwitting allies of God—since the Jews are now God's enemies—so in the 1960s and 1970s a powerful psychological and ideological affinity is manifest between Christian predispositions and the annihilationist designs of the Arabs. "The churches do not act effectively or courageously to oppose today's political campaign against Israel because their own repressed enmity toward the Jewish people is too powerful an inhibiting force."[37] What, after all, do the lives of a few million Jews matter to the pagan that lives within the Christian soul? The annihilationist designs of the Arab states against Israel have

---

[36] Ibid., p. 256.
[37] Ibid., p. 223.

quickened the lingering Christian desire to circumscribe, persecute, and even destroy Jews.

In contrast to Jews (so the covert Christian rationalizing goes) Arabs, as a people, shape up rather well. They are, when all is said and done, a rather innocent, abused, and needy lot, perhaps something like children. And, of course, multitudes of them are refugees. Refugees from what? From Jewish sophistication, Jewish intransigence, Jewish power. The appeal to the plight of the refugees, repeated a thousand times, can be so powerful and convincing because the anti-Jewish impulses involved are furnished with seeming integrity —this being accomplished by simultaneously assigning culpability for the refugees to the Jews, and justifying the anti-Jewish impulses by recourse to what appear to be the very highest humanitarian concerns.

Furthermore, is it not so that the Arab peoples never really spurned Christ? They can be fitting instruments of divine judgment upon *those Jews,* who *have* rejected and crucified the Lord. And the Jews of Israel are a stiff-necked bunch if there ever was one. They are so self-righteous, so willful, so *militaristic.* Once upon a time, the Assyrians could be the rod of God's anger (Isa. 10:5). In our day there are such men as Gamal Abdel Nasser and Anwar Sadat. We wonder. . . .

Again, in contradistinction to the minority which is Israel, there are untold numbers of Arabs in "great spiritual need." Perhaps we will be strengthened to save many of them for the very Christ whom *those Jews* despise. At the very least, it is most essential that we not overlook or jeopardize the safety of our Christian missionaries toiling so faithfully in Arab lands. . . .

Thus, explanations in depth are hauntingly and compellingly present for the recurring silence, "neutralism," and hostility of churchmen before the fact of Israel, revolting though these explanations are.

VIII

Insofar as Christian denigration of Israel cannot be divorced from the influences of Christian dogma and from historic Christian hostilities to Jews, the responsibility of Israeli Jews, of the Jewish world, and of Christians concerned for Israel may become clear. Responsible action will be determined by judgments, findings, and intuitions concerning the changeability or nonchangeability of Christian ideology and Christian behavior. It was entirely predictable that Christian denigration and persecution of Jews over so long a history would be revivified in adverse Christian policies and behavior toward the Zionist ideal and the reestablishment of the State of Israel. The anti-Zionist and anti-Israeli stance of so many nations and people appears simply inexplicable apart from the age-old influence of anti-Judaism and antisemitism within Western and Eastern Christendom. There is little in the story of dominant Christian attitudes toward Israel since 1948, and especially during and since 1967, to warrant any hope that the Christian world, and the American church in particular, will change.

We are met by the saddest truth of all: It was terrible enough when the Christian world betrayed the Jewish people in the Nazi Holocaust. That we should give our consent to efforts to produce *a second Holocaust* is an act beyond redemption, an unqualifiedly devilish act. Pre-Holocaust Christianity holds as full reign as ever.

11

On "Evenhandedness"

In Christian circles, the dishonoring of the rightful integrity of Israel is not limited to categorical opposition to her existence as such. Implicit or explicit alliance with those who would harass Israel, or endeavor to keep her in a threatened or insecure position, or ensure that Israel receives the short end of any political settlement reflects either conscious or below-conscious hostility toward the Jewish people. Particularly indefensible are cases where the hostility is masked by a third party's protestations of devotion to justice for the two sides.

I

Gregory Baum, the eminent Canadian Catholic scholar, offers a fitting expression. He speaks of the "false consciousness" of Christians. This phenomenon involves a "refusal to look at inherited ideological trends, and the denial that they are operative in one's views." False consciousness is "allied to a cheerfully good conscience." The man possessed by false consciousness respecting a class or group of people assumes a stance of objectivity toward them, refusing to acknowledge that his own history is interwoven with theirs. Such "objectiv-

152

ity" is not a genuine objectivity. "Objectivity is here a device for not looking at the whole historical truth." For Christians, it is false consciousness to adopt an objectivist stance toward Israel and other social manifestations of Jewishness. Christians who view the political situation of Israel without wrestling with their own ideological past, namely the anti-Jewish bias of the church through the ages, remain caught in their own inherited symbols. And they unconsciously perpetuate an anti-Jewish attitude. Inevitably, they are taken captive by prejudices and false judgments. Being unconscious, the ideology will express itself in unexpected ways. Thus, those who insist that they are "only" anti-Zionist and not anti-Jewish will eventually reveal the unconscious, ideological origins of their attitude. False consciousness can never be overcome by science, only by a willingness to change.[1]

To illustrate the above state of affairs, Father Baum cites the anti-Jewish ideology of A. C. Forrest and *The United Church Observer.* To further exemplify the phenomenon of false consciousness, Baum alludes to a communication in the *Observer* from the Very Rev. Ernest Marshall Howse. According to Howse, it is only overly sensitive people who discover "a secret hostility to Jews" in the *Observer,* whereas Mr. Forrest is merely trying to be objective. The critics are, Howse maintains, "pathological" in their sensitivity. From their standpoint, editors who criticize Pakistan must be secretly hostile to Muslims, those who criticize India are secretly against Hindus, and those who are alienated from China have a latent animosity toward Confucianists.[2]

Baum comments:

In these and in other explicit passages, [Howse] refuses to wrestle with the inherited ideology of the Christian church. The stance of

---

[1] Gregory Baum, "Salvation Is from the Jews: A Story of Prejudice," *The Christian Century,* 89:19 (July 19, 1972), 775–777. Copyright © 1972 by Christian Century Foundation. Quotations reprinted by permission.

[2] Ernest Marshall Howse, communication in *The United Church Observer* (Toronto), 34:9 (March, 1972), 12, 42.

objectivity allows him to look away from the actual historical link between his group and the various peoples and religions he mentions. To classify Israel . . . simply as one among several societies is to deny the entire ideological past. For accompanying Christian preaching almost from the beginning were hostile and prejudiced views, *not against Muslims, Hindus or Confucianists, but against Jews.* . . . To attempt to negate all this by recourse to objectivity is false consciousness. . . .

Since the Christian community has been totally insensitive to moral issues regarding the Jews for almost two millennia, a sociology of knowledge makes it highly unlikely that Christians will all of a sudden produce sensitive moralists on matters pertaining to Jews. It is sociologically unlikely that people who for centuries overlooked obvious injustices in regard to a particular group, slandered them and denigrated their religion, will quickly become sensitive moral guides as to how this group ought to behave. If, therefore, the Christian wants to express his own critical views of Israeli policies, he can do so with honor only if he reveals that he is also wrestling with his own ideological past.[3]

II

Much of what Father Baum has to say is illustrated in the "evenhandedness" of the Quaker Committee that prepared the study, *Search for Peace in the Middle East,* a 35,000-word document that constitutes the primary focus of this chapter. For Christian "evenhandedness" regarding the Middle East conflict is intimately linked to what Baum describes as "false consciousness." However, it is essential to note that the ideological component of false consciousness is, as we shall emphasize, closely associated with a refusal or failure to provide responsible, relative moral judgments with respect to the two sides, the Arab and the Israeli. The Friends' report has shown itself to be highly portentous, not simply for Christian–Jewish relations in the United States and elsewhere, but also for the possibility of a lasting peace between the Arab world and Israel. The document is also indicative of

---

[3] Baum, "Salvation . . . ," pp. 776–777 (italics added).

the hazards of separating anti-Israelism and anti-Zionism from antisemitism, at least antisemitism of a below-conscious sort. In sum, false objectivity is fuel for human prejudice and human strife alike.

The Quaker study was, in its words, "prepared by a working party, initiated by the American Friends Service Committee and the Canadian Friends Service Committee and acting in association with the Friends Service Council (London), the Friends World Committee for Consultation, and the Friends Peace and International Relations Committee (London)." Two editions have been published, the first under the imprint of the American Friends Service Committee, and a slightly revised edition by the Fawcett World Library.[4] Except where otherwise noted, cited references are from the latter edition.

The Friends' judgments are not atypical of what we have been getting from Christian quarters. Their statement has received considerable attention and acclaim beyond Quaker circles; it has often been described as "fair-minded," which, depending upon the source, can be a highly revealing judgment. The Friends are reputed to stand for peace, but a close inspection of their pronouncement raises the question of whether that description is accurate in terms of the specific conflict under discussion. That the study is not, in fact, the impartial analysis it claims to be is suggested in such various responses to it as its distribution, gratis, by Americans for Justice in the Middle East, an anti-Israeli organization located in Beirut; a book-length reaction by three American scholars entitled *Truth and Peace in the Middle East;*[5] a critique and analysis of the report's unconscious bias by the chairman of the Committee on Israel of the American Jewish Congress,

---

[4] *Search for Peace in the Middle East* (Philadelphia: American Friends Service Committee, 1970); *Search for Peace in the Middle East,* revised edition (New York: Fawcett World Library, 1970).

[5] Arnold M. Soloway, with Edwin Weiss and Gerald Caplan, *Truth and Peace in the Middle East: A Critical Analysis of the Quaker Report* (New York: Friendly House Publishers, 1971).

Judge Justine Wise Polier;[6] and, predictably, a strong editorial entitled "In Defense of Friends" in *The Christian Century,* which leaped to the side of the Quakers, excoriating Judge Polier for her reaction.[7]

Careful study of the contents of *Search for Peace in the Middle East* shows that Judge Polier's evaluation is substantially justified. The same is the case with the assessment by the authors of *Truth and Peace in the Middle East,* who affirm that the Friends' report displays a blatant bias, suppresses facts, distorts history, and presents a slanted and

---

[6] Justine Wise Polier, "Open Letter to the 'Friends,'" *Congress bi-Weekly,* 37:12 (Dec. 4, 1970), 3–6.

[7] "In Defense of Friends," editorial, *The Christian Century,* 88:2 (Jan. 13, 1971), 36. *The Christian Century's* method was quite remarkable: A Jewish leader, Judge Polier, spoke against what she believed to be an unjust document, and the *Century* countered by citing a passage from that very document in order to evaluate the critic! Does not the Quaker study warn us of those "leaders of the American Jewish establishment" who "identify themselves with the more hard-line elements inside the Israeli cabinet . . ."? Thus *The Christian Century* simply begged the entire question. With an assist from the Friends, the *Century* could at one and the same time seek to intimidate American Jewish spokesmen into silence, and obscure the truth that it is the Quaker preachment which is on trial and not American Jewry. How are we to fathom the behavior of the *Century* editors? They could hardly be so naïve or inept as to imagine that a document lamented by responsible Jewish leadership, and commended by many enemies of Israel and the Jewish people, is in fact fair to the two sides. How is it, then, that the editors identified the Quaker study as a "model of openness," an achievement that is "reconciling" and "unprejudiced"? One possible answer is that they are beset by the same unconscious bias that afflicts the Friends. This conclusion is strengthened by attention to the long history of *The Christian Century's* ambivalence toward the Zionist movement and Israel. In the latter connection it is revealing that on the occasion of Israel's twenty-fifth anniversary *The Christian Century* felt called upon to chastise Israel for its display of military might. The *Century* lamented "the mistaken impression that Israel's power to survive depends solely on its military power" and maintained that "Israel's strength stems primarily from its citizens' memory of Auschwitz and the realization of their ancient hopes, articulated in the Scriptures, of returning to their land" ["Israel at 25: Accentuating the Negative?," editorial, *The Christian Century,* 90:21 (May 23, 1973), 592]. Here is another instance of the familiar Christian dualism of matter and spirit. The *Century* showed a typical lack of sensitivity to the truth that Israel remains a state under siege. The very opposite of the *Century's* contention is the case: Israel's power to survive *does* depend solely on its military power, and this will be so for a long time to come.

one-sided set of conclusions.[8] Equally justified is Bettina Silber's critical analysis of the Quaker document.[9]

There follows a listing that extends to several major categories. Under each heading, representative examples are furnished from the Friends' statement itself.

III

The Quaker Committee backs one side in the Arab-Israeli conflict while denying it. One salient instance of this is the Friends' method of summarizing conflicting viewpoints and then following up with italicized counsel of their own. The summary of the Israeli point of view is succeeded by demands that Israel cease its policy of prolonging "indefinitely the military occupation of Arab territories," "of disclaiming responsibility for the plight of the Arab refugees," and of insisting that "some, if not all" of the lands "taken over" in 1967 are "now permanently Israeli." By contrast, the summary of the Jordanian and Egyptian views is followed by the judgment that while the Arab states ought to establish control over "commando groups," it is *Israel* that must "abandon its policy of massive retaliatory 'over-kill' strikes" against the Arabs.[10] Again and again the Friends range themselves on the Arab side and against Israel on specific issues, e.g., Big Power and United Nations intervention, border forces on both sides of demarcation lines, and the disposition of Jerusalem, which cannot be "the sole possession" of one national state.[11]

Clearly, the Quakers have a perfect right to assume these positions—but not while they continue to deny that they have taken sides. As a matter of fact, the Friends impugn the motives of Israel and question whether she is sincere about achieving peace—a stance they never assume toward

[8] Soloway et al., *Truth and Peace in the Middle East,* p. ix.

[9] Bettina Silber, "The Friends Fail in Their 'Search for Peace in the Middle East,' " *Near East Report,* 14:28 (Dec. 9, 1970), 186–187.

[10] *Search for Peace . . .* , pp. 72–82.

[11] Ibid., pp. 45, 47, 48, 87, 97, 99–100.

the Arab side. They try to get us to believe that the Arabs are infinitely more moderate than they sound. But the Quakers portray the Israelis as infinitely more militant than *they* sound.[12]

On the issue of sincerity, one stratagem is the Friends' claim that the Israeli Government has failed to allay "persistent Arab fears" by making clear that it entertains no "further" [*sic*] demands for "territorial expansion."[13] In point of truth the so-called expansion of Israel has resulted from the Arab states' wars and harassment against her. Apart from this condition of hostility, she has not made a single territorial demand. Israeli sincerity is further questioned by the allegation that "each side feels that force is the only language the other side will understand."[14] This is equivalent to saying that Israel's announced policy of seeking a final peace settlement with the Arab states is a subterfuge. The truth is just the opposite. If there is one thing that Israel has never claimed, it is that a "military solution" could ever resolve the conflict. Only the Arabs have taken that position.

Nowhere do the Friends question the justice of the all-decisive Arab charge that by her very existence Israel constitutes an unjust intrusion into, and an evil assault upon, "the Arab world." From beginning to end, their conceding of the reality of an Israeli state (though with very weighty conditions) is most grudgingly expressed. Nowhere do they even acknowledge as a valid issue the relevance of Arab behavior to the rightness or wrongness of the existence of *Arab* states. Only Israel's sovereignty is subjected to questioning.

The one positive ground allowed for the right of Israel to be where she is (apart from a reporting of Israeli and Jewish claims) is through an alleged fait accompli: the fact that Israel is *there*. Thus, the document urges Arab leaders to tell their peoples that "however unfair they may consider the manner of its creation, Israel is a reality which must be

---

[12] Ibid., p. 186.
[13] Ibid., p. 95.
[14] Ibid., p. 45.

accepted and lived with in their own long-term interest."[15] This is hardly a compelling or valid moral argument, or one that can counteract Arab ideology and prejudice. Unless Israel possesses a right to exist that transcends de facto power, no one is justified in demanding Arab acceptance of her existence. Unjust faits accompli must be fought against. Here is why we must assert that the Friends' demands upon the *Arabs* are immoral, within the framework of the Committee's own presuppositions and reading of history.

The Quakers' most questionable stance is in their assumption that the Middle East conflict is morally symmetrical. Again and again they offer false equations, e.g., that "the Arab paranoia over the prospects of unlimited Israeli territorial expansionism is matched by a Jewish paranoia toward the prospects of unceasing Arab determination to destroy Israel and to slaughter all Jews."[16] It is not correct to "match" the two cases, and hence it is unfair to try to do so.

"Evenhandedness" in regard to two opponents, one of whom condemns the other's claim to life, is not true evenhandedness but a commitment to the one side. The Friends endeavor to convince us that it is possible for party A to be morally evenhanded or neutral or reconciling within a state of affairs where, in plain fact, party B is dedicated to the abolition of party C. It is of no avail to take refuge in the attestation that "there are no devils and no angels in the Middle East."[17] This is an irrelevancy. It cannot alter the fact that "evenhandedness" and "neutrality" comprise a tacit alliance with party B. The Quakers would do well to search their consciences for the reasons their study has been welcomed enthusiastically among many enemies of Israel.

The Friends resort to a double standard, particularly in making demands upon Israel that are not made on the Arabs. The writers of the study tell Israel that she must "realize

---

[15] Ibid., p. 115.
[16] Ibid., p. 95.
[17] Ibid., p. 37.

the fruitlessness of rigid policies" (evidently the Arabs have not been rigid) and "recognize the obligation, as military victor in past combats" and as the "militarily dominant power," to make "the first moves toward peace." Even though the Quakers must be aware that Israel will not consent to certain demands, they continue to insist that Israel change, e.g., in respect to territorial adjustments associated with the outcome of the Six Day War. But when the item is something they know the Arab side will never accept (e.g., direct negotiations), they insist that such a stipulation is not feasible. Thus, while accusing the Israelis of inflexibility, they do obeisance to Arab inflexibility.[18]

In this connection it is no accident that the Friends enthusiastically endorse the U.N. Security Council Resolution of November 22, 1967 as the way to peace. Bernard Lewis has observed in *Foreign Affairs* that the Resolution demands one-sidedly territorial and strategic concessions from Israel (with force as the only redress should the need arise) and only diplomatic concessions from the Arabs, concessions that could be easily "reversed by a simple declaration."[19]

The Quakers' dedication to the United Nations and their continued calls for action by and in behalf of that body constitute the most damning evidence that their "objectivity" is anything but that.[20] As we have already noted, the United Nations follows a highly partisan line in the Middle East

---

[18] Ibid., pp. 114, 99; cf. p. 87.

[19] Bernard Lewis, "The Great Powers, the Arabs and the Israelis," *Foreign Affairs*, 47:4 (July, 1969), 643. We must go much further than Lewis. In point of fact, the only real concession explicitly demanded of either party in the U.N. Resolution is that of withdrawal applied to Israel by name. No tangible concession is actually required of Arabs, i.e., of *specific* Arab states. The technique employed here is to omit reference to any concrete Arab polity. Instead, refuge is taken in the abstraction "Middle East." Also, Arabs have an easy way out of the wording, "respect for and acknowledgment of the sovereignty, territorial integrity and political independence of every state in the area. . . ." Since when is Israel a legitimate state? [Alice Eckardt and Roy Eckardt, *Encounter with Israel* (New York: Association Press, 1970), p. 204].

[20] Cf. *Search for Peace. . .* , pp. 97–100, 113.

conflict. Professor Gil Carl AlRoy's description is highly apropos:

The direction of forces in the power arena is far from random; in fact, it is utterly predictable. Within the international community, the Arabs outweigh their foe to the point of crushing it in numbers, alliances, strategic resources, wealth, and other factors. The Arabs are highly desirable diplomatic agents. The Israelis are highly expendable—indeed, a negligible quantity. So extraordinary is this diplomatic disparity that it transcends completely even the ideological and cold war barriers in the world. Thus, aligned with the Arabs are India and also Pakistan; Spain and Greece but also Yugoslavia and the Soviet Union; the Vatican but also militantly anti-clerical Poland and Albania; Communist China but also Taiwan; the Common Market block but also the Warsaw Pact. It does not require much imagination to discover which of the sides in the Middle East conflict would urge big power and United Nations intervention, decision and imposition, and which would dread the very idea of this.[21]

A final instance of a double standard is that the Quakers give the case for the Arab refugees lengthy, central, and detailed attention, while in only part of a single sentence do they mention that Jewish refugees should be considered in compensatory processes.[22] As Bettina Silber points out, the original document included not a single word on Jewish refugees from Arab countries until *Near East Report* and other parties protested the omission.[23]

The Quaker Committee reverts to historic religious bigotry and resurrects the conspiratorial charge against Jews. The Friends inform us that the Israelis have practiced "two-eyes-for-an-eye" retaliation.[24] I refer to Judge Polier's response: We may ask why the Quakers, with the aid of a false quotation from the Old Testament, should want to give the

[21] Gil Carl AlRoy, "The State of the Mid-East and Mid-East Studies," *worldview,* 14:10 (October, 1971), 8.
[22] *Search for Peace . . .* , p. 101.
[23] Silber, "The Friends Fail . . . ," p. 31.
[24] *Search for Peace . . .* , p. 31.

impression that Israeli reactions to terrorist deeds stem from a religious commitment to vengeance.[25]

With respect to the conspiratorial charge, *The Christian Century* editorial mentioned earlier quotes with approval the Quaker warning of vague but insistent and widespread "pressures" upon American life brought by the American Jewish community, pressures that serve to "inhibit calm public discussion of the issues" in the Arab–Israeli conflict, and, on occasion, "induce public officials to endorse policies concerning Israel in which they do not believe. . . ." The Friends add that this "is not a new phenomenon in American politics . . . ," and then they utter a threat: Those Americans who are concerned with "inter-faith harmony and brotherhood" can hardly remain indifferent to the above kind of Jewish behavior. The passage cited is from the first edition of *Search for Peace in the Middle East.*[26] For *The Christian Century* to have proceeded publicly in this manner suggests that the Quakers can hardly plead that their later version has somehow annulled their accountability for the first version of their pronouncement. The earlier version is the one that has been circulated by proponents of the Arab cause.

In a sense, the Friends appear to have managed things two ways: the furnishing of one version for dissemination by the one side (75,000 copies of the first edition were distributed), and the circulation of a seemingly less harmful version that might be calculated to disarm critics of their generally anti-Israeli and anti-Jewish position. Editorial deletions of erstwhile charges against Jews and Israel hardly mean that the hostile sentiments behind them are no longer operating, any more than they mean the erasing of harm already done.

The first edition remains within the public domain. The only ethical way out of this state of affairs for the Friends would be a public repudiation of relevant parts of their

[25] Polier, "Open Letter . . . ," p. 5.
[26] *Search for Peace* . . . , 1st ed., p. 68.

original statement, a course they appear to have no intention of taking. The fact that primarily anti-Israeli and anti-Jewish passages are the ones that had to be changed—such changes were made at comparatively few places—is itself an index of hostility against the one side from within reputedly fairminded Christian quarters.

IV

The statement contains distortions, half-truths, and out-and-out falsehoods. Here it is hard to know where to begin. The Quakers seek to perpetuate the myth of Arab–Jewish amity in the good old days before the Zionist incursion. Those on the Arab side call Arab terrorists "commandos"; Israelis call terrorists "terrorists"; the Quakers call terrorists "commandos." By some legerdemain the *fedayeen* become a "resistance" movement. The June War of 1967 becomes "a war nobody intended to happen." No distinction whatsoever is made between terror as an entrenched, long-standing and perfectly acceptable policy within the Arab world, and terror as an exceptional Israeli act of the past. We are assured that injustice has been done to the Palestinians by Israel "and the world," though evidently not by the other Arabs. The pacification and reconciliation of Israeli Arabs to their Jewish neighbors become merely "supposed" developments. And Israel is guilty of ongoing territorial expansionism. The Quakers admonish us that "anti-Jewish prejudice, discrimination and persecution are not a problem the Arab countries must be expected to solve for the rest of the world by repeatedly trading away Arab territory."[27]

The following are illustrative of the simple falsehood category: continuing support of Israel by Western Europe (the Israelis might wish to be apprised of this!); the Arab leadership's agreement that Israel is a reality, political as well as

[27] *Search for Peace* . . . , rev. ed., pp. 13, 25, 27, 31, 36, 40–41, 46, 82, 95.

geographic (at this writing, there remains no unqualified evidence of any such change, and I include the position of the Sadat Government);[28] the function of the Arab "commando attacks" as serving "to unify a loose coalition government that would otherwise fly apart and bind an otherwise critical and peace-hungry people to the hard-line policies of the government"; the Israeli rejection of the U.N. Resolution of November 22, 1967 (the opposite is the case); and the official Israeli policy of seeking security "primarily through the annexation of Arab territory. . . ."[29]

The Quakers omit and suppress data. They show little comprehension of the role of the Soviet Union in the Middle East conflict, including its precipitating of the 1967 hostilities. In their strictures against Israeli refusals to trust or to accede to international and U.N. action, they fail to make clear past Israeli admission of and reliance upon such action, to Israel's own subsequent hurt. The study fails to note the creation since World War I of eighteen Arab states extending over 4.5 million square miles and, by contrast, the infinitesimal space allotted to Israel in the U.N. Partition, a decision accepted by the Palestinian Jews and rejected by the Arabs.[30] The document is totally silent on the thousands of Arab refugees already rehabilitated and aided by Israel, on her initiative alone.

The most egregious suppression of fact arises in connection with the reported position of Al-Fatah calling for a secular democratic Palestinian state where Arabs and Jews can live as fellow-citizens. The Friends suppress reference to the Palestinian National Covenant and accompanying resolutions officially adopted in 1968 by the Palestinian National Council, comprising almost all Palestinian groups and domi-

[28] See A. Roy Eckardt, "The Fantasy of Reconciliation in the Middle East," *The Christian Century*, 88:41 (Oct. 13, 1971), 1198–1202.

[29] *Search for Peace* . . . , pp. 24, 80, 86, 95–96, 108, 113–114.

[30] Polier, "Open Letter . . . ," p. 4.

nated by Al-Fatah. These pronouncements have never been abrogated. They stipulate that only Jews who lived in Palestine before 1917 will be permitted to remain. This would mean dispatching between two and three million Jews one way or another.[31]

Within cited materials, the Friends' study repeatedly phrases pure allegations in such a way as to suggest that they constitute unquestioned facts. Examples—all of them reflective of the straight Arab propaganda line—include the Quakers' simplistic historical assertion that the Christian West cooperated in forcing the Jews upon the Arabs and supported the establishing of Israel as a means of escaping "its accumulated centuries" of antisemitic guilt; the charge that American commitments to Israel are so totally dictated by a Jewish voting bloc that our President "has no real freedom of action to pursue an even-handed policy"; the allegation "that the Israeli state was born with the aid of Western political cynicism and achieved through the determination of the Zionists to take over all of Palestine"; the conviction of "continuing" Jewish expansionism as a fundamental cause of Arab fears and hostility; and the claim that until Jewish "injustice is admitted, both by the victorious Israelis and by the international community," steps toward peace are out of the question.[32]

Why is it that the Friends raise no objections whatsoever against the falsity and unfairness of these charges?[33] Similarly, the authors fail, or refuse, to offer discriminate moral judgments. Thus, they refer with total indiscriminateness to "a propaganda war that has never ceased." "Warlike rhetoric" is reputedly practiced equally "on both sides." The actions of Egypt and Israel leading up to the Six Day War were

[31] Ibid., p. 5.

[32] *Search for Peace* . . . , pp. 24, 56, 67–68, 94.

[33] In the revised edition, an attempt is made to provide a more balanced context for the second of the charges listed (ibid., pp. 55–56; cf. p. 30 of the May, 1970 version).

equally "provocative and precipitate."[34] American support for Israel is unqualifiedly equated with Soviet support of Arab states.

As a kind of climactic insult, the Friends include a summary of what they call a "remarkable" article by Nahum Goldmann in *Foreign Affairs* which advocates that Israel be neutralized as a special kind of state.[35] The Quakers here utilize a clever and now-frequent stratagem in anti-Jewish circles: the citing of a Jewish "authority" or representative as a means of showing that Jews are "with us," just as we are "with Jews." Yet surely even Friends must recognize the intolerable affront to Israelis, and to Jews, in any demand that Israel be put at the mercy of her foes. We are brought back to the double standard. The spectacle of an outside, pacifist Christian body practicing ideological imperialism upon Jews, and doing so with help from a Jewish leader's proposal, is before us. One is reminded of a certain cynic's definition of Christianity: the religion which teaches that Jews are to turn the other cheek. That demand is never made of the enemies of Israel.

V

The Quaker representatives are victims of false consciousness, as that condition is described by Gregory Baum, and their report contains the fruits of that unhappy condition.

The Friends' announced goal of human reconciliation was powerless to overcome their false consciousness as Christians. That high goal could not keep them from serving dubious forms of expediency and, indeed, from distorting and even suppressing truth. True consciousness, by contrast, makes for courage, and courage makes for truth-telling. The

[34] Ibid. rev. ed., pp. 36, 109.
[35] Nahum Goldmann, "The Future of Israel," *Foreign Affairs,* 48:3 (April, 1970), 443–459; *Search for Peace . . .* , p. 119.

Quakers' ideological taint prevented them from achieving authentic objectivity. Concretely, a result of their effort must only be to compound Arab fears of Jews and Israelis, and to aggravate Jewish fears of the Christian world. In the name of peace and justice, the Friends have erected barriers to peace and justice.

The false consciousness of the Quakers impels them to give voice to the same tiresome and evil accusations against the Jewish people (aggressiveness, inflexibility, vengefulness, conspiracy) that we have encountered a thousand times. False consciousness entices the Friends' Committee to make the same old insufferable demands of the Jewish people, including a resort to one set of moral standards for Jews and a quite different set for the detractors of Jews.

False consciousness fosters moral blindness. Landrum R. Bolling, chief architect of the Quaker pronouncement, was for one moment honest when, at a conference in Jerusalem, he expressed agreement that a pro-Arab presentation would be required in order to balance what he considered a pro-Israeli slant in the American mass media.[36] But Bolling was soon to betray this honesty, in the report and in other public statements, through an effort to hide a commitment to the one side on the part of himself and his group. The price of "reconciliation" contained in the Quaker study is an overwhelming refusal to evaluate ongoing Arab behavior critically and a diametrically opposite course in respect to the Israelis. The Friends are partisans who pretend—to themselves as much as to their public—that they are impartial mediators devoted to everyone's best interests. Their primary transgression lies in the infinite qualitative and quantitative difference between the contents of their declaration and the claims to objectivity and fairmindedness they make for themselves. Their false consciousness obscures to them, as to others, their prejudices and sins. Rather than boasting of the history of

[36] Soloway et al., *Truth and Peace in the Middle East*, p. 2. The date of the conference in Jerusalem was Feb. 13, 1970.

their good works as humanitarians,[37] the Quakers would have been better advised to take into their hearts the history of Christian maltreatment of Jews. This might have helped them somewhat to surmount the false consciousness that wars against true objectivity. Their "evenhandedness" might have become genuinely evenhanded.[38]

---

[37] See, e.g., *Search for Peace . . .* , p. 7.

[38] In light of the comment in chap. 9 on the altered editorial policy of *Christianity and Crisis,* it is not surprising that that journal, in which the chapter just concluded substantially appeared, should launch a concerted attack upon my critique of the Quaker report. A suspicious, though insightful, colleague suggested to me that in publishing my (noninvited) manuscript, *Christianity and Crisis* was simply setting me up for just such an opportunity. (It is true that just prior to my submitting the critique, I had published elsewhere a tribute to the journal's founding editor, Reinhold Niebuhr, in which I called attention to the marked editorial shift of *Christianity and Crisis* respecting Israel and the Jewish people.) The fact is that the journal refused to accept a revised draft of my assessment of the Friends' study and insisted on publishing (if anything were to be printed) the original draft—contrary, of course, to my wishes in preparing and submitting a substitute. Then *Christianity and Crisis* furnished immediate rebuttals and strong condemnations of my analysis, every piece having been specifically invited by the editor, as he subsequently acknowledged to me. My original article was answered by A. Denis Baly in the very same number in which it appeared ["The Search for Peace: A Modest Defense," *Christianity and Crisis,* 31:15 (Sept. 20, 1971), 186–191]. When I sought to respond to Baly, there sure enough was another answer from him, in that same later number [A. Roy Eckardt and A. Denis Baly, "More on the Middle East," 31:16 (Oct. 4, 1971, 206–208]. The journal's application of "evenhandedness" was: We must not print any critique of the Quaker pronouncement without a simultaneous rebuttal. To my knowledge, *Christianity and Crisis* has never followed a comparable procedure on any other topic. Normally, the dignity of readers in evaluating materials for themselves is respected. But then came the real deluge, an issue of the journal that included a long, invited reply by Landrum R. Bolling, chief author of the Friends' statement ["Mission Impossible?," 31:20 (Nov. 29, 1971), 253–257], together with five additional invited pieces, prevailingly condemnatory of my assessment. Finally, when I sent in a full rejoinder to these attacks, I was informed that any such piece would be out of the question—"on purely journalistic grounds"—and that only a 1200-word communication would be permitted. My brief piece was remanded to an inconspicuous place in the letters column ["Dr. Eckardt Replies," 31:23 (Jan. 10, 1972), 297–298]. An irony of this affair is that my critique of the Quaker declaration is relatively mild. Unlike the authors of *Truth and Peace in the Middle East* (pp. 1–6 and *passim*), I have omitted the more sordid elements in the story that lie behind the work of the Friends' Committee.

12

The Affirmation of Israel

No faithful Christian wishes to foster those evils of polarization that rend the human family and betray love. Yet we are not permitted to turn away from particular historical-moral contexts, from specific moral obligations. In these respects, if not in others, the point of view "situation ethics" takes is a proper guide. Apart from a contextual approach, our choices cannot be truly responsible; they may only contribute, in awful irony, to the polarizing and destructive consequences we seek to escape.

A Christian affirmation of Israel—and by this I mean an affirmation on the part of certain Christians—must pay careful attention to the political situation in the Middle East, and it must include responsible decision-making in that situation. But the affirmation of Israel also carries us beyond the Arab-Israeli conflict. Such an affirmation begins at the natural level and proceeds to the transnatural level. That is to say, it addresses itself to problems within the socio-political order, and then it moves to the domain of personal-communal faith. In the present chapter these two areas are treated in the order indicated.

I

Authentic evenhandedness is not impossible for Christians who respond to the Arab-Israeli conflict.[1] A great deal depends upon whether the assessors can control their false consciousness.

It is essential that we hear with sympathy, if critically, the woes and the pleas of both major protagonists, the Israelis and the Palestinian Arabs. It is equally essential that we be honest, especially with ourselves. It is not fair automatically to equate criticism of Israel with antisemitism. Yet that there are connections among anti-Zionism, anti-Israelism, and antisemitism is hard to deny. A fundamental link is found in the proclivity to reject Zionists, Israelis, and Jews not for what they "do" so much as for what they "are." And we must be alert to a stratagem that has become fairly widespread: when the suggestion is made that some opponents of Israel just may be antisemitic, the allegation is categorically denied and vigorously condemned as dirty pool. Superficially, it would appear that the opponent has fashioned a perfect piece of armor. But protestations to self-purity are seldom convincing. I suspect that the regnancy of antisemitism in our world has left few people totally free of the disease, and this applies even to those of us who fight antisemitism.

Those who contend that Israel is fully entitled to live in dignity and peace are many times accused of slavish assent to her every deed and every wish. They are lackeys of the Jewish cause and conspiracy. (This accusation is the other side of the coin just noted: the absolute denial that opponents of Israel could be antisemitic.) The stratagem has been utilized not only by Christian antisemites but also by antisemitic Jews.[2] Since this allegation of servility is not

---

[1] An effort in this direction is made in Alice and Roy Eckardt, "The Tragic Unity of Enemies," *The Christian Century*, 86:3 (Jan. 15, 1969), 73–76.

[2] I was once identified as a "house-Christian of the Zionists." The charge came from an anti-Zionist Jew.

often sustained by the facts, I am led to wonder whether the charge may not cloak a wish to discredit opponents and ultimately to foster the discrediting of Israel.[3] I have opposed many official acts of Israel, and expect to continue to do so, just as have unnumbered persons who do it with a probity I cannot boast: the Israelis themselves. Israel is not God; it is her foes who fabricate the evil fable that her supporters see her as divine, just as these same detractors strive to make the world believe that Israelis flaunt their "victories" as proof that the Lord is on their side.[4] I am afraid that some parties who condemn specific Israeli policies are impelled to do so not primarily because they consider the acts intrinsically wrong, but because they cannot really bring themselves to approve *any* Israeli policy, i.e., they cannot accept Israel. In other words, they do not accept Jews.[5]

---

[3] Landrum E. Bolling (see note 38 to chap. 11) tries to associate my name with "pro-Israeli hardliners" and with "the most uncompromising defenders of all aspects of the Israeli Government's policies" ["Mission Impossible?" *Christianity and Crisis,* 31:20 (Nov. 29, 1971), 255, 256]. I challenge Bolling to find a single hint of any such point of view in anything I have ever said or written. For example, where did he secure the ludicrous datum that my name is to be linked with those who demand annexation of all the Israeli-occupied territories? These are unconscionable charges indeed. The one person whose existence Bolling seems incapable of granting is a Christian critic of his who is not at the same time a blind *Stellvertreter* of Israel. The critic becomes, in effect, some kind of secret agent, an absolutist disciple. The man who would discern any presence of antisemitism in Bolling or the Quaker group has simply sold his soul to Israel and to an aggressive, expansionist Israeli government. Bolling's nemesis is that a number of us who are Christians and Americans have done no such thing. His accusation is comparable to those who, reprehensibly, identify criticisms of Israel with anti-Zionism and antisemitism.

[4] After the war of June, 1967 a well-known Jewish scholar from outside Israel delivered to an Israeli audience a ringing religio-patriotic sermon praising the victory of the armed forces as, in effect, a divine victory. He was at once challenged by an Israeli soldier who stood up and cried: "These hands of mine have been drenched in blood. With them I have killed many human beings. How can you talk that way?"

[5] Among the many sickening aspects of A. C. Forrest's anti-Jewish campaign is his repeated insistence that his critics must surely have been taken captive by the "Zionist conspiracy." Forrest does not appear capable of discerning that this tactic of his is one of the best proofs of his antisemitism.

II

The primary and fateful challenge posed by the Arab-Israeli conflict is how to avoid unrealistic sentimentality without falling into cynicism and the endorsement of a naked power contest. The latter are especially menacing consequences once the judgment is reached, as it must be, that reconciliation appears impossible in the foreseeable future.

There is a pitiable illusion—manifest today, for example, among some younger Israelis—that if Israel will only be kind and conciliatory to the Arabs, the Arabs will be the same in return. Something of this illusion appears in an engrossing, widely read, and informative study (though at base a misconceived one) by an Israeli Jew, Amos Elon. The author of this work—*The Israelis: Founders and Sons*[6]—rightly dismisses as naïve the hope among his countrymen "that the Arabs will come round to recognizing that their decades-old opposition to the return of Jews has been a horrible misunderstanding."[7] Yet Elon himself exudes something of the same moralistic idealism he exposes in his own people. He pleads, for example, that Israeli "compassion" can be a way to peace. This idealism would perhaps not be so unfortunate were it not combined with a *Realpolitik* that cannot avoid practical cynicism. (Reinhold Niebuhr taught us long ago the close kinship between idealism and cynicism.) The cynicism is made inevitable by Elon's seriously truncated understanding and exposition of the roots of Israel (a viewpoint found among other Israelis as well). Israel is largely reduced to the product of a modern nationalist liberation movement. In concentrating upon such modern "founders" as Leo Pinsker and Theodor Herzl, Elon only succeeds in making Fathers Abraham and Moses conspicuous by their absence. By focusing the case for Israel upon a presumed political fait accompli, in fulfillment of nationalist longings

[6] Amos Elon, *The Israelis: Founders and Sons* (New York: Holt, Rinehart and Winston, 1971).
[7] Ibid., p. 249.

that had come to pervade the Jewish communities off in Europe and Russia, Elon simply plays into the hands of Israel's foes. For the enemy is forced to respond, quite rightly: "How in hell did your nationalism ever give you the right to invade and steal our country?" Here we have the consequences of Elon's sacrifice of the historical-juridical rationale of Israel to power-political considerations—the reduction of today's confrontation to, in effect, one of naked power.

Elon is incorrect in implying that the moral idealism of Israelis has crowded out the kind of historical perspective that can save them from national foolishness. It is precisely their apprehension of the centuries-long presence and continuity of the Jewish people in their land that delivers the Israelis from the cynicism of *Realpolitik*. The whole Arab–Israeli encounter is at once moral and historical–juridical; these two categories just cannot be separated. As attested in Chapter 9, the legitimacy of Israel rests preeminently upon historical–juridical right (in common with other Palestinians), a right that is surpassed nowhere on our planet. This kind of right (which, with all human rights, is of course relative, not absolute) provides moral sanction to the Israeli–Jewish political claim, avoids the immorality of naked power assertion, and escapes the sentimentality of moralistic idealism.

It is one thing to concede, as I have done, that Arab opposition to "the return of Jews" combines with anti-Israeli prejudice among American Christians and others to make futile certain kinds of educational efforts. It is quite something else—and a failure of responsibility as well as of nerve —to permit such opposition and prejudice to govern national and international decision-making. For the opposition and the prejudice are sent to perdition by the judging voice of an ancient and abiding history.

Wherein, then, lies the value of Elon's work? There is an indispensable lesson in his book. In the very act of ignoring, in large measure, the objectively grounded rationale of Israel, Elon testifies obliquely and unintentionally to the element of fantasy in any hoped-for reconciliation in the Middle East. For, on their part, the enemies of Israel come along and insist that the pretended historical–juridical "justification" of Israel exudes immorality and nonsense. The "justification" is viewed as a contemptible ideological stratagem designed to hide the realities of brute coercion and theft.

Among our prevailing illusions is the idea that the situation in the Middle East is a "conflict" or "international dispute" that can be "resolved" to the "greater or lesser satisfaction" of the antagonists. The world is, of course, full of such disputes (e.g., territorial and boundary disputes) which can always be settled or at least "lived with," with the aid of mediation, compromise, or limited and temporary military operations. The Middle Eastern problem is a universe away from all this. It has nothing to do with border questions. Our overall fantasy includes the notion that by "withdrawing" from "occupied Arab territories" Israel could gain acceptance by her foes. In truth, every inch of "Israeli territory" is considered Arab land. Israel could "withdraw" to a half-acre settlement along the Mediterranean sands, and she would remain as "guilty" as she is now or as she would be, for that matter, were she to occupy Cairo or Damascus. Any temporary atrophy within the cancer that is Israel would only be preparation for a future metastasis. The obliteration of *all* Israel is a holy obligation.[8]

The infinitely sad conclusion to be drawn from all this

[8] A most disturbing condition is the refusal among Arab "sympathizers" to treat the convictions of Arab peoples and the literally normative Arab point of view with the seriousness that is deserved. To respond to the pledge, "it is our duty to destroy the enemy," by insisting that it is not to be taken literally or is merely "a manner of speaking," is to lack respect for those committed to the pledge. It means, in addition, a failure to admit the intimate relation between human words and human acts. The Arab rejection of the Jewish claim is anything but a purely "verbal" one; the history of the past fifty years effectively refutes any such notion. The deeds of men demand as much regard as their words. (The Arab sympathizer protests, of course, that Israel's stress upon the alleged Arab wish to destroy her is simply a power-political device to get her own way.)

is that Israel's actions are extraneous to the whole issue under discussion. It is the *being* of Israel that we see bound to the stake. True, the Israelis are repeatedly subjected to judgments upon their behavior: "Put aside your wrongful ways. Purge yourselves of your iniquities. Then we may accept you." John H. Marks offers the pretension that "an Israeli attitude of compromise and conciliation might quickly achieve" equal partnership in the Middle Eastern community of nations.[9] Such demands are spurious. For the truth remains that Israel is condemned for her good deeds as much as, if not more than, for her reputedly evil ones. To the enemy, Israeli "good" deeds are not really that; they are merely servants of dark, ulterior motives. No other nation is told to aspire to universal sainthood, no other nation is subjected to a trial that is never permitted to end.

So when all is said and done, Amos Elon and the Israelis and the Arabs and all the rest of us are left with the real state of affairs: a struggle to the death. There can only be, as at the moment I write, temporary lulls in the battle. Any objectively compelling moral–historical–juridical foundation of Israel becomes neither here nor there at the power-political level. Nevertheless, that very foundation provides us with moral undergirding in the eminently just war against the destruction of Israel. Here is our refuge from cynicism. But we must also avoid the equally powerful temptation of idealism, the confusing of earth with heaven. Were we ever to counsel Israel to rely upon the "pledged word" of others or upon vaunted "guarantees" from one or another party, rather than upon security measures and military power, we should have fallen victim to idealism. There is, by contrast, a common front between persisting Israeli policy and the application of the theological doctrine of sin to the

---

9 John H. Marks, "Israel—The Years Ahead," symposium, *worldview*, 16:5 (May, 1973), 20. Marks is actually devious here; he elsewhere denies that Israel has any moral legitimacy at all. She exists only by "sufferance" (idem.).

political domain. This doctrine teaches us that human promises and moral values are all too easily put to the service of human will-to-power and exploitation. (There is no implication of idealizing Israel here. If Israel must have the power to defend herself, so must the other Middle Eastern nations.)

III

Palestinian Arabs are possessed, with Jews, of comparable historical rights to the territory. Indeed, an insistence upon the compelling legitimacy of the Jewish claim to Eretz Yisrael also helps to undergird the independent political claims of the Palestinian Arabs, and is in a real sense a precondition for the latter claims. For once the objective justification of the rights of Jews were removed, the other Palestinians would be deprived of their claims as well. The consequences would be catastrophic, especially in view of the ongoing outside-Arab menace to the dignity of the Palestinian Arabs, and particularly the menace of the Transjordanians, who are "Jordanians" only by the rapacious conquest of the internationally authorized Palestinian state. Lack of independence for the Palestinians stems from injustices suffered by them in 1947–1950, when their Arab brothers and some of their own antecedents betrayed the singular opportunity of Palestinian sovereignty. The one overarching tragedy of erstwhile Palestine, and thence of the Middle East, remains the failure to institute the U.N. Partition Plan of 1947. The outcome was to be the dreadful plight of the Palestinian Arabs. (That their plight could have been easily resolved by the Arabs in power does not help now.) These unfortunate people simply want to return to their homeland, to be reunited with families and friends, to be adequately compensated for their hardships and material losses, to live with ordinary dignity. As the wife of an Arab pastor in the Lebanon put it to my wife and me: "We are not Palestinians, for Palestine no longer exists. We are not Jordanians, even though we hold Jordanian passports. We are not Lebanese, even though we carry Lebanese identity cards. Who are we?" The thousands of displaced Arabs in the pitiful refugee camps we visited are experiencing the fate met by countless Jews past and present. If, objectively speaking, comparison of their condition with the lot of Jews in Hitler's Holocaust does not hold, it is inhuman to expect these people to accede to rational moral distinctions.

On the other hand, the serious danger in preachments stressing Arab rights is a strengthening of those forces and interests that are bent upon the destruction of the Jews of Israel. Christians concerned about Israel will join the Israelis in a resolutely political program, fostering power structures that will make more and more inconsequential and futile the partisanship and hostility of the churches and other parties. But such a program is commended not just for the sake of Israel. It is offered in the name of the Arab peoples and of all humanity. For the moral paradox of the Middle East in the 1970s is that a categorical insistence upon the ethnic and national rights of the Jews of Israel—when that insistence becomes incarnate in power-political action—comprises the one telling resource we have for meeting our obligations to Arabs as much as to Jews. In truth, there is no other available way to heal the Arab world of its powerful impulse to self-destruction, no other way to preclude the terrible eventuality that future generations will have to remember Arabs along with Nazis as the wholesale slaughterers of Jews in the twentieth century.

Perhaps reconciliation begins to have a chance once we are reduced to full despair by the ineluctable barriers to it. The life-and-death moral paradox is that Israel may not endure (i.e., she may not live in peace and dignity) and yet that responsible Christians and other men must strive to prevent any such horrible negation. There is nothing original in this dialectical condition; the perennial human plight makes expressing the paradox even a little banal. There remains hope, but it is transrational. It rests upon the faith that some-where in this faceless and disgusting universe, where Jews are harmed because they are Jews while Arabs are harmed not because they are Arabs, a small voice has decreed that the Jewish will-to-live, and particularly the will-to-live in love and charity with one's neighbors, is right and good.

IV

Our affirmation of Israel has thus far concentrated upon political and moral issues. We attend next to the more per-sonal-communal domain, in association with relevant facets of the Christian faith.

I grope again and again for the meaning of the Land of Israel. The thoughts here set down reflect that search; they do not constitute a "final" interpretation.

When the Jews of Israel are threatened—as they were in the summer of 1967—Jews over the world experience the same threat. Yet, curiously, a few Christians feel the threat as well. How is this possible?

My thoughts upon Israel arise out of human and Chris-tian considerations alike. A visiting colleague insisted one time: "I was a man before I was a priest." I have to say, analogously, "I was a man before I was a Protestant Chris-tian." Hence, the phrasing above, "human and Christian," is not here introduced in order to supply support for Chris-tianity as, reputedly, the "true humanism" (*humanisme inté-gral*).[10] On the contrary, the concepts "human" and "Chris-tian" stand facing one another dialectically: the human ele-ment is a matter of simple fact; the Christian element is a fragile and highly problematic possibility. The two taken together comprise an acknowledgment of historical contin-gency.

Having been first a man, I became a Christian; I could

[10] Cf. Jacques Maritain, *True Humanism* (New York: Scribner, 1938).

have become something else. I am given to understand that Jewish reality is, in principle, quite another matter: to the conscience of the Jew, the duality just suggested has no convincing force. (Perhaps only Jews may speak of a *humanisme intégral*. In the measure that a gentile Christian dares to venture such a claim in his own behalf, his justification is that he must somehow have become part of Jewish reality.)

Having alluded to an inevitable duality within the life of a Christian, I suggest that the two dimensions referred to are brought together whenever the Christian is laid hold of by moral obligations. In the fateful days of May–June, 1967, I heard myself saying to a few groups: "Had the Israelis promised to annihilate one or another Arab nation, our duty would have been to oppose Israel." These words have haunted me ever since. For what condition could have been more contrary to fact? It has to be added that the context in which the words were originally offered was my lament and shame because the Christian churches I know had, for the second time in our century, remained silent or pretended to be "neutralist" before a diabolical intention and plot to destroy Jewish existence. I was arguing, in other words, as a human being, as one whose humaneness, weak though it was, was standing in judgment upon his own community of faith.

It is as a human being that I must also oppose philosemitism, for I am convinced that it is merely the other side of antisemitism. Philosemitism is antisemitism taken captive by remorse. Back in the summer of 1967, philosemitism was wearing, I fear, the mask of an indiscriminate enthusiasm for everything Israeli. Yet there persists the sickening gentile schizophrenia that in one moment judges Israel by superhuman standards (she is supposed to be ever-ready for greater sacrifices), and in the next moment judges her by subhuman standards (the Israelis are little more than militaristic secularists corrupted by self-interest). However, I remain as certain that Israel would not wantonly annihilate another people as I am of my wife's love, which is very far from utopian sentimentality. Why do I have this certainty? I do not know. Or, better, the certainty is part of my existence. As a Christian, I am convinced that men are sinful—all men. Yet it is very odd that some men can be trusted unto death. We all learned years back to cringe at the words, "some of my best friends are Jews." The reaction was right, granted the usual attitude covered up by the expression. *But must the presupposition here always be a philosemitic–antisemitic one?* Is it not possible, however incredible the testimony may sound, that the hope of Israel is the hope of mankind? Once or twice in a lifetime we may find ourselves forced to make affirmations that explode the ordinary canons of expectation. Some of our best friends *are* Jews! However, as a Christian— also as a man?—I have to insist on something, lest my "best friends" entertain delusions of grandeur: The moral stature of Israel and of the Jewish community as a whole is not a consequence of mere human accomplishment. It is an enigma of grace. As stated above, the idealization of Israel is forbidden.

V

The peoplehood of Jews is an axiom of Jewish existence. James Parkes applies to the Jewish people the fitting title "a natural community."[11] Yet can this axiom of Jews be affirmed by a Christian? Can it be avowed by one who must remain a Christian (since, to speak with the New Testament and even with the Jewish thinker Franz Rosenzweig, Jesus Christ is the Christian's way to God,[12]) but one who, for that very reason, makes the affirmation of Jewish peoplehood from out of his own inner being and not as a mere reporter of someone else's existence? This question transcends the purely "human"

[11] For example, in James Parkes, *Prelude to Dialogue: Jewish–Christian Relationships* (London: Vallentine, Mitchell, 1969), p. 217.
[12] See the citations in Nahum N. Glatzer, *Franz Rosenzweig: His Life and Thought,* rev. ed. (New York: Schocken, 1961), pp. 341, 343.

dimension. It leads us into another category (though not necessarily a totally different one qualitatively) from the issue of Israeli–Arab relations as such, relations that from one point of view simply involve politico-moral issues of the same genre as the dilemmas that were put to us by the Vietcong slaughter of civilians.

One answer is that just as moral demands sometimes succeed in marrying humanity to faith, and faith to humanity, so *belongingness* may have the same consequence. The question for the Christian is this: Does he not belong in some strange way to the family of Jews? (No question in the entire Jewish–Christian encounter can be more heartrending than this, for any affirmative answer must quicken—and justly so— objections from Jews.) Clearly, if the Christian is not part of the Jewish family, then for him Israel has no unique meaning whatever. The most that could be said is that he regards Israel from the standpoint of a man confronted by certain moral challenges. But these challenges can be duplicated at any time and at any place in the world. However, if the Christian does somehow belong within the family of Jews, then Israel is already alive in his heart and merely waits to become flesh through his words and deeds. The Christian scholar Krister Stendahl has expressed this second possibility: "We need to ask . . . whether they [Jews] are willing to let us become again part of their family, a peculiar part to be sure, but, even so, relatives who believe themselves to be a peculiar kind of Jew."[13]

It is Jesus who opens the way for Christians to be brought into the Jewish–Israeli family. Jesus was a man of Israel. (That we have to remind ourselves that the one whom Christians are supposed to follow was himself a Jew is a painful reminder of our false consciousness, of the silliness of our ideological maneuverings.) Living today, Jesus would be

---

[13] Krister Stendahl, "Judaism and Christianity II—After a Colloquium and a War," *Harvard Divinity Bulletin* (New Series), 1:1 (Autumn, 1967), 5.

called an Israeli. Through their involvement with a man of nineteen hundred years ago in a land thousands of miles away, American Christians are united to their American Jewish neighbors in the very next house.

I should be the last to propose seeking admission to a family that is alien to a man's own hopes and convictions. Here I must risk everything: If the people of the State of Israel belong in some singular way among the people of God, this cannot be merely because they are Israelis. And it cannot be because they are especially "religious" (which for the most part they are not). It can only be because the Jews of Israel constitute part of the abiding Covenant between God and his ancient people—the people of Abraham, Isaac, and Jacob, of Isaiah, Jesus, and Hillel. Without this attestation, one might have concern for Israel as a man, but not as a Christian.

A man can be quite honest in his family, perhaps only with his family. Hopefully, the sentences that immediately follow—addressed as they are to the Jewish community alone—are not crass exhibitionism. They are intended, at any rate, to point the way to our kinship (though, all too certainly, the Christian can claim family membership only by adoption, through Jesus the Jew). Does a writer prepare anything for publication apart from the wish, however submerged, that potential readers will approve what he says? Not very often. Does this usual state of affairs throw doubt, then, upon the integrity of his exposition? It may very well do so. On the other side I will plead that the wish for some kind of acceptance may also embody the longing of Christians (if only prodigal sons) to be taken back into the family. We should not come seeking acceptance were we not already committed to the being of Israel.

An American church official recently said that for Jews the future of the State of Israel "is the future of their people, but I'm not part of that people. . . ." This churchman was not right, I think. We who are Christians *are* part of the

Jewish people—by the very nature of our Christian faith. We do claim membership in the Jewish family. Therefore, Israel grasps us in our very existence, not merely as human beings (as men, we will simply try to be humanitarian), but as Christians. It is by virtue of our Christian existence that Israel can never be just another country for us. Of course, to the extent that it is on its own, Christianity is devoid of spatial ties. However, "through its indissoluble bond with the Jewish people and the Jewish faith, the Christian faith is yoked spiritually to Eretz Yisrael."[14]

The celebration of Israel is thus a celebration in my own Father's house; any derogation of Israel means gloom in that house. When again and again, on the occasion of the Six Day War and afterward, some men, reputed to be Christians, accused the Israelis of being "aggressors" and "like the Nazis," I was, as a man, repelled by the lying. I know these "Christians," with their hidden annihilationist designs, designs that are linked, both as cause and as effect, to the cancer of exterminationism that pervades the Arab world. As a Christian, I was ashamed. But I was more than ashamed, though my shame was deep. I also received the accusations as a personal insult, as though my own father were being maligned. Yet every gentile has to pray, steadfastly, that he be kept from the very same malignancy.

We poor pagans are called to give voice to the entreaty of Ruth of Moab: "Where you go, I will go; and where you stay, I will stay. Your people shall be my people, and your God my God. Where you die, I will die, and there I will be buried" (Ruth 1:16). The family is entitled to set conditions for the common journey; to lay these down is not in my purview. I can only yearn that Naomi's response before Ruth's importunity will be repeated: "When Naomi saw that Ruth was determined to go with her, she said no more" (1:18). And then the two went on together.

[14] Alice Eckardt and Roy Eckardt, *Encounter with Israel* (New York: Association Press, 1970), p. 262.

VI

I must try to anticipate an objection, one that derives from a nagging fear in the Christian conscience. Christians are taught to avoid idolatry—a lesson that, indeed, comes to us straight from Judaism. Is there not an inevitable element of idolatry in national adherence, and therefore in any unqualified acceptance of Israel? I offer three considerations: First, it was emphasized above, when we were reasoning politically, that support for Israel cannot mean an absence of criticism. The same is the case at the level of theological celebration. For love without judgment is not love. It is sentimentality. Second, we have to beware again of the affliction of a double standard. It is hard to imagine a more chronic case of idolatry than that besetting the Arab world vis-à-vis Israel—an idolatry so severe that it wills the very destruction of the other. Yet many of us seem scarcely disturbed by the spiritual condition of the Arab peoples, by their consuming hatred of Jews. Either we pay almost no attention to such hatred, or we take refuge in various methods of "understanding" it and even of excusing it. Third and most important, I believe that Reinhold Niebuhr is right in adjudging that of the two temptations, idolatry and irresponsibility, the second is the much greater evil.[15]

[15] Reinhold Niebuhr is cited on this matter in chap. 14.

Part Three
GLIMMERS OF CHANGE AND HOPE

13

Beginnings

I

The new "dialogue" of Jews and Christians has not arisen because of any positive alteration or development within Jewish life in its essence. For Jews living in a "Christian" milieu, the internal need to confront that environment in the 1970s is, in principle, no different from what it was in the 1920s or the 1870s. The peculiarities of the dialogue are largely a Christian problem. If nothing has changed for Jews, everything has changed for Christians. Christians have finally come under open attack by guilt. The dialogue is an effort to extricate ourselves from our Christian predicament. If Jews can never consent to sacrifice morality to "truth," certainly never to "truth" that is not truthful, Christians, if they work hard, can perhaps approximate the same ideal, as an act of courage in defiance of intolerable claims within their own historical life. The possibility of a real human relationship between Jews as Jews and Christians as representatives of a faith is thus primarily dependent upon Christian decision and action.

In Chapter 6 we referred to the way the traditional Christian threat to Jewish integrity serves to question whether

Christians can be considered the equals of Jews. We identified an authentic dialogic relation as the apprehension by each party of the other in his own self-understanding. Openness without self-identity violates the self; self-identity without openness violates the other. Genuine dialogue is never impossible. The potential for equality lies in the dignity of the partners, a dignity they possess simply because they are human beings, children of God.

Some Christians, furthermore, are committed to redeeming the past. All is not hopeless. Here and there, individuals and small bands have taken into their souls the conflict between the historic Christian defamation of the Jews and Judaism and the plain demands of righteousness. These Christians have made a choice. They are determined actively to atone, through deeds of justice, for the evils that have been done. There is also a gathering international partnership of Christian thinkers who are "possessed": men and women who simply will not tolerate Christian theology that means harm to the Jewish people.[1] Their standing ground is the truth, as voiced by Friedrich Heer, that "the greatest temptation to which Christians can succumb" is "to love God at the expense of human beings."[2] These new Christians are resolved to speak the truth in love (Eph. 4:15).

Part Three of this book would not be possible without the commitment to rectification that these Christians hold.

II

One of the hopeful signs of our times is that the evil forces that invaded the work of Vatican Council II have been counteracted by postconciliar trends. Catholic sin is being fought by Catholic goodness. To illustrate, I refer to a de-

---

[1] I hope some day to do a series of biographical studies of such Christians in different lands.

[2] Friedrich Heer, *God's First Love* (New York: Weybright & Talley, 1970), p. 393.

velopment within the Catholic Church in the United States, and, in doing so, I utilize, for contextual purposes, some contrasts with American Protestantism.

Within American Christianity, a noticeably greater practical contribution to understanding and solidarity among Christians and Jews has been forthcoming from the Catholic side, in comparison with Protestant effort or lack of effort. It is true that as human beings we sometimes idealize or overestimate contributions made by those beyond our own circle. In the present instance, however, the available evidence seems to bear out my judgment in favor of Catholic efforts.

Part of the difference in behavior between the two main branches of Christianity[3] is international and ecumenical in origin, reflecting nothing unique to the United States. The conciliar pronouncement on the Jews could have a positive effect, at least when not read too carefully. But certain elements more or less peculiar to American history and the American situation are undoubtedly of influence also. For one thing, despite their great numbers and the prosperity of their Church in this country, American Catholics have not lost their collective memory of what it is like to dwell as a minority within a dominantly non-Catholic land. By contrast, the American milieu has offered many opportunities for Protestant imperialism to assert itself, toward Catholics and Jews alike. In addition, the radical individualism of the historic American ethos has provided social supports for, and has compounded the force of, the decisive view traditionally shared by Protestants everywhere: The pearl of greatest price is the salvation of the individual soul. Nowhere has conversionism of the repent-or-be-lost type been as dominant within modern Christendom as in American Protestantism—in vast areas of the American South particularly, and to varying de-

[3] Eastern Orthodox Christianity in the United States is often ignored, and unwarrantedly so, in interreligious discussions. However, as yet not a great deal has been done within those churches in the area of Jewish–Christian relations. Nor does the future look very promising.

grees throughout the country. All in all, the relatively less individualistic spiritual resources within Catholicism have succeeded fairly well in combining with the tolerationist and pluralistic elements fostered by American culture and religion (elements that, paradoxically enough, have been largely the fruit of a broadly Protestant ethos) to issue in a somewhat greater concern for Jewish–Christian understanding within the Catholic Church, and more of a live-and-let-live outlook, than we find within American Protestantism.

There has been a marked contrast between official activity within the Catholic Church and that in the Protestant churches on the subject of relations with Jews. There is a Secretariat for Catholic–Jewish Relations, sponsored by the National Conference of Catholic Bishops, with a full-time director. A number of dioceses have created local offices for this same purpose. By contrast, the National Council of the Churches of Christ in the U.S.A., which represents shared Protestant and Orthodox church life, has been beset for years by the problem of how to forge institutional relationships with the Jewish people and Judaism. The direct and continuing consequence has been no provision for official leadership.[4] Significantly, the largest single barrier to establishing an effective organizational structure has been the persisting dispute over missionary efforts directed toward Jews. Protestant individualistic pietism dies very slowly. Most recently, the Protestant failure to meet the institutional challenge has been complicated by the influences of pro-Arab forces within the churches, particularly at the interdenominational level.

III

It was to be expected that together with the revolutionary Declaration on Religious Freedom,[5] the Vatican Council

---

[4] As I write, there is renewed hope of the appointment of a staff member within the National Council of Churches, with specific responsibility for Jewish–Christian relations.

[5] Declaration on Religious Freedom (Dignitatis Humanae), *The Documents of Vatican II*, pp. 675–696.

pronouncement on the Jewish people would, despite its shortcomings, be received and applied with considerable enthusiasm in American Catholicism. A preeminent example of American Catholicism's liberalization of dogma in the context of a search to advance brotherliness between Christians and Jews is the "Guidelines for Catholic–Jewish Relations" issued in March, 1967 by the Subcommission for Catholic–Jewish Affairs of the U.S. Catholic Bishops' Commission for Ecumenical and Interreligious Affairs.[6]

An inspection of the "Guidelines" quickly reveals how carefully its architects combed the Vatican Declaration of 1965 and passed over, or at least markedly toned down, those elements of the Declaration objectionable to Jews and others. It is equally evident that the American spokesmen were endeavoring to apply the Vatican pronouncement to specifically American conditions. Conspicuously missing is the conciliar assertion that with the coming of Jesus "Jerusalem did not recognize the time of her visitation" and "not a few" Jews opposed the spreading of the gospel. Gone as well is the Council's traditionalist allegation that "the cross of Christ" is "the fountain from which every grace flows." Instead, the American bishops' statement concentrates upon and develops quite different aspects of the thinking behind the Vatican Declaration: the importance of fraternal encounter between Catholics and Jews, Christian culpability for antisemitism, the ties that bind church and synagogue, the need for mutual understanding and respect, and the avoidance of all proselytizing. At one point the document goes decisively beyond anything in the conciliar statement: it commends common prayer by Catholics and Jews.

Such a highly selective rendering and application of the Declaration of Vatican Council II is not an accident. As proclaimed in the "Guidelines" themselves, the Catholic Church in the United States "has committed herself without reserve to the American ideal of equal opportunity and justice for

[6] The full text of this document may be found in *The Dialogue*, National Conference of Christians and Jews, bulletin no. 35 (June, 1967).

all." It is at once noteworthy and regrettable that no comparable pronouncement has been forthcoming from the Protestant side.

I do not imply that the "Guidelines" are beyond all criticism.[7] Further, as inevitably occurs within religions of authority, the extent to which directives from above will be implemented at descending levels of authority is contingent upon the degree of initiative and concern that is shown by the executive officials. There is, of course, great variation in interests and points of view among American diocesan bishops. It follows that in one diocese an active program of Jewish–Christian conversation and cooperation will go forward; in another, largely perfunctory acknowledgment of the need for such a program will be made; while in still another diocese, the entire subject will be ignored. Nevertheless, as observed in *The Dialogue,* a publication of the National Conference of Christians and Jews, "the Roman Catholic bishops of the United States have given their official blessing to a wide range of Jewish–Catholic activities, including the rapidly growing dialogue movement,[8] mutual scholarly studies (including study of the Scriptures), collaborative research in history, psychology, and sociology, revision of Catholic textbooks, common prayer, joint social action, and a wide variety of enterprises that will involve laymen, clergy, and scholars in what may well turn out to be the most significant event in Christian–Jewish relations in America."[9]

Catholic efforts toward Christian–Jewish understanding and brotherliness are receiving added support by the trend away from conversionism within the Roman Church. Monsignor John H. Oesterreicher, one of the framers of the Vati-

---

[7] Cf., for example, the dissatisfaction with the passage on the crucifixion story expressed by President Arthur J. Lelyveld of the American Jewish Congress (in a letter otherwise commending the "Guidelines") in *Congress bi-Weekly,* 34:8 (May 8, 1967), 3.

[8] Testimony to a "rapidly growing dialogue movement" appears rather dated, at least at this writing.

[9] *The Dialogue,* June, 1967, p. 15.

can Declaration and Director of the Institute of Judaeo-Christian Studies at Seton Hall University, has maintained that his Church sanctions "no drive, no organized effort to proselytize Jews, and none is contemplated for tomorrow. It may very well be that no such efforts will ever be revived." There will be "no movements, no centers for the winning of converts, however restrained."[10] On the whole, traditional Protestant evangelicalism in the United States lags far behind this Catholic affirmation. It is the case, however, that in American Protestantism—as in American Catholicism—attitudes toward Judaism and Jews have been influenced and, to a limited extent, bettered by Vatican Council II.

We may continue to hope that American Christianity will be increasingly delivered from the historic intolerance of the church, with aid from the countervailing force of religious pluralism, and may thereby serve as an exemplary witness in behalf of social, political, and religious freedom. A necessary way for Christianity to recapture its integrity in this age is through resisting the wiles of a "Christian state." Happily, in the United States a great many Catholics agree with a great many Protestants on this most crucial moral need.

[10] As cited in *The Dialogue,* June, 1967, p. 19.

14

Three Sketches

Individuals may induce historical change through their acts and through their thinking. If behavior has consequences, so do ideas. The meeting of Jews and Christians involves, of necessity, fundamental intellectual and spiritual questions, such as those confronted by the figures who speak to us through the following sketches. We return first to the time of Nazi Germany.

I

Kurt Gerstein. This man initially gained world attention through Rolf Hochhuth's play, *The Deputy.* In a recent historical biography, *Kurt Gerstein: The Ambiguity of Good,*[1] Professor Saul Friedländer of the Hebrew University in Jerusalem authenticates, corrects, and goes beyond Hochhuth's characterization. With Hochhuth, Friedländer focuses upon the anguish of moral choice, but he enables Gerstein to be his own living witness from within his own life situation.

As in Friedländer's earlier studies, *Pius XII and the*

[1] Saul Friedänder, *Kurt Gerstein: The Ambiguity of Good* (New York: Knopf, 1969).

Third Reich and *Prelude to Downfall,* the record is allowed to speak largely for itself. Sometimes I wished, as I read, that the biographer would cry out—Arthur A. Cohen calls the essay "brutally deadpan"—but then I would remember that Friedländer's very dispassionateness meant obedience to the passion of truth. (The more outraged one's description of monstrous evil, the more the account may have banality as its fate—a lesson I do not always succeed in remembering.) The power of Gerstein the man is thrust forward, paradoxically, by the biographer's very restraint. Had the chronicler pursued a different course, the truthful incredibility of his subject would have been lost.

The prevailing purpose of Friedländer's exposition is to trace the story of Dr. Gerstein's career and, thereby, to grapple with the dilemmas of a whole society and, indeed, of an entire world. The author's investigations lead him to consider as well the main aspects of the "final solution," including the attitudes and acts of groups inside and outside Nazi Germany. Friedländer gives us the fullest and most authoritative analysis yet possible of an unbelievable chain of events. At the same time, he impels us to face the haunting challenge to our own behavior in Kurt Gerstein's pattern of action.

Friedländer combs all the evidence (especially unpublished material) as a means of comprehending Gerstein's membership in Hitler's S.S. beginning in 1941, a deed described by the historian Gerald Reitlinger as perhaps the most astonishing mission of the Second Great War. We are advised that the veracity of Gerstein's long report on his endeavors (written shortly before his death) is, in essence, beyond all doubt. Accordingly, Friedländer does not question Gerstein's testimony that he joined the S.S. as an agent of the Confessing (anti-Nazi) Church.

The biographer's task is rendered difficult by two conditions: the powerlessness of available materials to answer some of our most fundamental questions (such as whether

Gerstein actually committed suicide or was murdered), and the massive enigma of Gerstein as a human being. Even in all the testimony from the latter's most convinced defenders, one feels "an inability to arrive at a full explanation of Gerstein as a person." Thus, Pastor Otto Wehr declared to the Tübingen Denazification Court that Gerstein's unearthly skill "in hiding his deep, inner, Christian life under a mask, for the sole purpose of helping others, defies judgment. It is impossible to do justice to this man . . . if one applies normal moral standards or if one attempts to explain him in political or psychological terms."[2]

Had he wished, Friedländer could nevertheless have marshaled a predominantly psychological explanation. His subject led "an existence full of contradictions."[3] Obstreperous as a lad, Gerstein in his youth exhibited a longing for moral and sexual "purity." It is probable that he never freed himself of the guilt feelings that ruled his adolescence and early years. While he gradually established what he called "a personal bond with Christ," his God always remained a God of wrath.

Although he turned against his authoritarian upbringing and tradition (his father had become an out-and-out Nazi), Kurt's very effort to "alert the world" against the Nazi menace does not appear totally free of desires to set himself up as the "right" authority. From 1942 onward, Gerstein's nervous state was increasingly aggravated, and he often conveyed an impression of intense depression and emotional exhaustion. His whole story reflects mental and spiritual turmoil. He became haunted by pictures of trainloads of Jews arriving to meet death. Despite an inner assurance that his chosen method of fighting the criminal regime was the right one, probably he could not surmount completely the dread persuasion of his own complicity in the exterminations.

As the official in charge of supplying the gas Zyklon B to the death camps, Gerstein succeeded in destroying a num-

---

[2] Ibid., pp. x, xi.
[3] Ibid., p. 45.

ber of shipments. But he could never have destroyed the entire supply under his jurisdiction. Obviously, he was obliged to cooperate in many murders. Toward the end he was tortured by fear and anxiety, including the fear of discovery. And ultimately he was to fall prey to terror. In referring to Gerstein's "most uncanny attempt to overcome his anxiety," Friedländer goes so far as to speak of "a real splitting of the personality."[4]

It is by virtue of his abiding stress upon Gerstein's moral agonies as a man and a Christian, and upon his moral stature, that the biographer finally escapes the psychologizing of his subject. Gerstein "was a unique personality by reason of the destiny he had freely chosen for himself, a man who . . . penetrated hell with the sole intention of bearing witness before the world and aiding the victims."[5] The guise of his challenge to us is the question of how we are to fight evil that is devilish. For some, to do any business at all with injustice is to fall into the devil's pit. Kurt Gerstein believed the opposite. However, he became so enraged that in the course of trying to alert the Western world and the Vatican to the truth of the death camps (foolishly, he expected a response), he shared his knowledge with many people he scarcely knew—so much so that Friedländer questions the recklessness.

From a quite different point of view, Günther Lewy has objected to the effort to justify those Germans who, by staying at their jobs for the purpose of ameliorating the horrors of the Nazi system, nevertheless enabled the machinery of extermination to grind away mercilessly. Had such men refused to comply at all, it is entirely possible that the extermination program would have been seriously hindered, as was the euthanasia program when some protested. Thousands of lives could have been saved.

The entirely justified controversies arising out of the

[4] Ibid., p. 178.
[5] Ibid., p. x.

foregoing dilemma can neither annul nor answer the question of whether I and my fellow Christians today would have come anywhere near the courage and the faithfulness of Kurt Gerstein. Vilmos Vajta's comment upon *The Deputy* is particularly pertinent here: "the real question is whether Christendom still believes in the path of suffering of its Lord, or whether it makes its witness depend on political considerations."[6]

Vajta's judgment suggests a possible response to Friedländer's conclusion that Gerstein was a tragic figure with a "tragic fate." In 1950 the Tübingen Denazification Court stooped to the wicked hypocrisy of placing Gerstein among the "tainted," condemning him posthumously for, allegedly, a failure to resist "with all the strength at his command" and for, in effect, the uselessness of his actions.[7] (It was not until fifteen years later that the Baden-Württemberg authorities agreed to review the case; on January 20, 1965 Gerstein was officially declared "not guilty.") Friedländer remarks bitterly that Gerstein was in a way punished "for not having behaved like the great majority of 'good' Germans and waited quietly until all the Jews were dead; paradoxically, the 'innocence' of such Germans is contrasted with the 'guilt' of a man who was obliged in some degree to accommodate to the crime in order to resist it." To Friedländer, "so much of Gerstein's tragedy lay in the loneliness of his action. The silence and passivity of the Germans, the absence of any notable reaction among the Allies and the neutrals, indeed, in the Christian West as a whole, in the face of the extermination of the Jews, invests the role of Gerstein with its true significance: his appeals having brought no response and his dedication having proved a solitary commitment, his sacrifice appeared 'useless' and became 'guilt.' "[8]

[6] Vilmos Vajta, "Vicar of Christ," *Lutheran World,* 10:4 (October, 1963), 410.
[7] Friedländer, *Kurt Gerstein,* pp. 225–226.
[8] Ibid., pp. 226–227, 228.

Yet it is the biographer himself who points us beyond tragedy by putting forth an essential criterion for defining moral resistance within a totalitarian system: the performance of acts that, once discovered, will cost the perpetrator his life. Kurt Gerstein belongs in this category. The real question is always whether a man or woman is going to endure to the end. Not only because of his readiness to suffer but because of his resolute will to do what was right, Gerstein could rise above tragedy. Every day he fought a terrible battle, not just against the system but against himself. His was a battle of will. And at the last he gained the victory. He won through —*in spite of* the powers that sought to capture him: family pressures, nationalist indoctrination, ostracism from friends, persecution, his pitiable psychic state, his natural human desire for solace and safety. The severest environmental–psychological forces are not always able to vanquish moral steadfastness.

On the basis of Friedländer's criterion, and on that alone—*absolutely not on the ground of any supposed "inno-cence" in Gerstein*—the words of this sketch may, despite their poverty, be offered as a legitimate dedication:

In homage to Dr. Kurt Gerstein (1905–1945), mining engineer, *Obersturmführer SS.,* relentless despiser of Nazism, servant of righteousness, in the end a faithful Christian who suffered and gave his life for the sake of the Jewish people.

II

Reinhold Niebuhr. We come next to the greatest political theologian of modern times. The childlike inability of Rein-hold Niebuhr (1892–1971) to recognize his own greatness always brought delight to those of us who knew him well. A saint, he had no comprehension of his saintliness. In the preserving of this ignorance, his anger was of indispensable aid. If Niebuhr was not a messiah, there was yet something messianic about him. I speak not alone of the deliverance he brought us, through his moral, spiritual, and intellectual attainments—he redeemed me from the vices of perfectionist–pacifist Christianity—but also, paradoxically, of his unexceptional insistence that no human being (or cause) can ever merit veneration as messianic.

Niebuhr's celebratedly bluff and reputedly derisive manner was utterly misleading as an indication of the man within. Of course, it is essential that authentic prophets act and speak as though they incarnate the very wrath of God. Probably no preacher will ever excel Reinhold Niebuhr as wearer of the mask of divine judgment. However, one test of true prophecy is the balancing of judgment by mercy. Behind Niebuhr's rough and forbidding exterior was a man wonderfully kind.

Professor Niebuhr's lifelong and valiant struggle against men's idolatries, and in behalf of human justice, together with his great stress upon the social obligations of religion, endeared him to Jews. They were natural friends of his, as he was the natural friend of the Jewish people. His fabled aphorism from the early years, "there are just two Christians in the entire City of Detroit, and they are both Jews," had as its background and inspiration the intimate, dreadful alliance between the churches and the forces of exploitive capitalism in the 1920s and 1930s. The maxim testified as well to Niebuhr's developing awareness of a quite different phenomenon: the ongoing commitment of the Jewish people to social justice. Reinhold Niebuhr was the Amos of American Christianity. Instinctively, Jews were drawn to him and his message.

The nature of their own tradition gave Jews further incentive for taking Niebuhr with great seriousness. Here was an American Christian leader whose intellect was staggering and whose scholarship and learning were prodigious, but who insisted that reason be utilized as the instrument of creative spirituality, in ways that avoid both dogmatic humanism and oppressive Christianity, while providing a firm foundation for practical social action.

Professor Niebuhr was deeply concerned with Christian–Jewish understanding. His unyielding enmity, as a Christian, to the churches' historic denigration of Judaism and to the obdurate effort to convert Jews to Christianity was especially noteworthy. He fought the missionizing stance on grounds of theological and moral principle. His unqualified respect for Jews and the Jewish faith earned him the gratitude of the Jewish community. How can there be respect for Jews as human beings without respect for Jewish convictions, including religious convictions?

Among Jews Reinhold Niebuhr will always be remembered for his courageous battle against Nazism and for his untiring endeavors in behalf of Jews under persecution. Indeed, much of the incentive behind his opposition to Nazism and his efforts to bring about American intervention in the war with Germany was his concern for the plight of the Jews of Europe. If, as I have long held, Niebuhr underestimated the unique force of Christianity in making possible the metastasis of antisemitism in the Western world (and, from there, to the Middle East), nevertheless he remained from start to finish a stalwart foe of antisemitism, as of other forms of human prejudice and exploitation.

Niebuhr's sympathy for the collective integrity and well-being of the Jewish people was bolstered by a general principle within his overall theological-moral position: In our less-than-perfect world, individual peoples—and small peoples especially—require political sovereignty as protection against those who would harass, oppress, or destroy them, just as they need freedom if they are to attain fullness of life. Of equal relevance here was Niebuhr's unrelenting opposition to the kind of Christian pacifism that leaves Jews, among others, the victims of tyrants and other oppressors. It was entirely logical that, early in his career, Reinhold Niebuhr became a

Christian Zionist—defined strictly as a Christian who supports the political freedom of Jews. Niebuhr was an ardent champion of a Jewish state in Palestine, and later of the State of Israel. To him, Zionism constituted one responsible and viable answer to injustices against Jews within and beyond Christendom, a concrete implementation of the survival rights of any people (for all its temptations, the collective will-to-survive is an authentic value within the divine "order of creation"), and a compelling recognition of the historic and moral claims of Jews to their homeland. Niebuhr contended that binationalism for Palestine was impractical. It must be emphasized, however, that his insistence upon the collective integrity of peoples extended fully to the rights of the Palestinian Arabs.

In one decisive way, Reinhold Niebuhr towered above the other theological giants of the twentieth century: through the unique and powerful unity he forged between theology and the politico-moral domain. I alluded in a previous chapter to Niebuhr's emphasis upon the intimate relationship between idealism and cynicism. An idealist is a future cynic; a cynic is an idealist who has learned something. The alternative to idealism and cynicism is realism.

Niebuhr's overall point of view bears the name "Christian realism." The thrust of his ethical position is disclosed in two passages:

I have spent a good part of my life validating the love ethic as final on the one hand, and trying to prove on the other hand that it must and can include all the discriminate judgments and commitments which we may broadly define as commitments in the cause of justice. . . . I am certain that an ethic of love which dispenses with the structures and commitments of justice is ultimately irrelevant to the collective life of man.[9]

---

[9] Reinhold Niebuhr, "Reply to Interpretation and Criticism," in Charles W. Kegley and Robert W. Bretall, eds., *Reinhold Niebuhr: His Religious, Social, and Political Thought* (New York: Macmillan, 1961), p. 450. Copyright © 1961 by the Macmillan Co. Reprinted by permission.

The moral crisis is ever changing, but all changes reveal one constant factor. The moral life of man is continually in the embarrassment of realizing that the absolutes of biblical and rational norms—which enjoin responsibility for the neighbor's welfare—can never be perfectly fulfilled, either by the use of or abstention from any of the instruments of community or conflict. Therefore, religious and moral guides must teach the necessity of discriminate ·judgment.[10]

Niebuhr disdained with equal force the practical cynicism of otherworldly spirituality and the utopianism and sentimentality that ever tempt the religious understanding—and especially the American Christian understanding—of the human condition. Cynicism and utopianism are, indeed, blood brothers. This world will never be the Kingdom of God. However, the dark that ever assails us is very considerably linked to our willful corrupting of our freedom. We remain responsible men, who can indeterminately transcend, though never totally vanquish, our sins.[11] By fashioning small kingdoms of proximate justice, we enable ourselves to bear and to counteract in some measure our own pride and idolatry. One such kingdom is political democracy, grounded as it is upon Judaic–Christian anthropology: "Man's capacity for justice makes democracy possible; but man's inclination to injustice makes democracy necessary."[12]

[10] Reinhold Niebuhr, "A Christian Journal Confronts Mankind's Continuing Crisis," *Christianity and Crisis*, 26:2 (Feb. 21, 1966), 13. Copyright © 1966 by Christianity and Crisis, Inc. Reprinted by permission.

[11] Those who take seriously certain anthropological presuppositions within the Judaic-Christian heritage—the understanding of the nature of man—will hardly be surprised by the depths to which human depravity descends. At the same time, they have to be aware that their very chronicling of man's inhumanity to man can itself sometimes contribute to and compound that very condition, in part through the defensiveness they may provoke in their public. The scholar who is obedient to historical truth is inevitably cast as something of a prophet who thereby tends, whatever the extent of his notoriety, to remain suspect within his own social and religious community. (This is one reason he may find a surrogate home in the university, for the free university constitutes a fortress against men's self-deceptions respecting their own history.)

[12] Reinhold Niebuhr, *The Children of Light and the Children of Darkness: A Vindication of Democracy and A Critique of Its Traditional Defence* (New York: Scribner, 1946), p. xi.

Niebuhr directed much of his wrath against the endemic moralism and pietism of the churches, with their witting or unwitting tendency to nurture complacent social conformity and serve the status quo. All too readily, the churches become special centers of self-righteousness and self-deception. Worse, the churches have all too little comprehension of the vast and inevitable gulf between personal morality and collective morality, between individual "moral man" and "immoral society."[13] At the social level, recourse must be made to essentially political decisions and action in order to approximate a balance of power among conflicting centers of self-interest. Order and justice are never attained by "pure love or pure reason but by an equilibrium of various forms of economic and political power."[14] Only in this way can human social life be made tolerable, only in this way can the weak be protected from the powerful. But the equilibrium is never stable; it must be continually reacted to in order to forestall a weighting of power on one side or an alliance of forces against powerless or relatively powerless parties.

Had Professor Niebuhr's long illness not prevented him from sustaining his earlier, powerful leadership,[15] the fortunes of American and world Christianity, as well, perhaps, as those of the Jewish people, would doubtless have been much happier over recent decades. The contemporary period is, in some ways, just as threatening as the terrible epoch that saw Niebuhr at the height of his powers. Lamentably, Christian realism is now largely in a state of disarray and eclipse. A younger generation of Protestant "liberals" has drifted away from the Niebuhrian "concept of constantly contending self-

---

[13] Reinhold Niebuhr, *Moral Man and Immoral Society: A Study in Ethics and Politics* (New York: Scribner, 1941).

[14] Niebuhr, "A Christian Journal . . . ," p. 13.

[15] Niebuhr's effectiveness was sharply reduced during the almost two decades of serious illness that preceded his death on June 1, 1971. In 1952 he suffered a serious stroke that left him considerably incapacitated, though he remained as alert as ever.

interest to revolutionary, third-world romanticism."[16] Our origins, history, and traditions as a nation are such that they forever tempt us into the sins of self-righteousness, isolationism, and neutralism. The specter of a resurgent Christian pacifism once again moves across the world, even within the circles that were once saved from the disease by Niebuhr's virtually singlehanded crusade. Once again, on more than one front, Christian idealism is showing its sweet and ugly face, with all the irresponsibility and naïveté of old, including the notion that the powers of darkness are really not all that bad. The perennial temptation of the churches to become irrelevant to national and international problems afflicts us with renewed force. The churches are markedly paralyzed by a failure to reach and to live by those relative moral choices that are among the few sure evidences of moral integrity and health. Instead, sentimental idealization goes blissfully forward. Once again we are being assured that if we will just be nice enough, and understanding enough, the aggressors of this world will either go away ("You must realize that A and B are primarily devoted to internal affairs") or will themselves prove to be nice gentlemen shepherding their nice, friendly peoples into international conciliation. Yet at the very same moment, cynicism, the companion of idealism, trumpets its absolutist, irrational conclusions—as in the repeated, indiscriminate insistence that no nation could be as pervasively rotten as the United States.

I referred in Chapter 9 to the recent fate of *Christianity and Crisis*. Reinhold Niebuhr helped to found that journal in 1941 and served as editor until 1966. The publication became an influential stronghold of Christian realism, especially during the Second Great War and on into the postwar period. Niebuhr's words at the time of the June War of 1967, in a commentary entitled "David and Goliath," were

16 *Time*, June 14, 1971.

as approving of Israel as they were descriptive of the real state of affairs: "a nation that knows that it is in danger of strangulation will use its fists." The all-decisive consideration remains, Niebuhr pointed out, that the Arab Goliath has "never accepted Israel's existence as a nation or granted it the right of survival."[17] Nor would Niebuhr tolerate the nonsense that uses Israel's success in defending herself thus far as justification for preaching equal right on both sides of the conflict. It was *after* the Six Day War that he stressed the centrality of the Arab nonacceptance of Israel. Shortly before that outbreak he had referred to "the complacency and irresponsibility of American neutralism in the face of the Nazi threat," a state of affairs intimately linked to our historic self-righteousness and idealism as a nation, and its concomitant perennial and powerful impulse to try to withdraw from the world.[18]

From a Niebuhrian perspective, requisite moral decisions in the Middle East conflict remain the same in principle as those necessitated in the confrontation with the peril of Nazism. Nowhere are the resources and lessons of Christian realism more in need of reaffirmation than in the Arab–Israeli struggle. But *Christianity and Crisis* has moved in a contrary direction. Eugene Rothman documents "the evolution of a Christian perspective" in successive numbers of that journal.[19] He shows the regrettable alterations that have taken place in its editorial policies since the Six Day War. Already in the same issue in which Niebuhr's "David and Goliath" appeared, John C. Bennett saw fit to revive the insufferable demands the Christian community has enjoyed making of Israel (as it has of Jews for centuries): "Now that Israel has the power and the initiative in the Middle East we hope that she will put her great gifts into creating something new in her relation with

[17] Reinhold Niebuhr, "David and Goliath," *Christianity and Crisis,* 27:11 (June 26, 1967), 141.

[18] Niebuhr, "A Christian Journal . . . ," p. 11.

[19] Eugene Rothman, "The Evolution of A Christian Perspective," *Midstream,* 17:2 (February, 1971), 3–12.

the Arabs."[20] How quickly some turned and helped betray David to his enemies! The about-face of *Christianity and Crisis* became total in the policy of "evenhandedness" demanded by the present editor, Wayne H. Cowan, in an editorial entitled "The Palestinian Time Bomb." As Rothman points out, Cowan strives to substitute an ideal condition of balancing between the antagonists for the real one of preponderance of right and wrong, with, as the inevitable outcome, total acceptance of the Arab case. The final stage of the evolution of *Christianity and Crisis* was "the inversion of previous priorities. . . . [The] justice of Israel's nationhood became merely one more element in the confused picture, and not a cornerstone from which other aspects of a solution might flow."[21]

Reinhold Niebuhr would have no part in this betrayal. Until the end, he remained true to his Christian realism. For his wife and himself, he wrote in his letter to us of September 10, 1970: "We share your concern about the present state of 'cease-fire' negotiations and are astounded that our government could expect Israel to persuade Egypt to rescind its 'cease-fire' infringements involving the Russian missiles." Wherever in our world there is no anxiety for the welfare and fate of the Jewish people, and no intervention in behalf of Jews, there is no Christian realism. In a sinful, fragmentary world we are left with no option but "to teach the necessity of discriminate judgment." As previously

---

[20] John C. Bennett, "Thoughts on the Middle East," *Christianity and Crisis,* 27:11 (June 26, 1967), 142.

[21] Rothman, "The Evolution . . . ," p. 11. The date of the editorial, "The Palestinian Time Bomb," was Oct. 5, 1970. See also Wayne H. Cowan's earlier plea for "evenhandedness" in a lengthy article entitled "The Elusive Peace," *Christianity and Crisis,* 30:8 (May 11, 1970), 95–101. The point of view to which Rothman refers was carried forward in the June 14, 1971 issue of *Christianity and Crisis,* in a piece called "Is Nixon Doing Something Right?" by Arthur J. Moore, a member of the editorial board. Moore wrote that "until a US president is prepared to exert really strong pressure on the Israelis about the border question and take seriously the question of the Palestinians, the present period will be remembered as only one of the ups on the Middle East roller coaster" (p. 114).

pointed out in this book, a third party who practices "even-handedness" in the presence of a first party dedicated to the abolition of a second party is doing the work of evil.

We cannot know, of course, when, if ever, the Christian realism of Reinhold Niebuhr will undergo the rebirth our world so badly needs. I see Niebuhr's position as comprising a theology of hope, not one of despair, but hope of a kind that transcends "hopes" that are ephemeral and deceive. Niebuhr exposed false hopes for what they are: temptations wanting in saving power. We may, by contrast, be set free; we may be granted a hope that endures. We will remain fallible and sinful men. But we need not deliver ourselves over to fate. We need not be defeated men.

Professor Niebuhr's dialectic moved resolutely and unceasingly from the horizontal dimension of human experience to the vertical dimension of faith, and then back again. Deprived of the motivations and power of faith, the human tale may fill itself with sound and fury, yet in the end it must signify nothing. However, any religious gospel that defaults in its worldly obligations and fails to honor righteousness and serve justice is mere sounding brass and a tinkling cymbal—once again, a signifying of nothing.

In the following passage, written in criticism of Paul Tillich, we find Niebuhr grappling simultaneously with three fundamental problems: idolatry, obligation, and meaning:

. . . the Christian faith is ultimately concerned . . . [with] the mystery of the reconciliation between the divine purpose and the fragmentary and idolatrous human purposes. In other words, it is concerned, not in evading idolatry, but in accepting historic responsibilities with an easy and yet uneasy conscience, since every form of human striving is bound to be idolatrous in the ultimate court. One might say that ideally the Christian faith enables men, not to escape idolatry absolutely, but to accept responsibilities, knowing that those responsibilities will involve us in idolatries from which no form of human perfection will redeem us. . . . The insistence on divine mercy as the final answer to the human predicament does not absolve us of responsibility but frees us for performing tasks in a world which never confronts us with clear choices of good and evil.[22]

Niebuhr was here seeking to resolve, or at least to live with, the agonizing dilemma of idolatry versus moral responsibility. There are evils worse than idolatry. Yet men still require deliverance from the evils that idolatry itself compounds. This can occur as they become beneficiaries of a peace that passes all human understanding, a peace through which the unrighteous are forgiven. Indeed, the essential power behind sustained political action is the divine forgiveness.

I have ventured to call Niebuhr's position a theology of hope. Much of the basis of this judgment is his summons to men to honor their indeterminate and God-given obligations as free, moral beings. The question, Is there hope?, is, in the present context, identical with the question, To what degree are we courageous enough to live as responsible men? I find some comfort in the tiny band of disciples who remain faithful to Christian realism. I find something of added hope in the recently founded group, Christians Concerned for Israel, of which Reinhold Niebuhr became a sponsor as one of his final public acts. And we must never underestimate the dimensions of hope within Reinhold Niebuhr's own politico-moral insights. Thus, if it is the case that the vital interests of nations remain "the hidden, but always potent, motivation of national policy,"[23] self-interest may nevertheless sometimes become an instrument of justice, as justice in turn can be an instrument of love. At least there is always a chance that genuine self-interest and the will-to-live may gain a tolerable victory within a nation over the impulse to self-destruction and self-punishment (as this latter infects, for example, the Arab world of today). There is the selfishness that does not in fact serve the self, and there is the selfishness that drives

---

[22] Reinhold Niebuhr, review of Paul Tillich's *Dynamics of Faith, Union Seminary Quarterly Review,* 12:4 (May, 1957), 112.

[23] Niebuhr, "A Christian Journal . . . ," p. 11.

men and nations into regard for others. We may hope that the United States will not destroy itself through the fantasy that it can betray Israel and yet emerge unscathed.

With Sören Kierkegaard, Reinhold Niebuhr insisted that humor is second only to faith as a way of living with life's ironies and contingencies.[24] However, laughter itself cries for redemption. Faith has to intercede for it. And then love must come to redeem faith along with hope. There remains, in the end, love's strange way with men: the symbiosis of righteousness and forgiveness.

III

Rosenzweig Despite Rosenstock. The Jew, Franz Rosenzweig, and the Christian, Eugen Rosenstock-Huessy, first met at the University of Leipzig. Rosenstock was a *Privatdozent* in medieval constitutional law, and Rosenzweig, though two years older, was his student. The men remained friends until Rosenzweig's death in 1929. Rosenstock emigrated to the United States, and in 1935 became a professor of social philosophy at Dartmouth College.

I introduce the volume *Judaism Despite Christianity,* which focuses on a series of letters between Rosenzweig and Rosenstock composed a few years after their initial encounter in 1913.[25] I place the present sketch third only because *Judaism Despite Christianity* was not published until recently.

The volume is beset by a number of literary shortcomings. Although we are not here engaged in the business of literary criticism, such faults as these cannot be passed by:

---

[24] Reinhold Niebuhr, "Humour and Faith," in *Discerning the Signs of the Times: Sermons for Today and Tomorrow* (New York: Scribner, 1946).

[25] Eugen Rosenstock-Huessy, ed., *Judaism Despite Christianity: The "Letters on Christianity and Judaism" between Eugen Rosenstock-Huessy and Franz Rosenzweig* (University, Alabama: University of Alabama Press, 1969).

Jewish–Christian communication in our time fairly cries out for a painstaking, creative grammar. An irony is that Rosenstock and, after him, Rosenzweig were earnestly committed to the moral urgency of "speech-thinking." Speech was held to be the essential revealer of truth and the very life-blood of human society. What a pity it is, therefore, that in a number of passages the correspondents seem to be competing to see who can win out as master of obscurity and turgidness. A proposition put forward by Rosenstock, later agreed to by Rosenzweig, and explicitly advocated by Harold Stahmer in his introduction to the volume—that history is a matter of passion, and that its problems and challenges cannot be "sorted out neatly according to the abstract, neutral, timeless categories and concepts" that textbook writers seem to find satisfying[26]—offers no warrant at all for the almost unbelievable opaqueness of much in the letters. Of course, the two thinkers were completely entitled to correspond privately in as enigmatic and tortuous a fashion as they wished. The issue is one of inflicting unintelligibility upon the public. Someone has said that human communication demands faith, hope, and clarity, and that the greatest of these is clarity. Without clarity, we play fateful tricks upon one another. Without clarity, intellectual and existential dialogue can scarcely come alive.

In one letter Rosenstock confesses: "I talk in such a way that only my partner in a discussion actually understands me." Rosenzweig replies: "Your letter has caused me half a sleepless night, because there was so much in it that I did not understand on first reading, and I do not on principle read anything the second time unless I have understood it"[27]—a rather bizarre "principle" for a scholar. The tragedy is that both men were quite capable of writing clearly and even inspiringly, as evidenced by many parts of Rosenzweig's

[26] Harold Stahmer, in ibid., p. 1.
[27] Rosenstock-Huessy, ed., *Judaism Despite Christianity,* pp. 151, 157.

letters as well as in his other writings, and by Rosenstock's letter to Cynthia Harris.[28]

To turn to more substantive issues, in these letters neither protagonist attains concerted or intensive originality, although both men achieve a certain pioneering candor. It would be unfair to judge the effort exclusively from vantage points of the 1970s (assuming we have such), and we cannot ignore the contributions of these thinkers in other works. Our immediate obligation is to ponder the value of *Judaism Despite Christianity*. For the Rosenstock–Rosenzweig confrontation, as chronicled in that volume, remains of the highest significance in the contemporary Jewish–Christian meeting.

In an accompanying essay, Alexander Altmann seeks to represent Rosenstock's position: "The 'word' (in the biblical sense) is superior to the logos of philosophy. The 'word' springs from meeting and response. It has the character of a dialogue, whereas the logos has the nature of a mono-logue."[29] But does not everything depend upon the quality

---

[28] Ibid., pp. 178ff. Much of the literary difficulty of the volume derives from a misleading title which, taken with the cast of the essays introducing the materials, creates expectations not fulfilled by a reading of the letters. Little of the material is devoted to the Jewish–Christian relationship. The discussion of that subject does not begin in earnest until Rosenzweig and Rosenstock are well into the exchange. Nor do they stay with the promised theme. Many passages consist of trivia entirely unrelated to that theme. Structurally, the book suffers from limited coherence and direction. There is too little meat on the bones. The only new contributions are Professor Stahmer's introduction (marked by considerable discursiveness), and two brief commentaries by Rosenstock-Huessy. The latter give only rudimentary guidance to an understanding of the letters, a lack compensated for to some extent by the longer essays of Alexander Altmann and Dorothy M. Emmet. However, both of these essays are readily accessible in the files of *The Journal of Religion,* as is the lengthy "Letter to Cynthia" composed by Rosenstock in 1944. Altmann's analysis is restricted to the history and background of the correspondence; it does not elucidate the letters. Dorothy Emmet's essay—she translated the correspondence—is much more helpful, although it is needlessly repetitive. She reproduces long citations from many of the letters; these passages are then repeated in the section containing the correspondence. Deletions ought to have been made at one point or the other.

[29] Alexander Altmann, in Rosenstock-Huessy, ed., *Judaism Despite Christianity*, p. 30.

and conditions of specific "dialogues" and "monologues"? Many of the philosophic systems of history have exerted powerful existential influences upon human beings, and have often given men comfort. Further, when Rosenstock finds the letters emphasizing "that only in the extreme necessity of spiritual self-defense is there a chance" to learn "the truth about the questions that touch one's own life,"[30] he ignores the repeated opportunities for self-deception such occasions offer. Altmann's contention that the relationship between Rosenzweig and Rosenstock was one of I–Thou rather than I–It is only partially vindicated by the correspondence. Insofar as genuine dialogue means accepting the partner in his own self-understanding, Rosenstock is often far from this goal, as is, more than once, Rosenzweig. Undue idealization has been lavished upon these letters, as in the insipience of Hans Joachim Schoeps, for whom the correspondence is "the purest form of Judaeo–Christian dialogue ever attained, perhaps even for ages to come."[31] Happily, the considerable impurity is finally made inconsequential through a developing bond that came to surprise even the protagonists.

The reputed triumph of "revelation" over "reason" in the letters is no more convincing than other such reported victories. Apart from some kind of reasoned expression and application, revelation can boast little or no practical meaning —even if reason, devoid of some form of revelation of truth, can marshal little or no power. In his allegation that history comprises a struggle, not between man's faith and man's reason, but between God and man,[32] Rosenzweig reduces all events to a single (rationalistic) form of treatment, and he loses the real dialectical tension between faith and philosophy. In this, Rosenstock's influence carries the primary responsibility. Fortunately, when Rosenzweig is at last readied to

---

[30] Rosenstock-Huessy, ed., *Judaism Despite Christianity*, p. 31n.

[31] Hans-Joachim Schoeps, *The Jewish-Christian Argument* (New York: Holt, Rinehart & Winston, 1963), pp. 129–130.

[32] Cf. Rosenstock-Huessy, ed., *Judaism Despite Christianity*, p. 33.

say a personal *Nein* to Rosenstock's Christian faith, he does so by pitting historic Judaism against Christianity—a decision that could never have been reached were "pure faith" left alone to adjudicate between the one religion and the other. Rosenzweig's historical and moral reason and experience as a Jew increasingly run to his rescue, resources that he calls upon again and again in his intellectual struggle with Rosenstock. A whimsical lesson is the way in which Rosenzweig, a formidable mind pretending to have been delivered from the wiles of reason, must in the very conduct of his warfare constantly resort to reason reinforced by historical knowledge and personal experience.

The dilemma of reason and revelation opens up fateful questions on the continuity/discontinuity of Christianity vis-à-vis Judaism and on "the myth of the Judeo–Christian tradition." Louis Ginzberg pronounced this myth untrue. Clearly, the discontinuities between the two faiths along with centuries of un-Christian and un-Jewish treatment of Jews by Christians forbid any elevating of the myth to "truth." Yet, toward the end of the correspondence, Franz Rosenzweig cries: "Can't you find any way at all between complete identity and absolute opposition?"[33]

Rosenzweig's ultimate vision meant preserving the divine "stubbornness of the Jews" while affirming that the Christian church serves to unfold the living Covenant with Israel. The crucible of Rosenzweig's own convictions in encounter with Rosenstock's position seems to have made this viewpoint possible. With regard to the fate of Rosenstock's polemic, in *The Christian Future* we find him referring to the Jewish friend who nearly thirty years before refuted his misunderstanding of Judaism.[34]

In the last letter of the correspondence we meet the Jew and the Christian in contrasting places, but it is a "comple-

[33] Ibid., p. 146.
[34] Eugen Rosenstock-Huessy, *The Christian Future: Or The Modern Mind Outrun* (New York: Harper & Row, 1966), p. 182.

mentary contrast" possessed of "something in common": opposition to paganism and natural religion, an objective oneness "determined by a common goal."[35] Incidentally, Professor Stahmer errs in placing the total thought of Rosenzweig within a Jewish–Christian relationship where, because the claims of the two sides are "universal in scope," they are therefore "logically irreconcilable."[36] Ultimately for Rosenzweig, Judaism and Christianity become reconciled, logically and in every other way, by their representation of two different kinds of universality.[37]

While I myself have argued for the above persuasion (though from the Christian side), I know that the obstacles to its adoption are weighty and manifold. From a Jewish perspective, we may refer to the moral and theological denial that the church's alleged universalization of Israel's witness is authentic. And from within the prevailing Christian tradition, we need only make passing mention now of Christendom's historic refusal to honor the divine particularity of Jewry. Judgmentally, we have to say that the church has never been healed of the endemic disease of Marcionism.[38]

I am fully aware that Rosenzweig's affirmation in *The Star of Redemption* that the gentile world can come to God only through Jesus Christ[39] must simply remain unacceptable to the Jewish community of faith. The most we can possibly justify morally is a Christian accommodation of the Rosenzweig view. In such an adaptation, it is declared that the divine

[35] Rosenstock-Huessy, ed., *Judaism Despite Christianity*, pp. 164–165; cf. Rosenstock's present-day attestation, pp. 74–75.

[36] Stahmer, in ibid., p. 22.

[37] Cf. Altmann, in Rosenstock-Hussey, ed., *Judaism Despite Christianity*, p. 38.

[38] Rosenstock comments negatively upon the "Old Testament" and upon Zionism (*Judaism Despite Christianity*, pp. 88, 140, 144). In one place Rosenzweig himself numbers Zionism among Judaism's "self-deceptions, attempts to take the Kingdom of Heaven by force," although he concedes that these efforts are nonetheless necessary in order to sustain the inner dynamic of Jewish life (ibid., p. 159).

[39] See Franz Rosenzweig, *The Star of Redemption*, trans. William W. Hallo (New York: Holt, Rinehart and Winston, 1971), pp. 336–379.

Covenant with original Israel abides and will abide. Yet, sadly, even in this restricted declaration there is estrangement—because many Jews can no longer believe in the Covenant.

Here arises the haunting query: Are the Jewish people to go it alone? Israelis concentrate upon determining their own destiny. Put differently, is the Jewish–Christian meeting any longer a justified effort? Does it still make moral sense? The answers each of us gives will depend upon his views on the relation between speech and deeds, and also upon his assessment of the contemporary historical situation.

The appropriateness of the publication of *Judaism Despite Christianity* in our day lies not in its intended celebration of the Jewish–Christian dialogue,[40] but more in its unintended post-mortem function: Is the dialogue that died in 1967 to stay dead? Harold Stahmer puts more at stake than he may realize when he agrees that the value of the letters is contingent upon their relevance "to the passionate concerns of real people now and in the future."[41]

Within the Christian churches, as we have seen, only small minorities show any disposition to stand with the world Jewish community in its continuing trials. Many apologists for recent church pronouncements upon the Middle East conflict have obviously wished their efforts to be received as aids to the "dialogue" of Jews and Christians. But it remains much more obvious that most Jews cognizant of the different pronouncements view them as acts of complicity in genocide, as falling within the same category as all other outside threats to the security and indeed the survival of the State of Israel and therefore of the Jewish people.

The "dialogue" could remain more or less a joke so long as the Christian side had all the advantages of power. Fortunately, Jews have equalized the situation—with their bare

---

[40] Stahmer, in Rosenstock-Huessy, ed., *Judaism Despite Christianity*, pp. 9–10.

[41] Ibid., p. 5.

hands. Even those Jews who physically remain in *Galuth,* in dispersion, are free now: through Israel they are blessed with an experiential, living cause that stands in judgment upon, and vanquishes, all the immoralities of Christendom. By virtue of Eretz Yisrael, aided by a burgeoning religious and social pluralism that is post-Christian, Jews can for the first time in Western history tell Christians to take all their antisemitisms along to perdition with them.

Let us, therefore, pose the acid question: Where does the religious doctrine of Jewish enduringness confront its most fateful challenge?

The relentlessness of Rosenstock convinces Rosenzweig that "rosewood is the hardest wood there is." Franz then responds that Israel is not a nation like other nations.[42] He is right of course: the world's hatreds are the stern, if reprehensible, proof. And, both theologically and morally speaking, the Jews are to remain separate. That is to say, they are to "stay with God." Yet the trouble remains: the "difference" is just what antisemites and anti-Zionists have obsessively preached ad nauseam. Is not Rosenzweig falling a victim to Christian (i.e., Greek) spiritualization? Is he not impaled upon a dreadful dilemma of either–or? And unless his "faithful remnant" of today can annihilate such dualism, with the aid of a doctrine of secularization, they (Jews and Christians alike) are as dead as the late, lamented dialogue.

Where does the Hebrew Bible ever conclude that the Covenant and political identity are incommensurate? The Covenant is with a people. To give this persuasion precise application today, the State of Israel, as I have sought to argue, possesses no rights that do not appertain to any and every state.

In a word, it is this *ordinary* nation, this *profane* people, that is the nation of the *Covenant.* Are we able to bear this *mysterium tremendum?* Are we prepared to *act* upon it? If

---

[42] Rosenstock-Huessy, ed., *Judaism Despite Christianity,* pp. 123–132.

not, the Jewish–Christian dialogue will know no resurrection from the dead. The Christian who would revive the dialogue must go to the Jewish people at the place where their hearts are. The meaning of Jewish existence in the United States, as elsewhere, is bound in a life-and-death relation to the survival and security of Medinat Yisrael, the State of Israel. Alas, I too only talk! Yet I do rejoice that at least a few Christians are living where their (accusing) consciences converge upon the existential requirements of the Jewish people as human beings. Who are these Christians? They are of the sort to be found living and toiling in the small Christian *moshav* Nes Ammim, north of Haifa. These people have come to the Land to express the fundamental solidarity of their Christian faith with Israel. Alternatively, and by identical logic, the Christian may find himself making his witness through a place in an Israeli munitions plant.

What does Franz Rosenzweig have to do with Tel Aviv? If the answer is "nothing," then there is no "Rosenzweig despite Rosenstock."

15

Toward Authenticity

In this chapter I work toward defining a positive, authentic Jewish–Christian relationship in a way that develops some points thus far made only in passing, and that brings to focus much of my overall position.

I

The Christian faith, together with Jewish thinking, receives the happenings of time and place with the utmost seriousness. The meeting of Jews and Christians in our time is conditioned, ineluctably, by two events and one threat: the European Holocaust and the accountability for it; the rebirth of the State of Israel; and the eventuality of a second Holocaust—Israel's possible obliteration. Yet it is one thing to say that these events and this threat determine the nature of the confrontation of Jews and Christians, and it is something else to ask: Are these events and this threat of decisive meaning for the Jew as a Jew and for the Christian as a Christian?

Dare we relate the Holocaust to the resurrection of the Jewish state? In some passages in *Israel: An Echo of Eternity,* Abraham Heschel seems to be filling a role rather like that of one of Elie Wiesel's madmen—or perhaps of one who replies to the madmen. Rabbi Heschel testifies that "Israel enables us to bear the agony of Auschwitz without radical despair, to sense a ray of God's radiance in the jungles of history."[1] Must we adjudge that Heschel is misguided?

The two events and the one threat lead us far away from a peaceful academic discussion or a pleasant study group. The setting in which the Christian community is placed is more in the nature of a trial. And much of our existential dilemma is to try to learn which role at the trial is ours: Judge? Defendant? Plaintiff? Jury? Witness? Onlooker? Who am I?

Among the major defendants at the trial is God himself. I do not think that the questions, *Is God dead? Is he not dead?* are the real ones. The excruciating question is whether, if God lives and is not helpless, ought he to go on living, he who has permitted the death of the Six Million? For an embittered Jakov Lind, in the Holocaust are "the flames of God's ever-burning love for his chosen people." The issue is perhaps less whether God can live in a human presence than whether he can live with himself. For, even after Auschwitz, God does not seem to be exactly working hard to prevent a recurrence of the Holocaust (not to mention that he seems to be ignoring the fate of many other people: the American Blacks, the American Indians, and on and on).

From a wholly opposite vantage point Emil L. Fackenheim asks: "Has [Hitler] succeeded in destroying the Jewish faith for us who have escaped?"[2] Now it so happens that I have not escaped from anything. I am *a survivor of nothing,* really. But there are survivors of the Holocaust. In behalf of them Zvi Kolitz, coproducer of Hochhuth's *The Deputy,* reconstructs the last thoughts of a pious Jew, Yossel Rakover.

---

[1] Abraham Joshua Heschel, *Israel: An Echo of Eternity* (New York: Farrar, Straus and Giroux, 1969), p. 115.

[2] Emil L. Fackenheim, *God's Presence in History: Jewish Affirmations and Philosophical Reflections* (New York: New York University Press, 1970). p. 71.

We have no actual document from Rakover. But we know that a Yossel Rakover did die in the flames. Kolitz has him addressing God in this wise:

You may insult me, you may castigate me, you may take from me all that I cherish and hold dear in the world, you may torture me to death—I shall believe in *you,* I shall love you no matter what you do to test me!

And these are my last words to you, my wrathful God: nothing will avail you in the least. You have done everything to make me renounce you, to make me lose my faith in you, but I die exactly as I have lived, a *believer!*

Eternally praised be the God of the dead, the God of vengeance, of truth and of law, who will soon show his face to the world again and shake its foundations with his almighty voice.

Hear, O Israel, the Lord our God the Lord is One.

Into your hands, O Lord, I consign my soul.[3]

These, then, are the choices for Jews: the abandonment of God; the post-Auschwitz affirmation of God. Even the second alternative reflects, with the first, a measure of ambivalence toward God, dead or alive—on the unassailable basis that in such an event as the Holocaust the Jew is the victim. The alternatives for the Christian are different—because Christians (and I do not speak of them indiscriminately) have been among the executioners and the friends of executioners. Accordingly, the Christian's temptation is not so much contempt for God as it is contempt for himself (in contrast to self-acceptance). The question for me as a Christian is not so much "Does God live?" as it is "Do I still live, or have I destroyed myself?" Have we who are Christians despoiled our integrity? The prime question to Jews is suffering; the prime question to Christians is guilt.

[3] Zvi Kolitz, "Yossel Rakover's Appeal to God," *Trends: A Journal of Resources,* 1:6 (February, 1969), 32.

II

From the foregoing it is already manifest that two sorts of issues face us: the objective theological question of God's will, his righteousness—the question of truth—and the existential question of human moral responsibility and culpability. We have to keep grappling with both issues at once if we are to approximate an authentic Jewish–Christian relationship for our time.

Constructively, we may begin with a problem that Christians have but that Jews do not have, at least not to the same degree. From the Jewish side, to be a human being is to be a Jew, and to be a Jew is to be a human being. There is no separation between the two elements. In the Halachic tradition, a Jew is someone born of a Jewish mother. For the male child, circumcision is the symbolic acknowledgment and celebration of Jewishness; it does not create Jewishness. But in the Christian tradition, we would be incorrect to assert that a Christian is someone born of a Christian mother—or father, for that matter. If one is a Jew simply by being born, to be a Christian (by contrast), one must *do* something: he must make a decision, a decision of faith. Jewishness means peopleness. But Christianity is a religion. Without entering into the possible conflict between infant baptism and adult baptism, one has to say that in the Christian view, baptism represents a fundamental decision. The gentile child, for example, may say "no" to his parents' desire that he be a Christian—and then he is not a Christian. The child of Jewish parents may say "no" to his family's religious wishes for him, but this does not make him any less a Jew. He may be a poor Jew, from his parents' standpoint, but he is still a Jew.

One may inquire what all this has to do with the problem I said Christians have. It has everything to do with it. For me to accept the Christian faith is, for me, to be granted answers to questions that confront me simply as a human being. But when the Jew affirms the Jewish faith, he receives answers to questions that confront him as someone who is already a Jew. And there is all the difference in the world between these two states of affairs. A Jew can be an atheist without ceasing to be a Jew. But the idea of a Christian atheist remains a contradiction in terms.

Let us take a further step. The question to the Christian is how he may be accepted by God. Here the difference between the two sides is enormous. The question of how the Jew may be accepted by God as an individual human being is not a life-and-death matter for the Jew. What counts is participation in Jewish peopleness. And the Jewish people are, as Franz Rosenzweig would express it, already with God—at least once the stance of Yossel Rakover is taken. The Jews are already part of the community of God's people, participants in an age-old Covenant. As Jews, they do not have to "be saved" (as against what Christians say); Jews are already children of Abraham, Isaac, and Jacob. By being children of the fathers—the patriarchs—they are children of their heavenly Father. The Covenant with Abraham and his people is an abiding Covenant.

The claim of an elect nation of Israel is most delicate. Later I shall raise questions about it. For the moment, I only ask that my present intention be kept in mind: to point up the nature of the Christian's problem. In that context, I worry not so much about possible offense among Jews when the conviction of Jewish chosenness is expressed by, of all people, a Christian, as I worry over something else: If it is so that the Lord has pledged his faithfulness to Israel, the question is: How may his abiding Covenant be extended to us who are poor pagans?

Christians believe, or they hope (faith and hope are very close)—Christians *trust*—that through the grace of God in Jesus the Jew they are made fellow members with Israel in the Covenant. The Covenant is, so to say, opened upon the world. The writer of the letter to the Ephesians reminds his readers that before Christ came, they were, as gentiles, strangers to "the commonwealth of Israel," outside "the covenants of promise, having no hope and without God in the world." Yet through the grace that burst forth in Jesus they "are no longer strangers and sojourners, but . . . fellow citizens with the saints and members of the household of God, built upon the foundation of the apostles and prophets, Christ Jesus himself being the chief cornerstone . . . (Eph. 2:11–20).

III

Genuine dialogue is unwavering in its honesty. Earlier I attested that a Christian is a person who dares to hope that he belongs in some all-decisive way to the family of Jews— even when he is entirely aware that such testimony may very well have to be rejected by that family. A parallel here is that Jews testify, to Christians, that the Christ, the Messiah, has not come—even when they know that such a denial is against the deep persuasion of the Christians they face.

The Jewish community cannot accept Jesus of Nazareth as Messiah and Lord. The point of view of the Jewish people is represented movingly by Martin Buber, of blessed memory: "Standing bound and shackled in the pillory of mankind, we demonstrate with the bloody body of our people the unredeemedness of the world."[4] The Jew experiences most intensely "the world's lack of redemption. He feels [it] against his skin, he tastes it on his tongue, the burden of the unredeemed world lies on him." Because of this knowledge "he *cannot* concede that the redemption has taken place; he knows that it has not."[5] This is why we must understand, as Christians, that the Jewish nonacceptance of Jesus as the Christ

[4] Martin Buber, *Ereignisse und Begegnungen* (Leipzig: Insel-Verlag, 1920), p. 20.

[5] Martin Buber, *Israel and the World* (New York: Schocken, 1948), p. 35.

is an act of faithfulness to the God of the Covenant, and *not,* as in the historic Christian polemic, an act of faithlessness.

Dr. Buber, with characteristic charity, goes on to speak in behalf of the Christian side. He writes that the Christian is the "daring man" who insists that "the redemption of the world has been accomplished."[6] With this judgment we may both agree and disagree. At best, the redemption that Christians find in Jesus is only a start. The uniqueness of Christianity is its faith in the resurrection of Jesus as the Christ. The Christian religion affirms the victory of God over nature, through his victory over death. Yet, at best, Jesus is only, in Saint Paul's words, the "first fruits of the harvest of those who have died" (I Cor. 15:20). Death remains a stern reality —and so do human prejudice and war and disease and that evil of evils, loneliness. The Christian can only hope for the final redemption. In this he joins his Jewish brothers, who, as they rejoice in and obey the precepts of Torah, also live in expectation of the Messianic Kingdom.[7] At the Seder, the cup of wine is set out for Elijah, herald of the Messiah. So, too, in the Christian communion ritual, the words attributed to Jesus are repeated: "I tell you I shall not drink again of the fruit of the vine until that day when I drink it new with you in my Father's kingdom" (Mark 14:25). And so the Jew and the Christian wait together. They look ahead. They are the people of tomorrow.

Frank M. Cross, Jr., a Protestant New Testament analyst, applies the Pauline teaching in Romans 11 to the sphere of Jewish–Christian relations in this way: The church affirms "the validity and eternity" of the election and vocation of Israel. Christians are never permitted to "refer to Judaism as 'another religion,' or as a false form of the biblical faith." It is into the eternal Covenant with Israel that Christians are grafted, as a wild olive branch is grafted into the

---

[6] *Ibid.,* p. 40.

[7] A. Roy Eckardt, *Elder and Younger Brothers* (New York: Scribner, 1967), p. 160.

root of a domestic olive tree. "The two covenants are one covenant just as the eternal covenant of Israel is identical with the new or rather renewed covenant" of the church.[8]

With the above persuasion in mind, I should like to reaffirm my opposition to any avowed effort on the part of the church to missionize the Jewish community as such. I do this not on moral grounds, although there are moral consequences here, but on strictly Christian confessional–theological grounds. For if the Jewish people are not already a part of the family of God, we who are gentiles remain lost and without hope. The Covenant into which Jesus of Nazareth ostensibly leads us would be revealed as an illusion. By seeking to do away with the Jewish community as an indissoluble union of faith and people, missionizing is, in truth, a veiled, and perhaps below-conscious, attack upon the integrity of the Christian faith, for it assaults the very foundation of Christianity: the Jewish people and their Covenant with the Living God.[9] André Lacocque, Professor of Old Testament at Chicago Theological Seminary, is therefore correct in writing that those organizers of "Key 73"[10] who singled out Jews as objects of their evangelizing zeal revealed a frightening and deeply rooted illness, namely, a misunderstanding of the Christian church's testimony and nature.[11]

A revolution in the church's dogmatic presuppositions is required if there is to be a new beginning. We Christians have not rested our hearts upon God's grace; we have looked upon "the Jews" as raw material for "conversion." We have oscillated between the imperialistic, gentile compulsion to

[8] Frank M. Cross, Jr., "A Christian Understanding of the Election of Israel," *Andover Newton Quarterly,* 8:4 (March, 1968), 237, 240.

[9] Eckardt, *Elder and Younger Brothers,* pp. 157–158.

[10] As described in a Cokesbury (United Methodist) promotional piece, "Key 73" was "a massive attempt [in 1973] to reach every person in North America with the challenge of the Gospel of Jesus Christ."

[11] André Lacocque, "Key 73, Judaism, and the Tragedy of Triumphalism," *The Christian Century,* 90:22 (May 30, 1973), 630. To Lacocque, "Key 73" was "at least in part a dangerous and perhaps essentially non-Christian undertaking" (idem).

make Christians out of Jews, and a pagan, antisemitic diabolism. By smuggling ulterior motives into the meeting with
Jews, we have, in effect, told the eternal Thou to keep silent.
In denying the Israel that makes God live, we have practiced
a form of deicide.

Whenever the Christian church opens itself to the divine
sovereignty, it comes to honor its calling to add the *world* to
the Covenant with the Holy One of Israel. Jesus is the Savior
of the world. Coos Schoneveld, Jerusalem-based adviser on
Jewish–Christian relations to the Netherlands Reformed
Church, rightly attests that the basic meaning of Christian
missions is "the invitation to all people in the world, who
stood outside the Covenant between God and the people of
Israel, to enter into that Covenant."[12] The church can in no
way expect Jewry as a whole to agree that the gentiles may
come to God through Jesus Christ. But insofar as the church
empowers *Christians* to commit themselves to this assurance,
as against the travesty and even the blasphemy of seeking to
make Christians out of Jews, the Christian community will
thereby be enabled to live out the real dialectic between
itself and the Israel of God. And the church will be giving
full homage to the unique truth and integrity of the Christian
faith. If as the world's real prodigals we will return to our
Father's house—the dwelling of our elder brothers—perhaps
our Father and they will accept us. Perhaps then will begin
a new Christian–Jewish dialogue, a new covenant sustained
by forgiveness and joy and peace. There are already a few
signs that the Christian church has started its long journey
home.

IV

Having affirmed a covenantal theology, I must now share
some of my misgivings, or at least questionings.

[12] Coos Schoneveld, book review in *Christian News from Israel*, **new**
series (Jerusalem) 22:1 (5) (1971), 36.

I have elsewhere suggested that Christian intervention in the doctrine of Israel's election easily opens the way to immorality. For Christians, things come to a terrible impasse: We must speak of God—because we claim to be members of his family, if only by adoption—yet we have despoiled his household. The Covenant is broken—not by the Jews, not by the Lord—but it is broken. We Christians have broken it. Jewish suffering is Christian guilt. And so much of the guilt remains unappropriated. We would feel our guilt more if we *knew* more. At this point, I think that the educationists are partly right. If only we Christians knew our Christian history, knew it in the sense of appropriating it into our own existence. I refer, of course, to the long years of Christian denigration and persecution of Jews and their faith. Ignorance is a drug that deadens the pain of guilt, and thereby deprives us of any effective catharsis.

Elie Wiesel's *Beggar in Jerusalem* testifies that at Sinai, God gave Israel the Torah, and then in "the kingdom of night," the Holocaust, he took it back again.[13] Why should God have done that—or, more circumspectly, why should the beggar have claimed this about God? One answer is that we heathen brought God so much grief. Therefore, this is the age after the Covenant, this is the post-Covenant time. Prophecy has ceased; revelation has stopped; the Torah is, in a sense, gone. Perhaps all that is left is for the Jewish people to tell tales. It may be that we Christians cannot do that. For us to tell the tale is only to speak of our shame. Perhaps all that we have left is the tale of a meeting, between those who have survived and us who have survived nothing.

How, then, are we to speak of the Covenant? How, then, are we to speak of election? How, then, are we to speak of the God of Israel? Near the beginning of this chapter I alluded to an issue that is joined in current Jewish thinking. On the one side, there is the negation of God *because* of the

---

[13] Elie Wiesel, *A Beggar in Jerusalem* (New York: Random House, 1970), p. 200; Samuel H. Dresner, "The Elie Wiesel Phenomenon: 2. Witness for Judaism," *Conservative Judaism*, 25:1 (Fall, 1970), 36.

Holocaust. Richard L. Rubenstein, for example, views the God of "the kingdom of night" as a "cosmic sadist" who is beneath our contempt, or at least unworthy of our worship. On the other side, there is the affirmation of God, *despite* the Holocaust, as in Emil L. Fackenheim. What is the Christian theologian to say?

If historical events can never demonstrate faith, neither can history (including the most horrible evils) disprove faith— though, to be sure, history may compel the refining of a given faith. *Theologically,* therefore, the Christian may side with Professor Fackenheim, the believer. Yet, *dialogically,* the Christian does not contradict Rabbi Rubenstein, the non- believer. For while Christian atheism is out of the question, Jewish atheism is not. And because of the peculiar relation between Christians and Jews—specifically, Christian com- plicity in the genocide and harassment of the Jewish people —there exists one place where the Christian travels the road with Rubenstein. In this time after the Covenant, it may be that Christians are forbidden to speak of Jewish election in the traditional sense—yet for an entirely different reason from the arrogant judgment in the churches that Jewish election is annulled by the inauguration of the "new Israel."

The reason we may be forbidden now to speak of Jewish election is that there is no way to immunize the traditional, historic testimony to that election against satanic culpability for the incredible suffering of Jews. At the Holocaust, the Covenant went up in flames. God took back the Torah.

This reasoning does not have to conflict with Emil L. Fackenheim's assertion that it is blasphemous to find any positive purpose or justification in Auschwitz. Such reasoning is further consistent with Fackenheim's plea that Adolf Hitler not be granted a posthumous victory. For if the doctrine of Jewish election is to be retained in some form, perhaps this can only be done through its detheologization, its total morali- zation and total secularization; that is to say, through the avowal of election-beyond-suffering, of election-to-live, of un- qualified Jewish normality. We are left with a 614th commandment: the command to survive.[14] Professor Fackenheim asks: "Is not, after Auschwitz, any Jewish willingness to suffer martyrdom, instead of an inspiration to potential saints, much rather an encouragement to potential criminals? After Auschwitz, is not even the saintliest Jew driven to the inexorable conclusion that he owes the moral obligation to the antisemites of the world not to encourage them by his own powerlessness?"[15] Martyrdom was once a Jewish way of sanctifying the name of God. I do not see how this is any longer possible.

We may celebrate the resurrection of the State of Israel, yet *never* justify the crucifixion of Auschwitz as *any* kind of exchange for Israel. Even to think of such justification is to gaze into the abyss of the Evil One. The way of reasoning proposed here is vindicated, I am emboldened to say, in and through a contemporary caveat: While the eye of faith may discern an ultimate correlation of Auschwitz–Israel—Israel as a "ray of God's radiance in the jungles of history"—this correlation can *never* be applied to the historical–political domain without playing into the hands of those who demand the destruction of Israel on such a moral ground as that many non-Jews have been made to suffer for the sins of other non-Jews. In contrast to the correlation argument we may attest, with James Parkes, that "the moral right of Jewry to an autonomous community in the Land of Israel has nothing to do with atonement for Europe or with the survival of Auschwitz." As we have emphasized, and as Dr. Parkes continues, that right "rests on solid historical evidence—the continuous presence of a Jewish community from Masada to Balfour, and its place in Jewish history."[16] Had there been no Auschwitz, the right of the Jewish people to Israel would not be one wit lessened.

In some such way as the foregoing we may begin, perhaps, to represent Professor Fackenheim as protagonist

---

[14] In traditional Judaism there are 613 commandments.
[15] Fackenheim, *God's Presence in History*, pp. 75–76.
[16] James Parkes, review of Alan T. Davies' *Anti-Semitism and the Christian Mind, Jewish Chronicle* (London), April 3, 1970.

before Rabbi Rubenstein, and Rubenstein as protagonist before Fackenheim. And all the meanwhile we represent another Jewish protagonist, Jesus of Nazareth, who suffered before his resurrection but does not suffer after it.

V

I have declared that the State of Israel determines the nature of today's meeting of Jews and Christians as much as does the Holocaust. The reconstituting of Eretz Yisrael presents us with at least three major and related moral lessons: First, the reemergence of Israel is living refutation of the centuries-old Christian fantasy that only the Jews' "recognition" of Jesus as "their" Christ could put an end to the "dispersion" of God's erstwhile people. If historical events neither prove nor annul the affirmations of faith, we can hardly claim that our own historical pretensions are immune to correction by the plain facts of history. Second, the dreadful epoch of Jewish martyrdoms is finished. Soon after the Six Day War the father of Anne Frank wrote that the events recorded in his young daughter's diary were to become "part of the national memory that built the State of Israel," and were also to kindle the spirit behind the June War. There would be dead *heroes* if need be, but no more Anne Franks. She and her generation were the last. "There would be no more martyrs." Insofar as Christendom may wish to condone, and even help to find, Jewish pariahs and martyrs, it will have to be informed (how many times before it listens?) that the god behind this wish is dead, that his sentence of death was given not alone in Dachau, Belsen, and Auschwitz, but with the massing of Egyptian tanks in the sinai in the spring of 1967, the firing of Syrian guns upon the *kibbutzim* beneath the Golan heights, and the Jordanian shelling of Jerusalem. The Israeli voice is the voice of Jews everywhere: "We will not accept annihilation as our fate. If you refuse to acknowledge our dignity as human beings, you must expect to take the consequences. You will have to decide, tomorrow if not today, which of us is on his way to hell." Perhaps the final tragedy of the Christian church is that it appears prepared to let this voice be the voice of any and every people except the Jews.

The third lesson is that the eternal minority is no longer a minority. Again I cite Richard Rubenstein: The State of Israel means "the massive refusal of the survivors of Auschwitz ever again to live as a part of Christian Europe." (A parallel judgment may be made with respect to Jews in the Muslim Arab world.) These survivors resolved, in effect: "We may die on the sands of Palestine, but we will never again accommodate ourselves to your good graces or your prejudices. There may some day be another Masada. . . . There will never be another Auschwitz."[17] The State of Israel brings singular deliverance from the temptations that habitually afflict Christians as a majority in the presence of Jews. I refer back to a point made in Chapter 14. In Israel Jews can be what they *are*, free from the sufferance of anyone. Here is a place where the Christian duality of "human" and "religious" is advised to hold its tongue and keep its distance. It is a good thing for the Christian soul to be made to live without power, especially power over Jews. Perhaps Israel—yes, a *secular* Israel—can help teach the church the meaning of trust in God.

Is the same to be said for the American scene as for Christian Europe? In principle, here too, the minority days are gone. Because of Israel, the Jews of the United States are at last emancipated. True, Jews who are *forced* to remain beyond Eretz Yisrael live in unrelieved exile. They are in captivity. But for those who can freely choose, and who choose to pass their days in a land other than Israel, the Diaspora gains authenticity. It is the State of Israel that makes the choice possible. Without Israel, there is no such freedom, and every Jew is held in exile. With Israel, the Jew

[17] Richard L. Rubenstein, Foreword to Davies' *Anti-Semitism and the Christian Mind* (New York: Herder & Herder, 1969).

of the Diaspora is sustained in every moment. He knows that he can be welcomed home—unconditionally. He is free—not to return or to return.[18]

Is there, then, nothing of exile in free Diaspora life? Unhappily, we must answer no. Israel herself is not spared the threat of obliteration. Nevertheless, she grants Jews courage to be responsible men *despite* the reign of the devilish powers. Are only Jews given courage? No. For, as David Polish writes: "The capacity of a people to face the demonic in man and to overwhelm its own fate is a vindication not only of this people, Israel, but of the spirit of man. . . ." Because of Israel, Jews in the Diaspora–exile may stand tall —and so may every man.[19]

Yes, the State of Israel changes the whole nature of the erstwhile Jewish–Christian relationship. We Christians are finally defeated, and this is very good for us. We are defeated by the sovereignty of one tiny land. The Jewish–Christian confrontation of almost two millennia is totally transformed.

All that needs to be said by way of completion is that the judging and potentially redeeming bond between Israel and Christians extends to every dimension of the Jewish–Christian relation. David Demson of Emanuel College, Toronto has observed that the Christian "does not merely notice Jewish existence (as a sign of God's promise), but is committed to be a *defender* of Jewish existence. The Christian is committed to the defense of the Jew, just as a brother is committed to defense of brother in the house of their father. . . . [If] the Christian repels the Jew from the house, the Christian will do well to remember that he is also repelling the will of the Lord, who has invited both Jew and Christian into his house."[20]

[18] Alice Eckardt and Roy Eckardt, *Encounter with Israel* (New York: Association Press, 1970), p. 252.

[19] David Polish, "The Tasks of Israel and Galut," *Judaism*, 18:1 (Winter, 1969), 15; Eckardt and Eckardt, *Encounter with Israel*, pp. 252–253.

[20] David Demson, "Christians and Israel," *The Ecumenist*, vol. 7 (November/December, 1968), 14.

16

Reconsiderations

In a recent number of *Religion in Life* Rabbi Levi A. Olan, former president of the Central Conference of American Rabbis, takes to task several Christian theologians, including James Parkes, Reinhold Niebuhr, and myself.[1] "Eckardt, Parkes and Niebuhr have one thing in common—they find Judaism inadequate for man. The first finds Christianity as the better salesman for the covenant to the Gentiles; the second sees Judaism as having the answer to social problems but needs Christianity to meet man's personal needs; and the last finds Judaism nationalistic and suffering from *hubris,* and suggests that the answer is God's mercy through Christ."[2]

I shall leave it to spokesmen for the Parkesian and Niebuhrian positions to respond specifically to Olan's charges at those respective points.[3] With respect to his overall critique, Olan is partially wrong and he is partially right. He is wrong

---

[1] Levi A. Olan, "Christian–Jewish Dialogue: A Dissenting Opinion," *Religion in Life,* 41:2 (Summer, 1972), 154–178.

[2] Ibid., p. 170.

[3] I shall also pass over the rather amusing misquotations and misspellings of my works and name in the Olan piece (cf. ibid., pp. 155, 166, 170, 178). In one quotation from me, the German word *"Auseinandersetzung"* becomes, strangely, *"Asein-Anderzetzung."* Again, the very least courtesy we owe our adversaries is to take the trouble to spell their names correctly.

in that he not only distorts and recounts onesidedly my published theological point of view—as well as to some degree that of James Parkes, and to a lesser degree that of Reinhold Niebuhr—but he largely misstates the historical and factual relationship between the Jewish and Christian faiths. Yet he is partially right in his criticism of me and my past work, together with the work of other Christian theologians, and he is to be taken with especial seriousness in his insistence upon the necessity for a most radical reformulation of the Jewish–Christian relationship. For he is quite accurate and convincing in his observation that the Christian church, in its official expressions and the efforts of many of its theologians, is, lamentably, not ready "to come to a dialogue with the Jews free of the hope of ultimate conversion of the Jew to Christ." The notion that Jews must sooner or later "recognize" Jesus as Lord and Savior continues to pervade the churches. Furthermore, we can hardly fault Rabbi Olan for his piercing reminder of "the awesome silence of the Christian church at Auschwitz, and the more deafening silence when the Arab world set out to hurl the Jews of Israel into the sea."[4]

I

In the matter of Rabbi Olan's errors, a prime issue is whether Christian integrity is founded upon a denial of Jewish integrity. Olan endeavors to have me claim that it is so founded. He tries to make me declare that the elder brother, the Jew, does not have "what it takes to attract the Gentiles." Against my (alleged) position, Olan protests that Christians "should reject the role of being the supersalesman who has a snappier line than the boss to corral the natives into the covenant of the Jews with God. This relationship is demeaning to both Christians and Jews."[5]

Olan is correct that the relation as described is demean-

---

[4] Ibid., pp. 154, 159–160.
[5] Ibid., p. 167.

ing. But his account of my viewpoint is also rather demeaning
—to him as to me. For it does not accurately portray my
position. It is untrue to say that I find Christianity a "better
salesman" than Judaism. I have always affirmed that the
Jewish people and the Jewish faith are possessed of an integrity that is entirely independent of Christianity and the
Christian church. I have always celebrated the Jewish faith
for its steadfastness and truth. This position was already
offered in my initial study of the late 1940s, *Christianity and
the Children of Israel*. I maintained that Jews are uniquely
representative of the God of universal justice (in ways that
often put the Christian community to shame), and that the
church can never supersede the synagogue in the struggle
against paganism (because the church is peculiarly subject
to pagan distortions). I also raised serious questions concerning the missionary stance toward Jews.[6] On the other hand,
it is quite true that at that early stage of my thinking I had
not been liberated from a certain spiritual imperialism. To
some extent I was subjecting Jewish reality to Christian conceptions. Thus, I spoke of the ultimate reconciliation of all
men to God through Jesus Christ.[7] Further, and of immediate
relevance to Olan's criticism, I tended to reduce the worth
of Jewishness to its critical function within an essentially
Christian universe of meaning. While I did avow in *Christianity and the Children of Israel* that it is illicit to call upon
the antipagan role of Jews in a way that menaces their
particularity as a people,[8] nevertheless I had not wholly overcome a propensity to treat the Jews as a means to a particular Christian theological scheme (and even to a particular
Jewish theological scheme), rather than approaching them
as ends in themselves, as Jewish human beings whose dignity
must remain wholly uncompromised.

[6] A. Roy Eckardt, *Christianity and the Children of Israel* (New York:
King's Crown, 1948), pp. xiii, 26, 39ff., 50, 55ff., 117, 146–151, 159, 163.
[7] Ibid., pp. 150, 177.
[8] Ibid., p. 166.

Rabbi Olan's critique involves a considerable misstatement of my more recent writings. It is not right to say, and to have me say, that Judaism is "inadequate for man." Contrary to Olan's charge, the conviction expressed in my work *Elder and Younger Brothers* that the Jews "stay with God" (while the Christian "goes out" into the world) is *never* offered as an adverse value judgment.[9] The distinction there drawn (following Franz Rosenzweig) is conceived in a totally functional way: Jews and Christians are regarded as having been called to differing vocational responsibilities. In reinterpreting and reapplying the Rosenzweig viewpoint, I have never intended to exalt the Christian view above the Jewish view. On the contrary, the testimony that Jews "stay with God" means preeminently that they remain *loyal* to him and that Jewish integrity and inner vitality must be honored against any and every external threat, including that of Christendom.[10] In my affirmation of a single, unfolding Covenant there is a categorical denial of any subordination of Israel to the church; the Covenant with original Israel is in no way annulled by its having been opened to the church and the gentile world. Finally, I have long since rejected the Christian missionizing attitude toward Jews—and this not at all on utilitarian or prudential grounds (in contrast to some other Christian spokesmen). As stated in Chapter 15 of this book, my opposition to the missionizing stance is grounded in the conviction that the conversionist effort is an attack, however unwitting, upon the Covenant of God and his people. It is the height of presumptuousness for the Christian to imply that the Jew is not already a member of the household of salvation.[11]

To Rabbi Olan, "Judaism cannot accept the judgment that it has no word for the modern world. The prophetic faith

---

[9] Cf. A. Roy Eckardt, *Elder and Younger Brothers* (New York: Scribner, 1967), pp. 145, 159ff.
[10] Ibid., p. 159.
[11] Ibid., pp. xx, 129–137, 143, 151–159.

is not only relevant to the present human condition, it is, religious Jews believe, at the heart of it."[12] Olan is entirely within his rights here. And he is entirely wrong—when he alleges that I deny what he says. I have always emphasized that to "stay with God" means anything but parochialism for the Jewish community. Yet where is the justification for contending that the Covenant with Israel precludes an extra-Jewish embodiment of the Covenant?[13] The real issue at this juncture, then, is not whether *Judaism* has a contribution to make, but whether the *Christian faith* has any word for the modern world and is relevant to the human condition. As made plain elsewhere in these pages, I have come to be highly ambivalent on the latter question, at least with respect to erstwhile empirical Christianity. But I have no doubts on one score: the right or lack of right of Christians and the Christian faith to have a place in the world is not different, as a moral issue, from that of the rightful integrity of the Jewish people. The problem of the rights of Christians is, in this respect, as much a problem for Rabbi Olan as for anyone else.

Nevertheless, it is still incumbent upon believing Jews to hold that the Christian faith, whatever its moral contribution or pragmatic social worth, is, in essence, false. Olan completely ignores this acknowledgment throughout my thinking. Christianity is grounded upon the coming and the resurrection of Jesus as the Christ. But from a Jewish point of view the Christ has not come and was not raised from the dead. This means that the relation of a Jew to a Christian is fundamentally different from that of a Christian to a Jew. As a Christian, I can and do believe in the essential truth of the Jewish faith—in an infinitely more positive way than the mere noninvolved assertion of the spectator that such a faith is true "for them," the Jews. As a Christian, I can and must affirm, unreservedly, that the Jewish faith is true *for me*. But a Jew

---

[12] Olan, "Christian–Jewish Dialogue," p. 167.
[13] Eckardt, *Elder and Younger Brothers*, p. 146.

simply cannot take an equivalent position with respect to the Christian faith. (The thinking of Franz Rosenzweig is just not typical of the Jewish viewpoint.) We gentiles can accede to the messiahship and lordship of Jesus in a way that would simply be forbidden to us were we Jews. For the Jew, Christianity is the prematurity of prematurities. I have always stressed that Jews find it most difficult to look upon Christianity as the valid unfolding of the Covenant to the gentiles. Rabbi Olan confuses, in a fuzzy way, my acknowledgment of the Jews' position with what is a strictly Christian confession: the opening of the Covenant to the pagan world through Jesus. Whenever, as a Christian, I have spoken in the latter way, I have implied *nothing* whatsoever about what Jews ought or ought not believe or do. It is difficult to think that Rabbi Olan would wish to deny the right of Christian confession. Olan's viewpoint is anti-dialogic in the sense that he does not honor Christians in their own self-understanding. His position is strongly reminiscent of Christian imperialism against Judaism and the Jews—though of course from the other side.

Rabbi Olan argues that "unless Christians are prepared to understand Judaism as a self-contained religious community, wholly unrelated to Christianity, dialogue is meaningless."[14] This is exactly what I have argued for years, and it is inexcusable that Olan should seek to associate me with Christian apologists who maintain otherwise. Where Olan himself is mistaken is in failing to acknowledge the opposite side of the matter: that Christianity is *not* self-contained, but is fundamentally related to Judaism. Olan's difficulty is exemplified in his subscription to the universal proposition, "the uniqueness of any religious community demands that it be understood in complete freedom from any relatedness to another community of faith."[15] He is right, of course, in speaking this way with respect to his own Jewish faith. Judaism

---

[14] Olan, "Christian–Jewish Dialogue," p. 176.
[15] Ibid., p. 164.

is sui generis. But Olan's faith-perspective prevents his seeing that the proposition is turned into a misleading half-truth when it is applied to Christianity. The Christian faith is, to be sure, marked by certain characteristics that are sui generis. But along with the discontinuity with Judaism, there is an essential continuity—so much so that when we speak of the Christian faith, the proposition cited could with equal force be altered to read, "the uniqueness of the Christian community demands that it. be understood in its relatedness to the Jewish community of faith." While Olan propounds well the essential discontinuities between the Jewish and Christian faiths, he has no comprehension of their essential continuities —or, better, of the continuity of Christianity with Judaism. The latter condition forces him into a peculiar position that resembles Marcionism. He concludes that the contemporary Christian emphasis

on the Jewish origins of the church, on the Jewishness of Jesus, or the foundation of the Hebrew Scripture for the New Testament is totally unimportant to Jews. It is an accident which has become an item in history. . . . For Jews, Christianity is not part of the original covenant which Israel made with God; it is not the New Israel or any Israel. Christianity is for Judaism a wholly new and different religion, totally unrelated to the covenant. Its Jewish origin is an accident of history. If Christians can accept themselves in this role, then dialogue can be fruitful between Christians and Jews, as between Moslems and Jews, Buddhists and Jews, and all other religious communions.[16]

Olan's attempt here to dispose of important historical events by reducing them to mere accidents is quite un-Jewish. The price of Jewish–Christian dialogue becomes a violation of historical integrity. Significantly, Olan falls into the same condition as that of the Christian ecclesiastic Ernest Marshall Howse, as we noted in Chapter 11: he destroys the historical link between Christians and Jews. As would be expected, then, Olan introduces, with Howse, the usual and tiresome

[16] Ibid., p. 177.

irrelevancies: Buddhists, Muslims, Hindus, et al. In a comment upon Olan's article Carlyle Marney properly observes that to concede the rabbi's argument "would be to call for the triumph of a Marcionism pronounced dead but not buried seventeen hundred years ago." And then Marney adds: "We Christians are not Marcionites, we are Jews."[17] Within Christianity, Marcionite influences have had disastrous effects upon the well-being of the Jewish people. It would be tragic if these influences were now to be fostered from within the Jewish community itself. If the history of the Christian treatment of Jews is evil—even, indeed, devilish—we can hardly rectify the matter by trying to obliterate the actual historical and human relationships between the two communities. If there is no truth without love, we do not serve love by distorting truth. To speak the truth in love requires truth as well as love.

II

The fact remains that my study *Elder and Younger Brothers* is not wholly free of Christian triumphalism, and hence Rabbi Olan's critique of me is in some measure justified. Even in that volume I do not wholly surmount a temptation to read Jewish reality through the eyes of Christian, or at least "religious," utilitarianism. Thus, I single out as a function of Jewry and the Jewish faith their necessary elements of judgmental action upon Christianity. Again, I refer to the duty of the Christian to help strengthen the faith of his elder brother in the living God.[18] One Jewish response to all this might well be: Why cannot you Christians, at last, just let us alone? Further, there has been something of a failure in my thinking to receive Jewish existence as an unqualifiedly

---

[17] Carlyle Marney, "Editorial," *Religion in Life*, 41:2 (Summer, 1972), 153.

[18] Eckardt, *Elder and Younger Brothers,* pp. 150, 153.

normal, human reality.[19] (Some counsel and teaching by Jewish leaders may have been blameworthy here as well, but that is a matter for Jews.) Along this same line, I now believe that the concept of "mystery" as applied to the people of God—a whole chapter in *Elder and Younger Brothers* is devoted to that theme—is unfortunate. It can be counted upon to play into the hands of detractors of Jews.

Where are the positive reconsiderations promised by the present chapter title? I should like to carry forward now, if only inconclusively and heuristically, the task of reformulating the Jewish–Christian relationship that is initiated in earlier pages and especially in Chapter 15. I have expressed the conviction that Rabbi Olan's critique must be taken with utter seriousness, particularly for his strictures against Christian imperialism. Here, in fact, is to be found the great worth of his essay. But I believe that the reformulating of the relationship of Christians and Jews will have to take rather different directions from the one proposed by Olan and will have to be much more radical.

The covenantal idea demands revolutionary rethinking. Over the years I have found myself moving progressively away from what is, in effect, Christian imperialism toward the confessionalist kind of faith that my great teacher H. Richard Niebuhr espoused. Dr. Niebuhr was convinced that "self-defense is the most prevalent source of error in all thinking and perhaps especially in theology and ethics." A radically confessional theology finds "the great source of evil in life" to be "the absolutizing of the relative, which in Christianity takes the form of substituting religion, revelation, church or Christian morality for God." A critical historical theology cannot be "an offensive or defensive enterprise which undertakes to prove the superiority of Christian faith to all other faiths. . . ."[20] But I have come to believe that a confessionalist

---

[19] Cf. ibid., p. 43.

[20] H. Richard Niebuhr, *The Meaning of Revelation* (New York: The Macmillan Company, 1941), pp. viii–ix, 18. See also, Niebuhr, *Radical Monotheism and Western Culture* (New York: Harper & Brothers, 1960).

standpoint must even exceed the bounds observed by H. Richard Niebuhr. Dr. Niebuhr remained absolutist, after all, at the point of declaring that the unity of the human race is to be found in Christ.[21] The issue is whether the church, in our time, can serve humanity unequivocally until the Christian gospel is redeemed from every trace of absolutism.

I look forward to a rampant secularization and humanization of the Covenant. (I speak exclusively from the Christian side; what the Jewish people and Jewish thinking do with the Covenant is their business and their problem.) I believe that covenantal theology is going to have to be thoroughly demythologized. I am now persuaded that the all-essential identity of moral standards in the honoring of Jews and in the honoring of other men requires that all our Christian theologizing about the Jewish people be somehow transcended. Although I came to this conviction before I read Rabbi Olan's essay, it is at this point that he is absolutely right. The almost unbearable question is whether Christian humanization can be achieved other than at the expense of teachings central to historic Christian faith—including a confessional-type faith—and yet other than through total self-liquidation. The question of whether Christianity can bear humanization is, of course, assailing and indeed shattering the entire Christian world of today. An extreme reflection of this state of affairs appears in the recent judgment of Friedrich Heer that the present Vatican establishment is "a sect that has excommunicated itself, closed itself off from the process of progressive humanization of mankind."[22] Parallel and no less controversial indictments of non-Catholic communions are to be found everywhere.

For Norman Podhoretz, editor of *Commentary,* the Six Day War represents "the recovery, after a long and uncertain convalescence, of the Jewish remnant from the grievous and

---

[21] H. Richard Niebuhr, as cited in Eckardt, *Christianity and the Children of Israel,* p. 130.

[22] Friedrich Heer, "The Catholic Church and the Jews Today," *Midstream,* 17:5 (May, 1971), 31.

so nearly fatal psychic and spiritual wounds it suffered at the hands of the Nazis. . . . The Jews, who had so often violated the commandment to choose life, now obeyed that commandment and chose life. It was a thing to celebrate."[23] The reminder need scarcely be made that the Deuteronomic command to choose life, to which Podhoretz makes reference, explicitly equates life with the loving of God and the keeping of his commandments, with death as the opposite of all this (Deut. 30:15–20). What Podhoretz has done is to detheologize Jewish reality. The election of original Israel is transmuted into, and concenters upon, the 614th commandment we identified in the previous chapter. The new commandment proves to be nothing more nor less than the sheer command to live, nothing more nor less than the free choice and right of Jewish existence as such. The commandment means *unconditional normality*. This is another way of saying that it is not a commandment. It is a declaration of independence, a celebration of the utter sanctity of life.

To what is the Jew a witness, after the Holocaust? He is, testifies Emil L. Fackenheim, "a witness to endurance."[24] Thus, it is the Jew who becomes Torah. The Jew is incarnation. Insofar as the notion of "a kingdom of priests and a holy nation" (Exod. 19:6) has turned into a guarantor of human suffering and degradation, and the bearer of impossible demands, it must be fought with resolution. That notion is inseparable from the erstwhile divine immorality, inseparable from God's self-revolt against his own creation, a condition against which Richard L. Rubenstein's protest is unconditionally justified.[25] When God takes on to himself functions

---

[23] Norman Podhoretz, "A Certain Anxiety," *Commentary*, 52:2 (August, 1971), 6.

[24] Emil L. Fackenheim, *God's Presence in History* (New York: New York University Press, 1970), p. 95.

[25] Cf. Richard L. Rubenstein, *After Auschwitz: Radical Theology and Contemporary Judaism*, (Indianapolis: Bobbs-Merrill, 1966); Richard L. Rubenstein, "Cox's Vision of the Secular City," in Daniel Callahan, ed., *The Secular City Debate* (New York: Macmillan, 1966), p. 142.

of the devil, he is no longer God—or, less contumaciously, he can scarcely continue to be honored as God.

I have often said that if the State of Israel is a Jewish declaration of independence from the Christian world, the Christian from his side cannot consent to a breaking of the tie. He is only an adopted son, true, and a prodigal at that, yet he is not prepared to be put out of the House of Israel. Buber assures us Christians that we are the "daring men." We may even dare to call upon the name of the Jew Jesus of Nazareth to intercede for us against banishment. But the great danger is that such insistence upon the retaining of the tie will only perpetuate the phase of prehumanization. Can this Christian claim continue to stand *after* humanization? I now believe that part of the "coming of age" that Dietrich Bonhoeffer envisioned (though he failed to apply his own principle to a Christian understanding of the Jewish people) entails the unconditional readiness within the Christian community to enable the Israel of God *to be whatever she will be* —even without us. Insofar as I comprehend my motivations— who ever does that, sufficiently?—I think that my erstwhile insistence upon membership in the Jewish family has been determined in considerable measure by the necessary warfare against Christian supersessionism, the fantasy that the "new Israel" has replaced original Israel. Hence, that insistence has been provisionally justified. But suppose that the fantasy is at last overcome! Must the family stay together? I am not entirely certain how to answer. I do know that loved ones part from one another and go their different ways—though they need not thereby cease their loving or their caring. Indeed, it may be that the parting must take place by the very decree of love and for the very sake of love. Love suffers. So Rabbi Olan may be right. It is just that he has not given the right reasons for being right.

I have to confess that the whole question of a post-Covenant theology (if "theology" it could still be called), including the challenge to a secularization of the Covenant, continues to baffle me in a number of ways. I have many more questions with it than I have answers. While I have no brief for Harvey Cox's massively mistaken characterizations of Pharisaism and "the Law" of Judaism,[26] I do agree with Cox, as with Paul Lehmann, that those today who determine to come out of the religious ghetto and to relate themselves meaningfully and constructively to the contemporary world are summoned to speak and to act in politico-moral ways, with politics understood as "the sphere of human mastery and responsibility." It is proposed that "what God is doing in the world is politics, which means making and keeping life human." Politics is also "man's role in response to God," with the same goal as that attributed to God himself. Theology today is that "reflection-in-action" through which the church strives to learn "what this politician God is up to" and thence to imitate him. "In the epoch of the secular city, politics replaces metaphysics as the language of theology." The church is called—*with* the Jewish community?—to center upon "none other than the life-and-death issues of a secular world."[27] In this connection, it cannot be insisted too often that political democracy and social righteousness are essentials of justice for the Jewish people. Wherever and whenever these essentials are threatened, antisemitism sooner or later asserts itself. The evils of poverty, unrest, alienation, and authoritarianism are —in our unredeemed world—invariably transmuted into the oppression of Jews. Those Christians whose concern for Jews is vital will do all in their power to help approximate an open, prosperous, secure, and equalitarian society—including, particularly, emancipation from all forms of religious pressure and privilege.

26 Cf. Rubenstein, "Cox's Vision . . . ," pp. 131, 137; Steven S. Schwarzschild, "A Little Bit of a Revolution?," in Callahan, ed., *The Secular City Debate*, pp. 146ff.

27 Harvey Cox, *The Secular City: Secularization and Urbanization in Theological Perspective,* rev. ed. (New York: Macmillan, 1966), pp. 217–223.

However, the really salient point in the context of this book is that we Christians speak of God and we serve God, as in a sense we permit God to speak and to serve, simply by letting the Jewish people alone, simply by working and praying for the Jews to be—*themselves.* In such ways as these the Christian church may yet "come of age."

III

It is highly doubtful whether in these late days Christianity is *any* "salesman" to the gentiles (to go back to Rabbi Olan's wording), much less to anyone at all—unless we mean a salesman of sin and death. I am forced into the following question: Is the Christian faith really so invincible to history, to world events, as I have, over the years, often depicted it in my writings and work? I have great doubts now that it is so invincible. Emil Fackenheim makes a heartrending judgment: "This is a generation in which even a God dying in history is more significant than one who dwells, unmoving, in eternity."[28] And yet, even an acceptance of the remorselessness of history conveys no unalloyed benefits. I refer to one tragic eventuality: An overcoming of the sin of Christian imperialism may itself contribute to new forms of antisemitism, through its implicit opposition to the doctrine of election that is insisted upon by believing Jews. Here is one of the very great dangers in the death-of-God movement, from the Christian side. There is also the unbearable force of the boy Benjamin's question in André Schwarz-Bart's *The Last of the Just*: If God does not exist, where does all the suffering go? "It goes for nothing. Oh my God, it goes for nothing!"[29]

Dr. Fackenheim has confessed that his own erstwhile

[28] Cf. Seymour Cain, "Emil Fackenheim's Post-Auschwitz Theology," *Midstream,* 17:5 (May, 1971), 73.

[29] André Schwarz-Bart, *The Last of the Just,* trans., Stephen Becker (New York: Atheneum Publishers, 1961), p. 69.

effort to make the Jewish faith immune to "secular" history meant a betrayal of the victims of Auschwitz.[30] Does not this dreadful judgment apply, and with infinitely greater pain, to proponents of the Christian faith? For we are not the *victims* of Auschwitz, we are the *cause* of Auschwitz. So just what are we trying to defend now? To protect? To preserve? Is it worth it? What *counts,* in the final reckoning? To what is a Christian theologian of today a witness, one who is marked with the terrifying self-identification, "theologian of the Holocaust"? Have I not also betrayed the people of Auschwitz, and especially the children there, in the very act of witnessing to the Christian faith? *Do I, in fact, speak for the devil?* My religion is riddled with antisemitism! Yossel Rakover could stay with God even in the moment of castigating him. But how can we Christians do that? There is a renowned Talmudic verse: "Would that they had forsaken Me, and obeyed My commandments." Can *Christians* take on that same yoke? Perhaps. I do not know.[31]

I do know now that the dialectical–existential obligation thrust fatefully upon me is how to live amid a simultaneous acknowledgment and denial of the power and necessities of history. Certain paradoxical demands appear inescapable: to deplore Christianity, in the name of Christian faith; to announce the death of the Christian God, in the name of the living God; to proclaim the death of the resurrected Christ, in the name of the Christ who may one day come.

Rabbi Olan is inerrant in implying that history can become a tyrant, the enemy of righteousness. But he is mistaken if he imagines that human beings can emancipate themselves from their histories and rise into some kind of ahistorical deliverance. We men expend our lives at the agonizing nexus between history and a dimension that transcends his-

---

[30] As cited in Cain, "Emil Fackenheim's Post-Auschwitz Theology," p. 73.

[31] The apostle Paul seems more than to flirt with the possibility: see Romans 9:3.

tory. And it is in that given place, penetrated as it is by unbearable anguish and a few glimmers of joy, that we may be, hopefully, grasped by the saving power of God.

The most terrible of all questions remains: Does the affirmation that the task of the Christian church is to bring the world into the Covenant through Jesus the Jew contribute in and through itself to a perpetuation of antisemitism? In the measure that the answer must be Yes, the Christian gospel can no longer be preached. (Is not this a time of the silences of God?) In *Christianity and the Children of Israel* I wrote that if the message of Jesus as the unique revelation of God gives evidence of compounding antisemitism, the true Christ is not being proclaimed.[32] I here reaffirm that persuasion. How relentlessly the dialectic of truth and love follows after us! In its completeness, the dialectic is expressed in two interconnected ways: (a) If there is no truth without love, nevertheless love devoid of truth is blind. (b) If there is no love without truth, nevertheless truth devoid of love is heartless. This is the time after the Holocaust. God has had to take back his Torah. Has he not also had to take back the Cross and the Empty Tomb? There are years when the first part of the above dialectic must be sacrificed to the second, lest our humanity be captured by the devil. Such, I believe, are the days of our years. We have to choose—between blindness and heartlessness. Blindness is a lesser evil than heartlessness, is that not so?

[32] Eckardt, *Christianity and the Children of Israel*, p. 155.

17

Deeds

Professor Heer asks: "How is this Church of ours to answer, today and tomorrow and the day after, for what she has done over these two thousand years to Jesus the Jew, to his people, to Mankind, and to herself?"[1] We must confess our sin; we must ask God's forgiveness and that of the world community of Israel. But we must also perform deeds of reconciliation.

I

One battle for today has to be waged against the maneuver—sometimes by well-meaning "liberals" who wish to bury the past for the sake of mutual Jewish–Christian acceptance in the present, and sometimes by unconscious antisemites—to bar the subject of past and present antisemitism from primary study and analysis. Such a policy would only mean cutting off the possibility of penitence and corrective action. Harvey Cox writes: "Psychiatrists remind us that the loss of a sense of time is a symptom of personal deterioration. . . . The same is true for a civilization. So long as it

[1] Heer, "The Catholic Church and the Jews Today," *Midstream*, 17:5 (May 1971), p. 31.

can absorb what has happened to it and move confidently toward what is yet to come its vitality persists." But alienation from its past means decline and ultimately death.[2] The tacit pretense that history never happened does not, unfortunately, ever make history go away. And the church will hardly change her behavior effectively or enduringly until she faces up to her past and present sins.

It is difficult to find a way to work through or with self-defensive Christians who resent or at least oppose any raising of the issue of continuing Christian responsibility for antisemitism. Are we left with nothing to say to Christians today who honestly or consciously feel no guilt for this disease? Much depends upon whether they consider them selves an integral part, and therefore in a real way a responsible part, of the total, historic Christian community. Are we or are we not our brothers' keepers?

Thus, another way to put the matter is to ask whether Christians have any truly deep sense of their own history. At the very least, Christians ought to ask themselves whether a denial of all responsibility for antisemitism is a morally justified conclusion, or whether it is in truth a temptation, one that is not unrelated to the machinations of the devil.

We ask once more: How, if at all, may Christian antisemitism be put to flight? A collective–pathological state, such as the one we have analyzed, cannot be separated from either the idealism that demands perfection or the cynicism that awaits nothing good. I believe that we are not yet so far gone that we can no longer distinguish between pathological cynicism and the reasonable cynicism that is an objective response to the fatefulness of the pathology. However, to discern the locus of antisemitism in the devil's work is a beginning for us: we then neither underestimate the terror nor overestimate it. The devil's summons is a most tantalizing

[2] Harvey Cox, *Feast of Fools: A Theological Essay on Festivity and Fantasy* (Cambridge, Mass.: Harvard University Press, 1969), pp. 12, 13.

one. Yet he remains, after all, a sniveling, cowardly bastard: he cringes in horror before the truth.

Sentimental idealism and unreasonable cynicism are common flights from the real world. But the Jew is *here*. He is the world, he is reality. The only end to antisemitism is a revolutionary transformation of the world. Beyond erstwhile Christianity and the nemesis of the Christian's own devilish condition stand the Jewish people. We are left with a choice between hope and despair. In the end, we may testify on the side of hope. This conclusion is made possible because Jews do not surrender to us, who have been the devil. That is to say, the Jewish people do not hate in return.

II

How are we to respond to instances where human acts excel the legitimate demands of justice and rise above the legitimate assignment of moral responsibility? The one available means for redeeming the cheapness of talk and the self-centeredness of guilt "feelings" is a deed of love that costs something. Whenever it takes upon itself that burden of guilt which undeniable culprits have either thrown off or only partly assuaged, such love points the way to the character and work of God.

Is there a path out of the cynicism that is the ineluctable outcome of our own history? Is there a way for the Christianity that killed itself to be raised from the dead? Another hope for the future lies with a remnant of Christians: those who do not directly carry the guilt for Christian antisemitism, but who are called to wage war upon a past that is as yet unredeemed.

It is morally necessary, it is spiritually blessed, that there be groups which give expression to, and keep alive, awareness of common complicity in sin. But much more is involved than this. There is a deeper lesson. Morally speaking, identification with evil has two opposite meanings. There is guilt in the act of identifying oneself with a malevolent community or nation, through "dedication" and committed behavior. But there is the beginning of an answer to guilt in that quite different identification with evil which willingly bears the punishment and the distress that ought rightly be the lot of others.

Someone must redress the evil, lest righteousness be made a mockery. But who is to do this? Those who look with derision upon all human repentance are asked to reflect upon such an enterprise as *Aktion Sühnezeichen,* the German Reconciliation Movement. Initiated in 1958 by two church leaders, Lothar Kreyssig and Franz von Hammerstein, the program involves teams of German young people who give up paid employment for a year to engage in constructive work. Their purpose? Forgiveness for their fellow-countrymen's crimes against Jews and other "enemies" of the Third Reich. Work projects have been carried out in various countries, including Israel, Holland, Norway, Greece, Great Britain, France, Belgium, Yugoslavia, and the Soviet Union. Included are a children's home, a youth center, a home for the blind, irrigation facilities, and the like. At Villeurbanne, near Lyons, the young people erected a synagogue. When asked how he came to the work, one young man answered that he had read of the horrors committed in the concentration camps: "It is hard to admit what happened. We can never wipe it out. The division of Germany, the wall of Berlin—here are the consequences of our guilt. We must obtain pardon so that never again will Cain kill his brother."

Three queries may be addressed to the cynic: First, how recently has your body been bruised and your muscles made sore by the handling of stone and mortar in the free service of other human beings? It is a mean thing when someone who is himself doing little or nothing is prepared to censure those who are performing deeds of mercy. Second and more important, can you really dismiss out of hand the voluntary bearing of guilt by people who in all justice deserve no blame? Third and most important, where do you stand on the question of God's judging and redeeming power to use and transform the unrighteousness that lives within the most righteous human acts?

An overwhelming moral fact is that the great majority of the participants in *Aktion Sühnezeichen* were not even born when the Second Great War started. No one can accuse them of perpetrating the Nazi program of destroying Jews. The penitence of these young people is entirely vicarious; they have taken upon themselves the sins of the fathers. They would be the first to grant that their efforts are not devoid of a wish for national self-respect, and even of an element of self-interest. The plain truth still stands that they are actively engaged in the search for human reconciliation.

Youth of today are expending marvelous energy in behalf of many social causes. They seek to redeem the past, a past that carries many evils for which they are obviously not blameworthy. Christian students and other young people in this country and abroad may be challenged by the example of such a movement as *Aktion Sühnezeichen*. (A marvelous Catholic counterpart to that movement is the younger nuns of the Sisters of Zion, who also work in many lands.)

Who in fact builds for the future? The person who desires to bury the past, refusing to allow any real link between his present behavior and that past? Or the human being who dedicates himself to redeeming the present consequences of the past? A "no" to the last question constitutes an ironic indictment of the detractor.

Is the act of moral judgment merely human or is it also divine? The ultimate issue is whether the confession that "all our righteous deeds are like a polluted garment" (Isa. 64:7) can be accompanied by an openness to the grace that transforms human lives. Where the confession is honest, the grace of God is already making its way. Indeed, that grace moves to purge away any lingering dishonesty. It is exactly here that human love and divine love meet. Love penetrates with the light of redemption into the dark world of human depravity. Through deeds of vicarious suffering—necessarily cleansed and sustained at every moment by the forgiving grace of God—the fateful power of guilt is at last broken.

Index

257